# WALKOUT

# WALKOUT

**HENRY C. WOODRUM**, Lt. Col. USAF (Ret)

# WALKOUT

*iUniverse books may be ordered through booksellers or by contacting:*

*iUniverse*
*1663 Liberty Drive*
*Bloomington, IN 47403*
*www.iuniverse.com*
*844-349-9409*

*Because of the dynamic nature of the Internet, any web addresses or links contained in this book may have changed since publication and may no longer be valid. The views expressed in this work are solely those of the author and do not necessarily reflect the views of the publisher, and the publisher hereby disclaims any responsibility for them.*

*Any people depicted in stock imagery provided by Getty Images are models, and such images are being used for illustrative purposes only. Certain stock imagery © Getty Images.*

*ISBN: 978-1-4502-3990-5 (sc)*
*ISBN: 978-1-4502-3991-2 (hc)*
*ISBN: 978-1-4502-3992-9 (e)*

*Library of Congress Control Number: 2010909473*

*Print information available on the last page.*

*iUniverse rev. date: 11/18/2021*

# CONTENTS

Prologue. . . . . . . . . . . . . . . . . . . . . . . . . . . . . . . . . . . vii
Chapter 1   Stansted . . . . . . . . . . . . . . . . . . . . . . . . . .1
Chapter 2   Shot Down . . . . . . . . . . . . . . . . . . . . . . . .9
Chapter 3   First Night . . . . . . . . . . . . . . . . . . . . . . 27
Chapter 4   The Second Day . . . . . . . . . . . . . . . . . . 34
Chapter 5   The Bar at Carrieres-sur-Seine . . . . . . . . . 57
Chapter 6   Lisa. . . . . . . . . . . . . . . . . . . . . . . . . . . 68
Chapter 7   Leaving Carrieres-sur-Seine. . . . . . . . . . . 78
Chapter 8   Versailles . . . . . . . . . . . . . . . . . . . . . . . 94
Chapter 9   D-Day and The Dogfight . . . . . . . . . . . .105
Chapter 10   Henriette and The Belgian . . . . . . . . . . .117
Chapter 11   The Bombing . . . . . . . . . . . . . . . . . . .126
Chapter 12   Roadblock . . . . . . . . . . . . . . . . . . . . .134
Chapter 13   The Other American . . . . . . . . . . . . . . .152
Chapter 14   The Terrorists . . . . . . . . . . . . . . . . . . .171
Chapter 15   On the Lam . . . . . . . . . . . . . . . . . . . .196
Chapter 16   Nanterre . . . . . . . . . . . . . . . . . . . . . .219
Chapter 17   Countdown . . . . . . . . . . . . . . . . . . . .249
Chapter 18   Liberation . . . . . . . . . . . . . . . . . . . . .261
Chapter 19   Pierre's Childhood Memories. . . . . . . . .287
Postscript . . . . . . . . . . . . . . . . . . . . . . . . . . . . . . . .293
Addendum 2021 . . . . . . . . . . . . . . . . . . . . . . . . . . .299

# PROLOGUE

### Redding, California

Almost forty-five years ago, 10 days before the D-Day landings at Normandy, German flak shot my airplane out of the sky over the northern suburbs of Paris. I expected to be captured. Suspended in my parachute, I looked down upon some of the world's most famous landmarks signaling my arrival in Nazi-occupied France. The likelihood of evasion seemed remote; but I did have hope.

In the ensuing years, numerous books have been published about life in German prison camps and of bold escape attempts, some successful. European authors have described their evasions from the Germans. Others have written about the Underground. A book written by a man responsible for devising escape routes for downed flyers, revealed the scope of planning necessary and the danger of involvement by civilians in the occupied countries. I have read many of these accounts with interest. All stress the importance of Underground contacts.

Some accounts written by men famous for war-time exploits, or those who gained fame since then by performing some particularly amazing feat, have outlined the event of their own "walkouts" via Spain or by boat across the English Channel. Each of them described the heroic acts of French, Dutch, or Belgian men and women, without whose assistance many Allied airmen would undoubtedly have been captured.

In my case, three months passed before I returned to safety in London. Talking with other evaders through the years has confirmed my feelings: without the help of the Underground, many more of us would have been caught. Only with luck and the help of the French Resistance did I avoid capture on several occasions.

I am telling this story more than four decades later, to explain how they helped me. I do not wish to dramatize my role. I just rode along with the Underground. As a young American pilot who couldn't speak a word of French, certain events presented very tense moments; but there were also frustrating periods of waiting and wondering. Many days were filled with apprehension, when all I could do was try to stay aware of the events that were unfolding around me. This book is written in the sequence in which the events occurred and is based entirely on my personal experience.

I want to pay tribute to those wonderful people in the Underground who gave me every possible measure of assistance, always at great risk to themselves. Many of them paid with their lives. I remain in contact with some of those who are still alive, and I corresponded with others before their deaths. But there were many I could never contact. I have used real names whenever possible, although at the time I deliberately tried to forget names to avoid inadvertently revealing them if I was captured. This is for all of them. They have my everlasting gratitude for everything they did for me and other airmen who were shot down but didn't make it back.

Henry C. Woodrum
Lt. Col. USAF (Ret.) October 1989

# Chapter 1

# STANSTED

We switched off the Quonset hut lights and stepped quickly outside into the cold English fog. It was 4 a.m., May 28, 1944, too early to be out of bed. Bud Morgan went first, angling the blue-lensed flashlight downward as we picked our way toward the latrine. Although it was just 15 feet ahead, it was invisible—as were the trees, thickly shrouded in the blanket of fog swirling around us. As we reached the latrine, the early morning silence of the 495th bomb squadron's hutment was suddenly shattered by a sputtering B-26 Pratt-and-Whitney engine on the flightline several hundred feet away. It coughed and wheezed like an old man stumbling out of bed in the morning. At last, the engine caught and settled into a dull roar.

Inside the latrine, I made a useless attempt to shave with the lukewarm water. The razor pulled raggedly through my overnight stubble, leaving patches of whiskers behind. But I didn't care what it looked like – and where we were going; no one else would either. Ah, another day at Stansted, our 9th Air Force base. Smitty had just roused us from desperately needed sleep with the news that we would be replacing another crew with a sick pilot on an early morning flight. Our other hut mates had already left for the briefing.

I might have figured: Bud and I were supposed to be free on a three-day pass in just a couple of hours. I hoped the fog would linger just a little longer until a regular stand-by crew could be organized. Back at the hut I pulled on a pair of green slacks and a green shirt—we never wore insignia on missions—then topped the ensemble with a leather flight jacket. As I pulled on my fleece-lined flying boots, I saw Bud was already dressed and waiting for me at the door. We headed to the club, still using the blue flashlight as we inched our way along the edge of the road to the creek where we both stepped gingerly along a rickety plank to cross the waterway. Bud led; flashlight pointed toward the narrow wooden board. I followed with a hand on his shoulder.

"You know Bud, some morning we're going to fall off this damned plank, our luck can't hold forever."

He glanced back at me and grinned in agreement. We'd been together almost a year, having flown a bunch of training missions in the States before crossing the Atlantic via the southern route over 20 countries before reaching Land's End in England, a 52-hour trip even when traveling at an average ground speed of 231 miles an hour along most of the 12,000-mile course. Now we flew combat missions together.

Entering the club, we spotted a lone cook sitting on a small stool, hunched over a pulp magazine, in the warmth of a crackling wood stove. Bud and I had just left the club three hours earlier. It had been packed and, anticipating our three-day pass, we had stayed until closing, hoisting drinks with the others. Now my queasy stomach and aching head told me that perhaps I'd hoisted a few too many.

"What's for breakfast?" Bud asked as the cook glanced up.

"Spam and eggs, that is if you're on a mission," he said, friendly enough, considering the time of the day. Only mission crews were allowed precious fresh eggs. He started frying them, along with the canned meat as we helped ourselves to some coffee from a huge urn on the other side of the room. It helped the queasiness a little, but I still hoped a replacement crew could be found. We sipped the coffee silently until the cook slid the greasy plates in front of us. Just then, our squadron navigator, Lou Offenburg, and a new navigator I hadn't met yet came in. Apparently the briefing was over.

"Where are we going?" Bud called across the room. Lou poured a cup of coffee, and then walked over to join us. He glanced toward the kitchen, making sure no one would overhear.

"You guys were on the one yesterday, weren't you?" We nodded. "Well, you won't have to strain to see the tower this time."

"Damn." Bud swore softly, but with a lot of feeling. I knew what he meant; we were going to Paris again.

The Jerries were moving every 88-millimeter gun they had to the coast of northern France, convinced that the invasion was near. Most of the weapons were centered in Paris where the country's numerous transportation routes converged.

We finished breakfast in silence, and then went to the briefing room where I pulled on a pair of tan-colored bib overalls that had just been issued. But I decided to keep the leather jacket I was wearing instead of taking the tan cloth jacket that completed the set. It was actually a tank corps outfit, lighter than our winter flying clothes that were too warm now that summer was near.

My overalls were baggy looking. Bud's seemed tailor-made, but I was tall and lanky at 6-foot-2 and 152 pounds. I glanced at the mirror and winced at the sight of my thoroughly mussed blonde hair, worse than in my escape photos when the photographer did the mussing deliberately. Bloodshot eyes glared back. All in all, I looked awful.

I slipped a Mae West over the jacket and felt to make sure my escape kit was in place. Then I felt for my escape photo in the left pocket of my shirt. As always, my dog tags dangled around my neck and my class ring was in place on my left hand. I checked everything else in at the counter, including my wallet, for safekeeping until I returned.

I met up with Bud again in the briefing room with two other pilots and a navigator. The major, who had been waiting for us, drew the curtains covering the big operations map to reveal a red line that traced our route from Stansted to the Channel and across a point near Le Havre, then into Paris. It was almost the same route we had flown the day before, but this time our target was much closer to the city. Again, we were aiming for a bridge.

Suddenly I felt nervous. Paris was rougher now than ever. There was no way of telling how many guns were moving to the west wall of Fortress Europa. The day before they'd briefed us that it was about 500. We were assigned as number five in the first flight. A guy I knew and respected was deputy lead. I'd be on his right wing in number five. He'd joined us after 25 missions with another group and was now nearing a total of 60 completed missions. I was always glad to fly with someone like that—someone who knew his stuff. This would be my 35th.

There wasn't enough time for a full briefing, but the major did give us a weather forecast and warned us to expect more flak this time.

"Your target is closer to Paris than it was yesterday. You may be getting hit from new areas as well, so watch out." He paused, waiting for questions that never came, and then added, "One more thing. Intelligence reports indicate that evasion from Paris would be nearly impossible now; the Germans have been picking people up off the streets. So, if you get in trouble, avoid Paris at all costs."

"Jesus Keerist, major," muttered the skinny pilot sitting next to Bud. I couldn't have said it better myself. It just didn't make much sense: we'd be flying into a 40-knot wind, giving the Jerries just that much more time to shoot. Now they were saying that if you were hit and had to bail out, fine, but just don't land in the city below.

Personally, I never worried about bailing out, but about getting blown up without a chance to jump. I'd already seen that happen to enough pilots on other missions. Some planes blew to smithereens, while others ignited like 100-octane torches. We seldom talked about it, but everyone thought about it. The Germans had a technique of firing an overlapping barrage with their mass of weapons. They were bound to hit something.

The major interrupted my thoughts. "Woodrum, we have two propaganda bombs today, and you'll have one of them along with your 2,000 bomb. Your gunners should be able to see it come apart as it falls away from the plane."

He jerked his head toward the door. "Okay, that's all, now get out to your ships."

Our group commander was Col. R.F.C. Vance, and one of my buddies coined the group's motto: "See France with Colonel Vance." I knew for sure we would get to Paris again long before we saw London.

I wanted more coffee, so Bud and I headed to the canteen where two British Red Cross volunteers served us. The sweet-looking American girl dressed in Red Cross garb was there too, but she didn't look up from her work when we entered. We knew why. Her fiancé, a pilot, had recently been shot down. Now she seldom talked to crewmembers. But the British women bubbled. "Give 'em 'hell,'" they told us as we left.

I grabbed my steel helmet from my locker, checked out a chute, then jogged over to one of the trucks. As I slid my chute onto the tailgate, I heard someone calling.

"Hey, lieutenant, wait a minute." I looked up and saw my bombardier coming out of the hut. It was Griffith, a staff sergeant and one of the last graduates from the enlisted bombardiers' school before the war. I was surprised to see him.

"What happened, Griff? You look terrible," I asked, as he reached the truck.

"Hell, we weren't supposed to fly today, lieutenant." I couldn't blame him. I didn't feel all that great either. He climbed in beside us. He was tall and blond, with a ruddy complexion and usually a cheerful grin. Today he just looked plain sick. The pouches under his eyes were red and puffy.

"Where's Burton?" I asked.

"He's out at the ship."

"You guys tie one on last night?"

"We were going pretty good, but don't worry about me, I'll make it, but I'll bet I'm a lot sicker that the guys we're relieving." He leaned back and closed his eyes as the truck slashed through the fog.

When we reached our revetments, we climbed out and saw a shadowy figure approaching with one of the blue-lensed lights. It was Rogers, our crew chief. We gathered around the nose of the aircraft; our shoulders hunched into our jackets for warmth. Another figure appeared as I was about to climb into the aircraft.

"Morning, lieutenant." It was Burton, our regular engineer. I returned the greeting. Burton and Griffith looked at each other but didn't speak. Burton grinned and Griff snorted. I figured they'd had another squabble, probably over a woman—as usual.

"She ready to go?" I asked.

Rogers nodded. "I pulled a 'mag' check 30 minutes ago, everything's okay."

"Good, where's the rest of the crew?" I wanted to brief them on the phony bomb. Rogers scrambled through the nose-wheel hatch to call the others. When they gathered, I passed the word. Just as I finished the instructions, someone poked his head through the hatch.

"Lieutenant, it doesn't look like you'll be flying for a while. How about joining us for some coffee?"

It was the first sergeant from the anti-aircraft artillery unit. His company had a position a few yards from our revetment. I told him we'd be right over. There was a new man with us this trip, so I introduced myself and asked if he had any questions. He'd be flying tail gunner this mission. I asked him to stay on board and monitor tower frequency, that we would bring him some coffee. He seemed eager. Since he was new, he was probably the only one excited about flying that day.

We followed Rogers to the partially underground gun crew's dugout. It was 12-foot-square with overhead timbers covered with plywood and several feet of dirt tamped into place. The furniture was strictly GI, fashioned from old packing crates. Coffee was brewing in a two-gallon percolator.

"By golly that smells good," Griff said, inhaling deeply. "I can sure use a cup."

"It's just about ready," he told Griffith. Then he turned to me.

"You weren't supposed to fly again today, were you lieutenant?"

It was more of a statement than a question, and I wondered suddenly if the gunnery crews followed our schedules just as the bunch of GIs I'd served with at Wheeler Field followed individual fighter pilots after the Pearl Harbor attack of December 7. I'd been transferred from the infantry to the Air Corps in Hawaii in September of "41 and was stationed at Wheeler, the fighter base for the islands. After the attack, I worked in the ground defense battalion and lived in a dugout similar to the one I was in now. I'd applied for aviation cadets, leaving Hawaii the following June with dreams of becoming a fighter pilot. And now here I was, waiting for the fog to clear to fly another mission piloting a B-26.

The NCO was still talking. "Hell, lieutenant, you guys have been flying a lot lately, we thought this was your crew's day off."

I shrugged. "It's only one mission. We can start our leave this afternoon."

The gunner who had been making the coffee filled four heavy crockery mugs with the steaming brew and brought them to the table. I reached for one and added a little cream and sugar, watching the lazy swirl of colors. I was feeling better and tipped my chair against the wall. The gunners were kidding with the flight crew. One of them was saying how he wished he was going on the mission—that he'd love a chance to hit the Germans.

"Be thankful you don't have to go, kid," Griff was saying. "Keep your ass on the ground while you have a chance."

"Just the same," the kid argued, "I always liked the looks of a B-26—it looks fast just sitting on the ground." I'd heard that before. It was in Hawaii, not long after the war started. A lot of GIs from Wheeler were sent to Hickam to reassemble B-26s shipped from the States to Pearl Harbor. The pilots were all fighter pilots reassigned to Marauders. With little training after they checked out, they flew from the East Coast to Southern California and were getting ready to fly to the South Pacific. When they came back from Hickam, one of the guys told me the B-26 looked fast just sitting on the ground.

Those Marauders quickly earned two nicknames, "The Baltimore Whore" and "The Flying Prostitute." It was a different bird alright; after growing up with aircraft that had wings longer than the fuselage, you blinked twice the first time you saw a B-26 with its short wings and negative angle of attack. It was the first American combat aircraft with a wing loading that required a mile-long runway.

We were in the dugout about an hour before we were told the weather would clear shortly. Bud and I walked back to the ship with Rogers. As we stepped closer, I could hardly make out the Y-5-T on her fuselage. It was our second bird, assigned after Lou Clay belly-landed our "Shopworn Angel" on its 13th mission when the gear hung up.

Hickey, the new guy, was still monitoring tower frequency.

"What's up?" I asked.

"Lt. Christenson just came by and said they expect the fog to lift within the hour. He wants us to roll the moment it clears."

I climbed in and called the rest of the crew back. I glanced at my watch: 8:30 a.m. and they'd roused us out of bed at 3:45 a.m. Same old army, I thought—hurry up and wait. From the cockpit, I could see the ghostly shapes of trees looking wobbly in the fog. Within a few minutes, the fog lifted, and we could see a hundred yards.

I gathered the crew and said, "It looks like we've been blessed with good weather. When you see the blue flare, we'll start to taxi." I felt pretty good considering the lack of sleep the night before, and was glad that I'd had a chance to relax with some coffee before takeoff. We were ready. I settled back into the cushioned confines of the pilot seat and waited for the flare.

# Chapter 2

# SHOT DOWN

During the next few minutes, the fog melted and the ceiling lifted. Scud floated over the airfield in patches as the breeze grew into an 8 mile-an-hour wind. As it cleared, a blue flare arched up from the tower. Across the airfield, engines coughed as pilots nursed the first faint sputterings into full-throated roars. Flight commanders reviewed mission notes as all of the crews completed taxi checks. As the pilots eased in their throttles, each ground crew offered a thumbs-up.

We taxied at 1200 RPMs, steering with our brakes, throttles, and rudders. When the leaders reached their positions, they stopped on the diagonal and eased their ships into place, babying them until they were precisely parked. The first two Martin Marauders took the runway; the leader was on the left of the number two plane, with both running at near full power as final engine checks were made. Brakes held back wings straining to become airborne. A green flare arched upward, signaling the lead pilot to take off. The mission was underway.

Ten seconds later, the next ship followed, its nose wheel lifting and holding until the plane became airborne. The main gear was retracted and the ship stayed only inches above the runway for an instant before beginning its ascent. The other planes followed suit. Only the 497th practiced a different style, keeping their noses high after gear-up, straining for altitude.

Morgan and I preferred speed, so when our turn came, I held the nose down after Bud retracted the gear, letting our air speed build. Then I eased the throttles back, climbing at 160 miles an hour and started a left turn, noticing the flight commander's aircraft completing its 180-degree turn.

I steepened my turn, judging the precise spot I would intercept the formation: about mid-point on the down wind leg. The first three planes were already tucked into a tight V and number four was slowly easing into his slot, below and behind the leader. I adjusted the throttles and slipped into formation, a moment before the sixth ship took its position. The deputy leader, in the number four ship, leaned across his co-pilot and gave me a thumbs-up. I was glad to be flying on the wing of such an experienced pilot.

Although I wanted to be in London on this particular day, it felt good to be part of a formation that proceeded so flawlessly. I relaxed in the armor-plated, bucket seat and framed the number four aircraft in my left window. We were the first six-ship flight in a cluster of three that would form an 18-ship box when assembled. Another box of 18 followed us closely. When the 36 planes were finally massed beneath the overcast, each in turn climbed out on course in the looser formation designed to get us through the overcast by completing timed 45-degree turns, resuming parallel courses, and climbing on course at 180 mph. Our flight broke through the clouds at 8,000 feet into blindingly brilliant sunlight, rejoining the formation in a marvelously blue sky.

We turned toward the coastal beacon east of Brighton, which marked our departure point. As we passed near London, the raucous warning of barrage balloons filled our headsets. The clouds were solid below us and I hoped that the weather forecast had been right in predicting clear skies for our return.

As we headed across the channel, our gunners could see fleets of B-17s and B-24s heading toward their targets in Germany. The plodding heavies left billowing white vapor trails, criss-crossed by thinner streaks from fighter escorts throttled back to stay with them.

"Want me to fly a while, Woody?" Bud asked.

I nodded and he took over while I leaned back, pulled a pack of Luckies out of my jacket pocket, and lit up. I pulled off the light silk gloves that were starting to make my hands sweat and stuffed them into my pocket. Halfway across the channel I instructed the crew to clear their guns and felt the aircraft shudder as the short bursts were fired together. Shell casings fell away from the aircraft ahead of ours as they too cleared their guns.

When I checked the intercom, each crewmember answered in turn with an "OK." I watched Morgan fly formation. He did so effortlessly, seldom adjusting the throttles. We were so close I could see the deputy lead grin at me and wave.

When the enemy coastline became faintly visible, I took off my jacket and shrugged into a heavy flak suit. I picked up my steel helmet and returned to my seat. I slipped the steel helmet over my cloth-flying helmet, and fastened the strap.

"Better get your flak vest, Bud. I'll take over now." I took the controls and relaxed, feeling good, remembering when I was a GI and thought I'd never have the chance to get near a plane. Now I was doing what I always wanted. I began mentally running through the flight plan, remembering every place where we took flak on the way in yesterday.

The nervousness took hold as we neared the enemy landfall. It always came on the same way: beginning with a subtle tenseness, then building until I spotted the first burst of flak. Suddenly it would release and I would concentrate on flying. Now, all I could do was wait for the inevitable. I thought about the percentages. To most of us that's all it was; just a percentage. If the gunners below are lucky, you've had it. But if they aren't, you go home and come back the next day to give them another crack at you. It was very impersonal.

Pilots never see the gunners on the ground who are trying to kill them, only the flak exploding, that is if they're lucky, because you never see the one that gets you. A pilot rarely sees his bombs exploding, buildings destroyed, or people killed. All he sees are those ugly, black blotches as the flak bursts, and he wished to hell it was all over so he could get back to the other side of the channel.

Our landfall was just south of La Havre. We took evasive action along a zigzag course that closely paralleled the Seine. We saw no flak until we neared Rouen where we bombed an airfield a few days ago. After the first burst puffed harmlessly nearly 200 yards away, I gave the airplane to Morgan to fly, suddenly realizing just how tense I was. I could clearly see the city, which seemed small from our altitude, and could make out the big cathedral. A few white, popcorn-shaped clouds were scattered below us.

Flak continued to burst around us as we moved upriver toward our target. A lot of it was from mobile units, not places where we'd picked it up before. As we approached our initial point, the air ahead suddenly blossomed with the barrages of a forewarned enemy. So much for the element of surprise.

Our flight leader failed to turn toward the target heading, but the deputy commander spotted the error and indicated with hand signals that I was to follow him. He started down the bomb run with me and number six on his wing. Flying straight and level, bomb bays open, we held 195 mph through the black, welcoming bouquets from German anti-aircraft gunners. The sound of laboring engines was accompanied by the thudding WHAM of exploding shells. Acrid smoke filled the cockpit, stinging our nostrils. Our ears were filled with the unsettling combination of deafening flak explosions, and an eerie silence in the headsets. In front of me, the flight leader was hit. His ship nosed down and pulled to the right, forcing me to throttle back and pull away. Smoke billowed from the rear escape hatches, and I watched the gunners' faces until the moment they leaped out, their bodies tumbling down and away until their chutes trailed out. At one point, the stricken aircraft nosed up slightly and I could see the pilot and co-pilot in the glow of the reddening cockpit, still trying to fly a torch about to blow.

Then the plane was out of view, but I could hear my gunners repeating "Bail out, bail out for Chris' sakes, bail out!" as they watched flames and smoke from the waist gunner's position leave a streaming trail.

But we couldn't worry about the other crew for long, we'd suddenly become the lead ship. Number six was way off to the left, so I flew the heading and told Griff to take over the run. The flak was intense, more than I'd ever seen. Griff fed me directions and I flew the heading as close as possible. Normally, Griff couldn't take over since the Norden bombsight is always in the lead ships only. But we'd flown some practice bomb runs two days earlier and a D-8 bombsight was still on board. I didn't know what we could hit with that from 9,000 feet, but we'd give it a go.

"You gonna be all right, Griff?" I asked on the intercom.

"Yeah, but I'll have to make it short," he answered. The flak remained heavy, rocking the ship. I concentrated on the instruments, my eyes flicking from airspeed to altimeter and heading.

Suddenly, three heavy bursts hit us simultaneously, rocking the plane sharply. The stench of cordite, or whatever it is that makes flak bursts stink, filled my nostrils. Man, that was way too close, I thought as another explosion twisted the wheel in my hands. I wondered where we were hit, but before I could ask, Burtons' voice announced, "Fire in number one!"

I turned my head and saw some damage, then leaned out to peer through the side window to see the entire engine nacelle. The cowling was loose, but still held together by fasteners on the bottom. Grayish-black smoke gushed from the cowl flaps while flames flickered from fluted openings. The slipstream held the flames inside the cowling, but I knew we had to douse the fire immediately.

"Feather number one!" I yelled. Morgan's hands flashed through the feathering sequence, and when the prop stopped turning, I called for cowl flaps closed and the fire extinguisher to be discharged into the burning nacelle. After a moment, I leaned around to get a better look. The nacelle was black, but there was less smoke now. Flak continued to burst around us. My mouth was dry as I glanced ahead, seeing numerous black puffs.

"How much longer, Griff?" I asked.

"Not far. Gimme two degrees left."

Just then, the ship gave another lurch and the wheel was wrenched from my hands. We both grabbed it. Burton's voice came over the intercom.

"They got us in the left wing. It's a hell of a hole but the shell didn't explode," he said. Again, I turned aside to check the damage while Morgan kept the ship on its heading. When I saw the hole in the wing, I was engulfed by a sense of helplessness. The shell had pierced the wing, leaving a ragged-edged hole the size of a volleyball. High-octane fuel gushed out, about three feet from what was left of the fire. Still, we were damn lucky the shell had burst harmlessly somewhere above us. If it had exploded on contact as was intended, our left wing would have been torn off and the whole plane set afire.

I turned back to the instrument panel as we took another burst in the bomb bays. Zagorski moved in to fight it. I glanced back and saw that his hand-held fire extinguisher wasn't doing much good. Just then I felt the ship lighten and Griff said, "Bombs away. Let's get the hell out of here!"

I began a turn away from the target, but our cockpit was suddenly filled with smoke and ear-splitting sound as the window on my left shattered and the controls felt limp in my hands. There was a burning sensation on my jaw and I gasped for air in the stench of the explosion. The smoke cleared quickly and I noticed a hole in the fuselage below my left foot. Rushing air filled the cockpit. Griffith appeared in the gangway in front of Bud, who slid his seat back so Griff could crawl out of the bombardier's compartment and into the cockpit. I eased back on the yoke until the wheel was almost against my chest, before I finally felt the elevator controls tighten. I tested the aileron and found only fifty percent use of the left aileron, but I had full rudder control. The fire in the bomb bay was blazing, and I knew we'd never get it out. I reached for the throttle and reduced power on the good engine, bringing the left wing down a little. We had to abandon ship.

"Bail out! Bail out," I yelled on the intercom, while wondering if I was doing the right thing. With the right engine churning, the other feathered and afire, we had another fire in the bomb bay. The hole in the left wing was still spewing fuel and my controls were shot. I couldn't even make a controlled turn. With all of the left aileron cranked in and power reduced to keep the left wing down, we were still in a right turn, heading right over Paris. All I could do was to try and hold it level enough for us to bail out.

Morgan turned on the alarm bell. Griff started for the bomb bay, but came back, shouting to Morgan. "Put the gear down! We gotta go out the nose wheel hatch. The fire's too bad in the bomb bay."

I glanced in that direction and saw flames and smoke. Morgan pushed the lever down and I saw a narrow slit of blue widen as Griff slid the nose wheel hatch cover open. The nose wheel fell away and the gear clunked into the down and locked position.

I thought about the props and kept the plane as level as I could to avoid hitting them as we bailed out. Griff climbed into the hatch and suddenly disappeared. Morgan stood up, ready to follow, but then leaned back and flipped on the destruct switch before stepping into the hatch, giving me a nod before he just disappeared. Now it was my turn. I peered toward the back of the plane, through the smoke, but couldn't see anyone else. As I leaned forward, I saw my steel helmet fall away. I'd forgotten to remove it. The mike cord gave a tug as it pulled free of the jack. The fuselage was straining and creaking with noises I'd never heard before.

I stood where Morgan had been just moments before, leaned down, pushed out, grabbed my knees, and left old Y-5-T forever. The sudden change was startling. I was surrounded by silence and lulled for a moment into an almost dreamlike unreality. It seemed as if I could stay that way forever, just floating along. It was a deeply satisfying feeling. I began counting, but then realized I'd already fallen quite a distance. I counted anyway, up to six or seven, before pulling the ripcord. I caught a glimpse of the ground, growing much closer now. Nothing happened. I pulled the ripcord again, the metal ring feeling cold and hard in my hand as I flung my arm outward, tugging. Then came the shock of the chute opening, not as violent as I'd expected. It was my first jump. Above me, I could see the whiteness of the silk canopy billowing in the air, fluttering with little noises as it formed into bulging roundness. I felt an overpowering sense of exaltation at just being alive, knowing that I would drift to the ground and go on living a little longer.

With that thought, I realized for the first time how strong my fear of getting hit and blowing up had been. Instinctively, I looked at my wristwatch. It was 11:43 a.m. I thought about the others and turned my head from side to side looking for chutes. I couldn't see any and wondered where they were. I twisted and turned my head and finally saw two chutes much higher to the east, then a third, beyond and above the other two. I counted again. There were only three; there should have been five. Where were the others?

I focused on the ground and spotted the Eiffel Tower and the Arc de Triomphe a mile or so to the south. The Seine curved and twisted its way through the city. Suddenly I remembered our briefing officer's advice—avoid Paris at all costs—and laughed aloud.

I looked around, craning my neck from side to side to find the plane, and finally saw it off to the north, below me. Smoke spewed from the fuselage, which was burning fiercely now, wild flames engulfing it. As I watched, it augured into a vacant area surrounded by buildings on three sides. It was the only open spot where it could have hit without demolishing something.

I guessed that I'd land on the northwest side of the city, most likely among some buildings. To the west, I saw a few open fields. I doubted I'd drift that far. The streets were empty. There were no people around; they were probably in air raid shelters.

Just ahead and below me, a burst of flak exploded with a loud WHUMP. It was so near I saw the burning crimson of its center as white-hot shrapnel screeched past me. Out in the open like this, the explosion was deafening, and my feeling of exaltation fizzled as I realized they were trying to kill me before I hit the ground. One man, alone, dangling helplessly in a parachute.

"You dirty, God-damn sons-of-bitches," I shouted. Another burst dotted the sky on my right and I shouted again, outraged that I might have survived all that flak on the bomb run, just to wind up a corpse in a parachute. Then another round appeared and I cursed them at the top of my lungs. The war was suddenly too damned personal, and I was furious.

Now, I was drifting faster. The arch was already some distance away and the open spaces I'd seen were closer. The ground was coming up fast. I began to relax again as the firing stopped, thinking I might have a chance to land in an open field. Out of habit, I reached for a cigarette, but I'd left my jacket in the plane along with my Luckies. I stretched against the harness and checked the terrain below, wondering how long I'd stay free after hitting the ground. I saw a few people below now. I then floated over a field and past a populated area with more people in the streets.

Small arms tracers whizzed toward me, but fell away just short of their mark. More tracers curved upward from the ground, red fingers reaching out greedily, and I wondered if I'd had it. The ground was rushing toward me now, and I could easily distinguish people below, all of them hurrying along, some glancing up at me before running toward the spot where they apparently thought I'd land. Tracers still whined past, closer than before, and I began pulling on the shroud lines in a side-to-side motion. Finally, I decided it wasn't doing any good, especially after I pulled too hard and spilled air from the chute, which caused me to very quickly drop for a few feet before the chute again filled with air. When I stopped swinging, the firing also stopped. Did the gunners think I was dead?

I watched the people running below me. I wondered how they felt; living in a country occupied by their enemy for four long years, and remembered a photo I'd seen. It showed a man standing in a street, listening to the Marseillaise being played for the last time before the Germans arrived in his city. His face was set, tears streaming down his cheeks, the skin around his eyes tightly crinkled and the muscles at the corners of his mouth clenched.

On impulse, I began shouting the tune of the French national anthem. It was a crazy thing to do, but it made me feel good. The ground rushed up quickly and I saw a vacant lot near a tiny railroad station. Up the street, two German staff cars and four trucks loaded with soldiers rounded a corner and headed toward me.

I pulled too hard on the lines and spilled some air, just missing a chimney, then slammed flat on my back, onto the concrete tiles lining the steep roof. Stunned, I began slowly sliding down the steep slope of the roof. The blow of landing knocked my breath away and even though I clawed feebly for a hold, I kept on sliding towards the edge. I saw my chute settle slowly over the chimney behind me just as I dropped over the edge, unable to prevent myself from falling to the ground. The shock I got when the slack in the shroud lines took up about two feet above the ground was tremendous.

As I gasped for air, my hand found the metal disk of the chute release and I pounded on it violently. As the harness fell away, I fell the last two feet, shrugged out of the Mae West life jacket and stumbled toward the back of the house, away from the street. My groin hurt like hell.

I heard German vehicles stopping out front. After a few steps, the pain in my groin intensified. It hurt like hell and I wanted to lie down and grab my crotch while I caught my breath. But as I came around the corner of the house, an old woman moved across the back porch and stopped suddenly, throwing up her hands with a startled look as I appeared. She turned and scurried into the house. I continued across the backyard and stuffed my pistol, still strapped in its holster, into one of the hollow-centered cement blocks stacked there. Our instructions were to ditch side arms in the event of imminent capture.

I heard German voices shouting out in the street. I saw no place to hide, so I walked on behind the next house, turned the corner, and headed for the sidewalk. I heard a strident German voice shouting orders. I noticed a canvas drop cloth spread on the ground with several cans of paint on it. I picked up a can with a brush in it.

Carrying the bucket, I tried to look casual as I crossed the yard to a low fence. I stepped over it to join a group of people gathered on the sidewalk and moved to the back of the crowd of people intently watching the Germans pile out of their trucks. They were milling around in front of the home where my chute still dangled from the chimney. I stood among the French civilians watching as German soldiers ran through the gate. A portly German officer stood in the backseat of an open staff car, gesturing directions. I was feeling pretty clever when a man moved up to my left elbow. He stood there for a moment before turning to give me a full-face stare. He knows who I am, I thought. I wonder what he'll do. As he turned back to watch the Germans, he pulled a pack of cigarettes from his pocket and offered me one without turning his head. I glanced quickly at the man, who turned and smiled. I nodded and took a cigarette. He struck a match and gave me a light. Again, I nodded my thanks. I smoked the cigarette and almost choked as I inhaled the strong tobacco.

The chubby German officer started giving his troops hell. Red-faced and screeching, his chest puffed out and he gasped for breath as he shouted—furious that they hadn't caught me yet.

The Frenchman nudged me with his elbow. He motioned with a sideways nod of his head for me to follow and we walked past the car, not six feet behind the German officer's back. When we reached the vacant lot I'd been aiming for, the guy turned and walked along a three-strand barbed-wire fence to a spot opposite a bunch of grape vines in full leaf planted in rows running parallel to the fence. Their leaves were bright green in the sunlight.

He pulled me close and mumbled, "Hide." He motioned to the vines. "Hide inna boosh." Then he took the paint bucket and walked away.

The little vineyard didn't seem to be much of a hiding place, but I stepped over the wire, snagging the bib overalls on a barb before I pulled free, picked out a grapevine in the second row, and lay down behind it. You guys are gonna have to look for me awhile longer, I thought, feeling fatalistic, but certain they'd find me in the next few minutes.

I heard the Germans moving. They began to fan out around the house and up the street, extending their search through the block. I rolled slowly onto my back so I could see if any of them approached. I heard troops milling around the streets, shouting orders as they dispersed the crowd. I remained silent, waiting, wondering what would happen next.

Something glittering in a nearby tree caught my eye. In the uppermost branches of the tree, I saw long foil strips reflecting the sun. I almost laughed when I realized it was an American product, a thing called "window." It came in bundles and was spewed from a machine in an airplane into the slipstream to reflect radar energy back to the antennas on the ground giving the appearance of aircraft on the scope. It was a highly effective radar countermeasure and here it was, used to scare birds away from a cherry tree. Suddenly, I remembered the propaganda bomb and the leaflet Rogers had given me at Stansted that morning. It was still folded in my shirt pocket, and I sure didn't want to be caught with that in my possession. I slid my hand under the flap of the coveralls, to fish it out of my pocket with two fingers, then crumbled it into a little ball and buried it in the soft earth.

I heard a German voice from only a few feet away, on the other side of the fence. I was disgusted with myself for not hiding better. I heard the same voice, then another. There were two of them and they were moving my way. I waited, staring up at the sky and trying to judge their distance. The voices were coming from behind my head. They seemed to be taking only a step or two at a time after which they would pause before continuing. I knew they were only a few feet away. I began taking deep breaths and holding them as long as I could, releasing my breath very quietly and slowly. Each beat of my heart hammered in my ears.

The first man appeared unexpectedly. I heard three footsteps, and with the third step, a German boot hit the ground just opposite my head. I kept my eyes fixed sideways without moving, watching all I could see of the boot, afraid to look up, but the strain began to hurt my eyes so I slowly allowed them to drift upward. Just then, the soldier moved again, one step this time, in a sideways shuffling movement so that he was facing the vineyard all the time. As he inched into the new position, I saw more of his leg up to the knee through the green leaves. I also saw part of his right forearm and hand, his fingers clenching the handle of a pistol. My eyes followed the length of the barrel and when the man's hand wavered, the muzzle lowered and I could see the bore. I stared at it, holding my breath, afraid to move, wondering how much longer I could remain motionless. My heart pounded in my chest until finally I had to breathe. I was sure they would hear me.

Then the first man spoke again, and the second answered. I realized they were standing next to each other. The German with the pistol took another sideways step. His companion moved with him and then I could see his boots also. The man with the pistol leaned forward, peering down the row of vines, but as he leaned, he turned his head to the left so that I saw his face in profile for the first time. He was just a kid, not more than 17 years old. He was thin-faced with bad acne. He wore a forage cap and was licking his lips nervously, his head moving from side to side as his eyes swept along the row of vines. He moved again, three more paces before stopping. The other man moved with him, but I still hadn't been able to see his face, just his right side, then the back part of his helmet and the upper barrel of the rifle he held at his side. They'll see me if they turn around, I thought. They were so jumpy they'd probably shoot me without thinking. Just a couple of damned kids.

The first soldier turned and talked to his companion for a moment, then, apparently satisfied, they walked off across the vacant lot. I took a long quivering breath. Too close, I thought. That was a real sweat job, but I had to grin at my good luck, I was still a free man. I've got to get away, I thought. After a close one like that, maybe I've got a chance. I suddenly felt exhausted, drained of energy, and remembered that I'd only slept a couple of hours the night before. I considered my next step carefully. Krauts were all over the place.

It all seemed pretty funny. I'd landed in broad daylight with German troops only a block away. They'd already spent a half-hour looking for me. During that time, I'd walked right past their commander, and two soldiers had walked past me practically lying at their feet.

I heard the Germans gathering in front of the house where I'd landed. I wondered what they were doing, so I half-rolled over and raised up to see above the vines. I saw an officer and two soldiers climbing a back stairway. At the top, the officer paused, motioning to the others and shouting instructions before he went inside. They were starting a house-to-house search. I could hear more soldiers entering other houses. When they were all out of sight, I decided I had to take a chance on finding a better hiding place. I checked my watch and was surprised to see it was already 12:35 -- I'd been down almost an hour.

I stood up and walked down the row past a wooden shed to the backyard of another house. I hurried around the side, and then cut across the yard to the front walk leading to the street. A young woman came out the front door of the house. When she saw me, she gasped, slamming the door shut as she ducked back inside, a shocked look on her face. I saw her pull a curtain aside to peer out at me. I motioned to her, but the curtain slipped back into place.

I walked to the front gate, a big wrought iron affair, and looked up and down the street. There were guards at either end of the block and atop a building across the street. I glanced quickly around the yard, saw several trees and a big bush in the corner of the fence, which was well screened by a hedge on the other side. I jogged over to the bush, and crawled in on my hands and knees until I came to the corner of the fence. I turned around, my knees tucked up to my shoulders, and leaned against the boards. I tried to relax, knowing I'd probably be there at least a few hours. I let my head fall back, and closed my eyes. Survival was now my only thought. Having been so lucky the first hour of my evasion, remaining free now seemed a reasonable goal.

Then I remembered the woman. I wondered if she'd turn me in, but decided that if she wanted to do that, she would have immediately run to the Germans. She seemed scared to death.

Just then, her front door opened. She looked around and stepped out pulling a baby buggy. She bumped it down the steps to the walk. She hurried back into the house, but reappeared in a moment, a whining toddler in tow. She dumped him into the buggy, then dashed back into the house, this time emerging with a baby tucked under one arm, and a large floppy hat in her other hand. She yanked the front door shut, and then stole a furtive glance toward the bush. She was really in a hurry. Apparently, she hadn't slowed a bit since her first glimpse of me.

She cuddled the baby, cooing softly, then laid him gently in the buggy. She wheeled the carriage toward the gate, her movements almost frantic. She banged her right palm against the latch which clanged as the gate swung open. She hooked the gate with one foot, and opened it far enough to push the buggy through to the sidewalk, then yanked it shut again, checking the lock. She straightened her hat and marched down the street.

She's one shook-up lady. But I realized she was terrified the Germans might find me in her yard. It was obvious that she was afraid something terrible would happen to her or her children if I was caught there. I began to realize the implications of getting French people involved. I wondered what the Germans would do to her, and decided she made the right decision by leaving. If I was caught, at least she wouldn't be around for the interrogation.

After her noisy exit, it seemed very quiet. I heard only the two guards occasionally, and muffled sounds of machinery across the street. I wondered what it was. I eased into a squatting position, and then stood facing the wall, trying not to shake the bush.

Through the concealing foliage, I saw a two-story building, set far back from the street. As I watched, a German soldier was patrolling the top of the building along a parapet encircling the structure. Near the back of the building, I saw the lattice frame of a radar antenna and guessed I was looking at an anti-aircraft predictor unit—very similar to the structures described by our Stansted briefing officers.

I laid back against the wall, talking to myself to stay awake. I desperately needed sleep, but was afraid that if I dozed, I could easily snore my way into captivity. I found myself reaching again for cigarettes and then remembered that my Luckies were long gone.

I reviewed everything that had happened, but the thing that worried me most was the fate of my crew. No one reported being hit and I was sure I'd been the last to bail out. I wasn't very well equipped for survival. A successful evasion with what I had would depend on luck and lots of help from the French. So far, I'd been really lucky. I could have been captured the minute I'd hit that roof. The coveralls I'd decided to wear, instead of my usual mission outfit, definitely helped. The unfamiliar uniform and the paint bucket made a nifty ensemble—for evasion. But now I was stuck in a bush. It was still a long time before dark. I tried to recall every remark made by our RAF briefing officers during escape and evasion lectures. One story in particular came flooding back.

A South African Hurricane pilot shot down on a Sunday rhubarb (a low-level fighter sweep during which it was claimed some pilots returned to England with debris in the air scoops) over Belgium, crash-landed near the edge of a village but climbed from the wreck unharmed. He was wearing a heavy, green, woolen turtleneck sweater, a pair of trousers of a darker color and heavy boots, but no insignia of any kind.

He trotted from the wreck into the village, reaching the town square ahead of the Germans who were in pursuit. He ducked into a café, walked to a wall, placed a chair under a light fixture there, and pulled a fountain pen from his pocket. As the Germans entered to search the place, they gave nary a second glance at the hard-working "electrician." After they left, a waiter motioned for the pilot to follow him. He was escorted to a safe hiding place for the rest of the day, placed with the underground that night, and later returned to England by boat. The paint bucket worked the same way for me. It gave me a reason for being there, so I was overlooked. I remembered hearing that if you could stay free the first 24 hours, your chances of successfully evading were about 50-50. Those seemed like pretty good odds to me. The more I thought about it, the more determined I was to remain right where I was—for the next two days if necessary.

But I was getting hungry. How long had I been under that bush? When I checked my watch, it wasn't as late as I'd thought. I guessed that it was about 6 p.m., but when I looked, it was just 3:30. It wouldn't get dark until nearly 10 since we were on double British summertime. Just before 4:00, the Germans in the building across the street called to their guards who climbed down and went inside. I took a good look around and saw nothing but homes along the streets.

The two guards posted near my fence were gone. Taking advantage of their absence, I stood and urinated against the wall, something I'd needed to do for some time. I moved around a little, stretching aching muscles.

Minutes later, an air raid alarm sounded, first from the building across the street, then joined by the clamor of public alarms a little farther away. I heard the rumbling of a large formation of aircraft and from my standing position, I saw two boxes of B-26s north of town, escorted by P-47s. The flak was heavy in the formation, but the fighters S-turned around the bombers, ignoring the bursts. The formation passed out of sight quickly and I wondered where they were going. The all clear did not come, however, and a minute or so later I found out why.

A formation of P-47s roared in from the west, dive-bombing a target along the river. I saw them slant in steeply, pull up abruptly, then fly off again. Flak and small-arms fire were heavy. Three Messerschmidts appeared just long enough to cross the horizon before they too disappeared as the all-clear sounded. I sat with my back against the wall again. Suddenly, I felt a tingle of apprehension. Somebody was watching me.

I looked into the next yard. An old man in a rocking chair was on the front porch next door, reading a newspaper. From time to time, he would hold the paper in front of his face, and then turn his head to stare directly at the bush, his eyes seeming to peer directly into mine. I was sure the old man knew I was there. A truck rumbled down the street and picked up the two soldiers who had resumed their vigil near the fence. I stared through the leaves at the face of the old man.

Can you see me? Do you know I'm here? I stared for a long, long time. The old man turned back to his paper several times, but always keeping an eye on my bush. Maybe he just thinks I'm here. Maybe he thinks he saw something and is going to holler for the Germans. I was sure that he knew I was there and wondered if the woman with the two kids had told him somehow.

The old man puffed contentedly on his pipe, rocking quietly. I looked at my watch at 7:00 just as someone came around the corner of the house from the backyard. Through the leaves, I couldn't tell whether it was a man or a woman, only that someone was there. I knew it could be a German so I waited until they came closer and I had a better view. The figure blurred as it stepped behind foliage that blocked my view. Finally, when the person was within ten feet of my bush, I saw the legs of a young woman and the lower part of her skirt. She stood silently for a moment, then crouched down on her hands and knees. A small cloth bag hung by a strap over one of her shoulders. She began to pull handfuls of grass, stuffing them into her bag.

Soon she began creeping toward the bush, then leaned forward to part the branches of my hideaway with both hands. Suddenly we were face to face. She drew back, startled to see my face so close to hers. I watched as her eyes flickered over me, and then turned away. The old man was peering at us from behind his paper. He gave a little nod and the young woman turned to me again, trembling as she reached out with a finger and poked me in the chest.

"Americain?"

"Yes," I said, "Oui, Americain." the girl fumbled for more words, passing a hand over her face in exasperation.

"Est-ce que vous allez bien?"

"I don't understand."

She smiled, remembering a key word, "Vous OK?"

"Oh, oui, OK."

She pointed to the blood on my arm and then to my face. I brushed the place on my arm and said "OK," then felt my face. I could feel dried blood on my cheek, and then fresh blood as the cut opened again. I shrugged at the girl and smiled. She spoke again in French that I couldn't understand. After several attempts, she made eating motions with her hands going to her mouth.

"Ah, hungry. Oui."

She made me understand that she would return at 9:00. She spoke several words slowly, but the only one I understood was "Allemand"— Germans. I realized that she was afraid to stay there very long while it was still daylight. She leaned toward me, grabbed my forearm and gave it a little shake. Then she picked up the canvas bag, looked back at the old man who nodded to her again, and she left. She was about 20, had long legs, a slim figure and was very attractive. I hoped that she'd return. I leaned forward in the bush, parting the leaves so the old man could see me. I clasped my hands together and shook them, smiling. He grinned and held up two fingers in a victory sign. From our distance, we smiled together.

# Chapter 3

# FIRST NIGHT

I jolted awake, instantly remembering where I was and what had brought me here. My back ached from leaning against the stone wall and the packed earth beneath me. Wailing air raid sirens, one blasting nearby, had roused me, but now their shrillness was overpowered by the short raucous blare of a klaxon sounding repeatedly from across the street.

A German non-com stepped outside, cupping his hands to summon the guards on the parapet. Two of them, clutching Mausers, trotted hurriedly down the steel stairway. Together they ducked inside the bunker.

From my bush, I peered up and down the deserted street. From somewhere came a baby's cry and a woman's voice calling out in French. Was it the lady with the kids and buggy? Probably not. Her door was shut tight.

But there was the old man, calmly rocking in his chair to some internal rhythm, and smoking his pipe. He'd become sort of an anchor for me and I hoped he'd stay. I poked my head out just enough to allow him to see me, and was rewarded when he turned slowly in my direction and nodded.

A box of B-26s appeared, flying northwest. That's good; at least they aren't coming back for the same bridge. Maybe our group hit it.

As the last B-26 disappeared, a dozen P-47s arrived, slanting down in a long arc before peeling off to dive bomb a target along the river. The explosions sounded impressive, and I recalled learning a few weeks ago that "jugs" dive-bombed the Pas de Calais with 1000-pound bombs. The aircraft disappeared and the evening quiet resumed. The "all-clear" sounded and enemy soldiers emerged like ants from a nest to patrol the parapet, their boots ringing sharply on the metal walkway.

My stomach growled. I was ravenous and wondered anxiously when the girl would return. I looked at my watch. It was only 7:30: I'd have to wait. I thought about my crew again, wondering if they'd been captured, hoping they were safe.

From my hiding place, it was impossible to tell if the Krauts were still looking for me. I didn't see them searching houses nearby, which was a good sign. Maybe they think I've already escaped or that I'm holed up, waiting for dark. Then I remembered I didn't have an escape kit; it was still in my Mae West. I needed the Benzedrine tablets to stay awake and first aid gear to clean my wounds. I cringed at the thought of dozing in the bush and snoring my way into captivity.

The map, though, was the most important thing. There was also a mirror, compass, needle and thread, and some other stuff I'd probably need sooner or later. But at least I still had my escape photos. One of the RAF evasion instructors had spent several days at our base and I talked with him one night at the club. He recommended keeping the photos on your person at all times, and I heeded his advice, placing them in my shirt pocket instead of in the escape kit. I was very glad I'd met that guy.

Remembering the gaping hole in my plane's wing that morning made me think how lucky I was. It seemed I had a lot of luck riding with me lately. A few days ago, we were flying a tight formation. Just at bombs-away when flak was heaviest, we were blown out of formation when several bursts exploded under our right wing. My plane was suddenly vertical, its belly facing the formation. I couldn't see a damned thing so I veered away from the group, descended to a clear spot, righted the plane, and rejoined the formation. That was more than just luck.

Another time, December 7 at Wheeler Field to be exact, a bomb with my name on it came screaming down out of nowhere. The explosion blew me fifteen feet through an open doorway and into a building. I walked away without a scratch that time also. Bud and I experienced a couple of engine failures on takeoff, too, but each time we set up single-engine landings without a hitch. Luck? You bet.

A motion near the house caught my eye. It was the girl, walking toward me. Slender, with a nice figure, she moved with an unaffected grace. Her blonde hair glowed reddish, and her complexion was ruddy. She wore the same print dress, but now carried a canvas bag. About ten feet from the bush, she watched the old man for a hand signal. Kneeling, she peered into my hiding place, handed me the bag, and smiled.

"Hallo. Est-ce que vous allez bien?"

I nodded, struck by how odd it was to be unable to converse with her. Shifting closer, she pulled a long, thin loaf of bread from the bag. It was sliced lengthwise, and then cut in half, making two, large sandwiches. I took a bite and, oh, it was so good! The cold sliced pork was seasoned perfectly. I gulped down the first bite, and then gobbled another while she stared in amusement. Then she handed me a big bunch of green grapes. Then came the final prize. A bottle of cool, white wine, the cork pulled and partially replaced so I could easily uncork it. As I tilted the bottle to sip, still holding half a huge sandwich in one hand, I thought of the Spam we usually ate after a late mission. This wasn't so bad after all, I thought to myself.

"Peelot?" she asked, watching me eat.

"Oui."

"Americain?"

"Oui."

She pointed to the sandwich. "C'est bon?"

I nodded again, then remembered another word. "Merci." She grinned, then abruptly took my left hand and pointed to my watch.

"Return." She pointed to 11:00 and repeated "Return."

She stood, taking the bag with her. She turned toward the old man, whom I'd forgotten all about.

"Bonsoir Monsieur Gilbert."

"Bonsoir mademoiselle, Tout va bien?"

"Oui, Monsieur, tout va bien." She walked to the rear of the house and disappeared around the corner. I sat relishing the gigantic sandwich and sipping the wine, dreading the end of my meal. I took my time, chewing slowly, and wondering when I would eat this well again. Finished with most of the second sandwich, I began nipping at the wine, relaxing for the first time. Although I sipped slowly, it wasn't long before I felt a healthy glow and slapped the cork back in the bottle. I was surprised to see that it was already more than two-thirds gone. I yearned for my cigarettes, but remembered they went up in smoke with my B-26. I wouldn't dare light up here anyhow, but I realized with a pain how great my craving for tobacco was.

My thought turned pensive as I began wondering about my family. How would I be listed, "Missing in Action" or "Killed in Action?" "Missing" wasn't too bad. My family would probably think I was a POW.

I heard German voices—nearer this time. They were posting street guards again, preparing for nightfall. I sat still, determined to stay free as long as possible. I heard German jackboots clatter as they marched along the sidewalk, past the bush. Gradually, the sound faded. Each time I heard fewer boots at they posted the guards.

This bush was my salvation, and I was ready to stay another day within its leafy solitude, remembering my instructor's words: "The first twenty-four hours are the most important." I heard the guards begin to make their rounds, meeting in the center of the block and marching slowly to the corners and back. I began timing the intervals because I was getting stiff and wanted to stand and flex my aching muscles. Finally, when I couldn't lie still another minute, I began to rise at the count of fifty until I was standing erect, stretching for all I was worth—a small luxury that felt really good. The top of my head was even with the highest leaves.

About an hour later, the moon came out and the old man returned to the porch. He stood learning against a post, puffing his pipe. After the guards made four or five trips, the old man went back inside. The street was dark, deserted, and still. Just me and the Germans.

I began to play a little game, silently talking to them as they walked past. "Right here, Kraut, within three feet of you is a big fat medal, maybe even an Iron Cross. All you have to do is point that damned Mauser at me." But they never stopped, walking methodically up and down, from the corner to the middle of the block and back again.

I set my first goal then: stay free through the night. I read my watch by moonlight. It was 11:00. The girl was still gone, but there were other visitors--the RAF.

I heard their four-engine rumble from a distance and wondered if they were Lancasters. Bud and I recently visited an RAF experimental station in Defford and rode in a Lank. The pilot, a Wing Commander, let me handle the controls once we were airborne, and I liked the way it flew. Later, he feathered the engines, first one, then two, then three, until we were flying on only number four. The air speed dropped to 120 kilometers, but remained steady through a 360-degree turn. I was astonished at the maneuverability of that big machine at such low speed.

The next day we took him for a ride in our B-26, which he seemed to enjoy, but it is an altogether different type aircraft. Our reason for going to Defford was to have a mysterious piece of electronic equipment designed to distort enemy radar installed in Y-5-T. When it was in place, we tested it successfully over the Irish Sea against a German radar unit captured by the British in North Africa. Then we crossed the channel to test it against the real thing.

An American civilian technician went along and he had a ball chatting with someone back in Britain on his own radio channel, but Bud and I had no luck locating our Spitfire escorts. In broad daylight, we flew within three miles of the French coast. As we turned up the coast toward Calais, our crew strained their necks looking for enemy fighters. It was really lonesome. Griff spotted some ME-109s inland, climbing parallel to our course. When they began a turn toward us, I added nearly full throttle and nosed down, accelerating to 380 as I headed back across the channel. I wasn't about to stay there without an escort. We crossed the coastline just north of Dover Castle and returned to Defford. The technician was convinced that the machine worked properly and was somewhat disappointed that we didn't stay longer. My crew was just relieved to be back over the English countryside. We asked about the non-existent escort and their official answer was a simple, "Sorry about that, old boy!"

Footsteps from the German guards interrupted my daydream as the roar of the RAF bombers faded.

It was already midnight and still no sign of the girl. I stood slowly and leaned forward to peer down the street, seeing only the two guards now standing motionless, one about thirty feet to my left. He turned and walked slowly down the street. The other turned away and began his trek to the far corner. They looked as tired as I felt. When I sat down again, I saw movement near the house and watched carefully. The girl! She walked quickly to my bush, a finger to her lips cautioning silence. As she took my hand, I crept out of the bush, still crouched over, and walked quickly toward the backyard. I straightened as we approached the little shed behind the house.

Inside was a trap door in the floor with steps leading down to a cellar. She motioned me down, and then followed me. When she reached back for the cover, I helped her tug it into place. It was dark there, with just enough moonlight filtered through a dirty half-window for me to distinguish old furniture, shelves stacked with boxes, bottles and all sorts of odds and ends. Years of accumulated dust covered everything.

"Est-ce que vous allez bien?" she asked her face barely visible in the dim light.

"Oui, bien."

"Attendez ici." Then in English: "A man comes."

We sat on a rolled-up carpet in the middle of the dirt floor. She made a quick motion with her hand as if she just remembered something. From her pocket, she handed me three cigarettes. I thanked her and lit one. It was strong, but good. While I smoked, she took a piece of cloth and a small bottle from her pocket. She poured some of the fluid, which had the unmistakable odor of alcohol, on the material. With a gentle touch, she turned my face and dabbed at the cut on my jaw. It stung like hell. It probably looked even worse than it felt. I was just finishing my cigarette when I heard three taps on the wall opposite us. She stood and tapped three times in reply. A narrow door I hadn't noticed opened from the outside, and a kid, even younger than the girl, came in, closing the door behind him.

"You are the American pilot?" he asked in perfect English.

"Yes, I am. Lieutenant Woodrum, 9th Air Force."

"Listen, we wanted to get you out tonight, earlier, but there is nothing we can do. There are too many German guards. They beat people up all afternoon, questioning them about you."

"Do they think I'm still in the area?" I asked.

"We think they believe you were already helped to get away, but they are holding people trying to find out something. The ones they hold know nothing. It's too dangerous to move you now. You will have to wait here and if they don't find you tonight, then you can leave tomorrow, after the guards leave."

"Whatever you say. I'll stay wherever you want."

"Here is best."

"Okay."

"Here are more cigarettes. I'll go now and come back, either during the night, or in the morning. I'll try and get you some suitable clothes, too."

"Okay, and thanks a lot."

"Bien. What is your first name?"

"Henry."

"Henri." He turned to the girl, pointing to me and said, "Henri" then for my benefit, he indicated the girl, "Nicole." He turned away and went out the side door which Nicole closed behind him. Then she started up the stairs.

"Bonsoir, Henri."

"Bonsoir, Nicole."

When she was gone, I sat on the rug, realizing how tired I was. I finished the second cigarette, took a sip of wine, and looked around for a cover. It was getting cold. I unrolled the carpet a few turns, then laid down and pulled it back over my body with just my head sticking out. It was very musty and I breathed dust for a moment or so before it settled. A sharp stab in my back reminded me of my rough landing on the roof. I stretched out, welcoming the sweet oblivion of sleep.

# Chapter 4

# THE SECOND DAY

I couldn't breathe and felt myself choking. Something was pinning me down! I panicked, why couldn't I move? I tried again, but my arms were bound to my sides. Awareness slowly returned. I opened my eyes, and even then it took a moment before reality came flooding back.

I was lying on my back, facing a cellar wall with a grime-crusted window draped with cobwebs. Faint light filtered through, casting a beam on my bedding. I realized that I'd rolled up in my rug another turn during the night—binding myself inside.

I rolled away from the window and felt the pressure on my arms release. Another roll and the rug sprang open, releasing me. I lay there, stretching full length to get the kinks out, right down to my toes. Then I rolled onto my hands and knees to stand on the dirt floor.

I brushed the carpet dust off my face, then found a rag on a shelf to wipe off the rest of the filth. I noticed the pack of Caporal cigarettes the boy had given me, and put them in my pocket, not wanting one just yet. What I really needed was coffee. My mouth was dry as sandpaper and I'd inhaled too much dust in my sleep. My back hurt even worse. My left arm ached, too, a kind of stinging sensation. I raised my shirtsleeve and saw that the inside was almost raw from the wrist to the elbow. The outer layer of flesh had been scraped away. I couldn't remember how that happened, only that I'd felt a sudden stab of pain as the last burst of flak had opened up the hole in the fuselage under my feet. How long ago was that?

I decided to investigate the basement now that it was light. An old dusty coat rack and a four-drawer dresser stood on one side of the room. I picked up a wire hanger to clear the cobwebs from the window. The sky was a swirl of orange and gray--just a little past sunrise. Outside everything was peaceful, no German voices barking orders. No birds chirping, no dogs howling, no roosters crowing. Nothing but silence. The cherry trees were silhouetted against the dawn, thin strips of tinfoil trapped there motionless. The streets were empty. That made me feel better. I hoped that they'd given up, after searching so long yesterday and posting extra guards. They probably thought I was out of the neighborhood.

I rolled the rug back into place, then picked up the butt of the cigarette I'd smoked the night before, trying to erase all traces of my stay. Only the cobweb-covered wire remained. I'd taken off my Justin flight boots last night, and now I sat down to put them back on. I stood up and did a few basic calisthenics, then began to inventory my possessions.

I had my wristwatch, not a GI issue with a sweep second hand, but a gold-plated Hamilton with a collapsible band. I put it in my shirt pocket. I also had a Zippo lighter, the pack of Caporals, my green shirt and pants, bib overalls, a comb and handkerchief, part of a sandwich and a couple of swallows of white wine remaining in the bottle. I drank the wine, the only thing to do.

My dog tags were around my neck. I remembered my class ring, Aviation Cadet Class of 43-D, April 12, 1943. I should have checked it in at Stansted. I slipped it onto the chain with my tags, wishing again that I had my escape kit. I would need some of those things, but mostly the map. I could use it right now to find out how long a walk it was going to be to Spain. That's where I intended to go as soon as I cleared this area. In training, they told us Spain would be our best bet; the Swiss border was too well guarded. Trying to remember my geography, I guessed Spain was about 500 miles away.

I lit a cigarette and sat contemplating everything I'd need to evade successfully. It was Monday, May 29, 1944 at 6:20 in the morning: the first full day of a successful evasion! Think positive, think positive.

I'd wait until people were up and about, but then, if neither Nicole nor the boy returned within an hour, I'd wait no longer. I'd go around the house to the street and walk out. I chuckled, remembering the expression, "Walk Out." There was a club, sort of like the Caterpillar Club, with a little pair of winged boots as an emblem for guys who evaded or escaped and walked safely out of the country where they were shot down. I decided I wanted a pair of those winged boots. I remembered our group's motto "See France with Colonel Vance." It looked like I was going to see it from the ground.

I began looking through the dresser drawers for clothes. I found an old beret and a couple of shirts, both too small. I dusted off the cracked and tarnished mirror, put on the beret and took a look. My God! My face was a mess, I was in need of a shave, and there were bulgy bags under my eyes that peered at me through a thick layer of sweat-streaked dust covering my face. Blood was smeared on my jaw.

I tried combing my hair, unsuccessfully because it was so matted. I tried cramming it under the sweatband of the beret, but long wisps protruded along the sides. The only other time I'd worn a beret was at the escape photo session back at Stansted, I looked much the same as I did now, because all the berets there were too small for me then too. My escape photo featured me in an old gray jacket, with no beret and my hair badly mussed. Now I was a dirty, beat-up, dissipated-looking blonde guy, appearing at least ten years older than my 25-years. I looked like a guy with a deathly hangover.

As I finished my personal inspection, I heard a noise from the stairs and looked up to see its cover being moved aside. Nicole peeked down at me and called "Hallo."

She descended, smiling. She was getting better looking each time I saw her. Someone else poked their head into the opening leaning down to speak. It was a frumpish woman in her fifties with gray hair that hadn't seen a comb this morning. She said something to Nicole who replied and then motioned me up the stairs. The woman handed me a baggy gray suit coat, tattered and worn, which looked much like the one in my escape photo.

The length was fine but it was made for someone with a much larger girth. I was skinny, with a 28" waist. All in all, it was perfect for somebody who looked like me. I'd have no trouble passing as a French bum.

"Bon," said the woman as I modeled. Nicole laughed. I was warm with the coat over the bib overalls and the green shirt. They gave me a larger beret, which fit better.

There was a small table and chair in the corner of the room with a bucket of water and washcloth, which I used to clean my face and hands. Then the woman motioned for me to sit down. She removed a napkin from the plate, revealing two pieces of toast and two hard-fried eggs. As I began to eat, she poured a cup of coffee for me.

At my first gulp, the kid I'd met the night before came in.

"Lieutenant, you must leave here alone," he said. "We cannot help you; it would be too dangerous. The search party is gone, but there are still guards on the block. We think they will soon leave. After you eat, you must go, too."

He seemed to be in a hurry, nervously glancing outside every few seconds as he spoke. As the woman fidgeted, I hurried through the meal, realizing she, too, wanted me out of the shed and away from her yard. I finished eating, then stood, asking the boy which way I should turn once I was in the street.

He pointed. "To the left from the gate. You will soon come to a main street."

"Okay," I said. "Merci." He did well for a kid his age, watching out for his family and helping an ally at the same time. He made his schoolboy English pay off pretty well too.

The old lady wiped her hands on her apron, then reached up, placed a hand behind my head and gave me a kiss—first on the right cheek, then the left, then the right again. The boy did the same thing. Nicole stood on tiptoes and kissed me on the lips. She followed me to the door and we went outside. I started around the house to the front yard. I turned once to see the little family crossing to the old man's place.

Nicole was still watching me, and I gave a little wave. She nodded in return.

I walked to the front gate, stopped to look up and down the street, then seeing no one, except a single sentry on the parapet across the way, I stepped out onto the sidewalk. I followed the boy's directions for a few feet before crossing the street diagonally to the other sidewalk. I walked several blocks without seeing anyone. But in the next block, I noticed a neatly dressed man standing on his front walk ready to pick tomatoes from vines growing there. I stopped at the gate and opened it, but he quickly trotted over and grabbed it to keep me out. We stood there for a moment holding the half-open gate between us. Then I pointed to my chest and said, "Americain."

He gasped, his face taking on a startled look and began a pushing motion, with his palms out, indicating in no uncertain terms that he didn't want a damned thing to do with me. I turned away and started walking, a little faster, grumbling to myself. He must have seen me yesterday and knew I was the parachutist.

I neared an intersection and slowed to a more normal pace, trying to remember to slouch as our instructor had advised us taller pilots. Slouching was easy, my back felt a little more comfortable that way. I wondered how far I'd have to walk today. Probably miles. I took it easy, glancing at the building and stores, most of them with empty display windows. It was 7:30 a.m. None were open yet.

Some of the homes I passed were built of stone, but most were wood-frame; all appeared to be more than thirty years old. There were vacant lots, full of trash. The street was rutted, with puddles here and there. Several German trucks passed, and a small open touring car, with square lines. The hood sloped down from the windshield to the front bumper. Two German officers sat in the back seat. I couldn't tell their rank, but one had a chest splashed with colorful ribbons. They didn't even glance in my direction.

Flower boxes decorated some windows and I heard chickens clucking. It seemed to be the kind of area our RAF instructor had described when advising us on making contact. "Go to a lower or middle-class neighborhood if you can, you'll be more likely to get help.

Try a café, garage, or other small business." I remembered those words as I noticed an old stone building set back from the street with a dingy, hand-painted sign proclaiming "GARAGE." There was a home nearby, with a walk leading to the door.

"That's for me," I thought, walking to the gate and trying to look as if I belonged there. I opened it and stepped inside. A small boy came onto the porch, watching curiously. I walked to him, pointing a finger at my chest, "I'm an American," I said.

An incredulous look came over his face and he repeated excitedly, "Americain?"

I nodded and his eyes grew larger, I knew he understood. Then, a little suspicious, he asked anxiously "Celui qui a atterri hier?"

When he realized I didn't understand, he pointed at me and asked, "Americain? Parachute?"

"Oui."

He jumped up and down excitedly, motioning for me to wait, then dashed into the house. He returned immediately with a frail old woman in a long, full-skirted black dress with a shawl over her head and shoulders. Her face was thin and wrinkled, her eyes watery but piercing. She looked like the portrait of Whistler's mother. Her hands fluttered as she groped for words, unsure, before she cocked her head to one side and asked, "Vous etes Americain?"

When I nodded, she motioned me into the house and I followed her, the boy right behind us. He shut the door while the grandma led me into the parlor, indicating I should sit. She left the room, telling the boy to follow, even though he obviously wanted to stay. They were gone only a minute or so before a pretty blond girl came into the room, smiling. I heard people talking in the next room.

"Vous etes Americain?" she asked the familiar question. I said "Oui," noticing, as she came to stand very close to me, that she had a smooth, almost porcelain complexion. Gorgeous.

"Tres bien! Tres bien." She gleamed, grabbing my hands and pumping them up and down. Then she leaned over and kissed me on the forehead. The door opened and another woman entered, followed by grandma. The fortyish woman brushed the blonde aside and faced me sternly, hands on hips as she gave me the once over. Looking me directly in the eye, she queried, "You are an American pilot?"

"Yes, I am," I told her. She was blonde too.

"Where were you shot down?"

"Near here yesterday, about 11:30 in the morning."

The kid came back, followed by a dark-haired man about the same age as the older woman, but stocky with sharp features and an aquiline nose. He stood silently while the woman continued her questioning.

"Where have you been hiding since yesterday?"

I told her about my bush, the old man, the family who helped me. I said it was six or eight blocks away, near a small railroad station. The man broke in, speaking rapidly in French. In a few short explosive sentences, the woman repeated what I'd said. The man apparently gave her some instructions because she turned to me and asked, "Do you have any papers?"

"No. No papers. But I have some escape photos."

"Show them to me."

I gave them to her. Then showed her my dog tags. The young blonde seemed convinced I was exactly who I said. She looked at the photos while the others talked together. The woman read my name aloud. To my relief they decided I was American.

"We have to be careful," she said. "You could be a German pretending to be an American. You could pass for German much easier than French."

I told them that two or three generations back, one of my ancestors came to America from either Holland or Germany, but most of my family was Scottish. Meanwhile, the old woman poured cups of coffee and pointed to a chair, telling me to sit again. Then more questions.

"How were you shot down?"

I told them it had been heavy cannon fire.

"What kind of airplane were you flying?"

"B-26, Marauder."

A young man entered the room from the garage, wiping greasy hands on a rag. He had a swarthy complexion, black hair and a pointed chin. The woman introduced him as Charles, her son-in-law and the younger woman's husband.

We shook hands, Charles grinning the whole time. The blonde's name was Yvonne. We heard someone call from outside. The English-speaking woman went onto the porch, cupped her hands, and yelled back. Through the window, I saw a dark-haired woman in a third-floor window of an apartment house across the way. She, too, cupped her hands and called.

About that time, Yvonne decided to do something about the cut on my jaw. She left the room, returning with a bottle of peroxide and some cotton. The cleaning stung a little, but I held still. Then, remembering how dirty I was, asked if I could wash my face and hands. She led me to a bathroom, gave me a bar of soap, and showed me where the towels were kept. I scrubbed as well as I could.

When I returned to the parlor, the boy was back, this time with another young man and the brunette I'd seen calling from the apartment window. Her raven hair glistened, and she positively glowed. I noticed she was also very, very pregnant. I heard them jabbering away at each other, but when I entered the clamor stopped. The brunette got up, walked over, and standing on tiptoe, kissed me. She stepped back and grinned, "Vous etes Americain?"

I couldn't help grinning back; the atmosphere in the room was pure joy. The two younger women bustled around as the older man kept asking "What did he say?" while grandma hovered on the fringe, absorbing it all. The English-speaking woman asked me if I'd slept.

"A little. I rolled up in a rug in an old, dusty cellar," I said, apologizing for my appearance. Then, curious, I asked where she'd learned English so well.

"In England. When I was young, my father worked in London."

"I'm supposed to be in London today on the second day of a two-day pass," I said wistfully.

"It's hard to believe that you just came from England. What is it like there now?"

"It's a major staging area for hundreds of thousands of troops: British, American and allied troops of many countries, including France. The island is overloaded with them. It's become a gigantic airbase—airfields everywhere—as well as a German target. There was a 200-plane raid last time I was in London."

The English-speaking woman, her name was Renee, translated for the others. As she explained, her husband, Antoine, walked over to the sideboard and pulled out a bottle and some glasses. He came back to the table and poured two drinks, handing one to me and leaving it to the others to fill their own.

"Vive l'Amerique!" he toasted.

We tossed them off. It was smooth cognac; I could feel it all the way to my toes. It reminded me of the three-star they made at Shewan-Jones winery in Lodi, California, which I'd visited many times before the war. Antoine filled them again. This time I made the toast. I held up the glass and said, "Vive la France." They nodded, pleased, and we clinked the rims of our glasses.

The brunette must have felt left out because she took the bottle, poured a glass, and drank both toasts, quickly and by herself, while the others laughed, kidding her. Charles went to the kitchen, came back with a water glass which he filled about half-full with cognac and sat there smiling, sipping it slowly. The boy was still grinning, thrilled about the sudden appearance of an American flyer in his home.

The two younger women pulled their chairs as close as they could get to mine. Jeanne, the brunette, leaned over and started combing back my hair with her fingers, smiling, humming a little tune, between frequent sips from her second glass of cognac.

Antoine began asking questions for Renee to translate. "How many sorties have you flown?"

"Yesterday was my 35$^{th}$. I guess it was really 34 1/2."

"Where do you live in the United States?"

"It's a small town in Northern California -- Redding, about 250 miles north of San Francisco."

"Ahhh. San Francisco." They all recognized San Francisco, even the way I said it. The brunette asked a question. Renee shot her a withering glance and said something, but the brunette only giggled. Then Renee gestured with a fluttering of her hands as if embarrassed, and asked, "She wants to know if you are married?"

I laughed. "No, I'm not."

I thought for a moment as Renee said "Non," then I asked, "What did you tell her when she asked?"

She grinned, "I said she should remember her condition."

I laughed, "Maybe she doesn't know mine."

Then Renee took charge. Leading me down the hall to the bathroom, she gave me clean towels and a razor. She said there was plenty of hot water and directed me to take a leisurely bath.

When she left, I put the stopper in the tub and started filling it. I stripped off my clothes and got in, easing down full length, absorbing the warmth, feeling good. I lay there soaking for several minutes before scrubbing. The white-tiled tub had a shower attachment with a flexible hose so I washed my hair.

My arm burned where it was scraped; it was still raw and oozing blood. I pressed toilet paper on it when I got out of the tub and the bleeding stopped. I also noticed a big, painless bruise on my left thigh. I probably hit it going out the nose wheel hatch. I toweled dry and lathered my face, being careful to leave a space around the cut on my jaw. The razor was sharp and when I finished, there was a little island of lather around the cut. I examined it in the mirror and saw only a thick, red line, crusting over. The alcohol and the peroxide had done the job.

I combed my hair and dressed in the green slacks and shirt. I stuffed the beret in my hip pocket. It was almost 11:00 when I started back down the hall, feeling a lot better. My first 24 hours of evasion were almost complete.

As I reached the room where the others waited, I noticed another man had joined them. I paused before entering.

"It's all right, lieutenant. This man is our friend. We thought you might be hungry, and he has brought something to eat."

The man stood and bowed. Awkwardly, I returned the greeting and we shook hands. He was about 5-foot-4 and had to look up at me. He wore gray trousers, black shoes, white socks, white shirt, black bow tie, and a white apron, its strings tied in front. He sported a thin black mustache and wore a straw hat with a flat brim, the kind popularized by Maurice Chevalier. They were also worn by butchers in the States, and I guessed this guy might be a butcher too. His apron was soiled with blood where he'd wiped his hands. He spoke slowly, Renee translating.

"He wants to know if you are really an American pilot."

I faced the man, maintaining eyeball contact. "Oui," I said, nodding, "I am an American pilot from California." His eyes widened.

"He says that if you fly airplanes you must see all sorts of preparations back in England. He listens to the BBC and the American station and they both say there will be an invasion soon. He would like to know about that."

I thought a moment as the man stood there attentively. I can't say too much, I thought. He's heard our propaganda, but I didn't know how far to go.

"Tell him the invasion will come. They say it'll be soon. General Eisenhower is the commander. What you've heard is true."

As Renee translated, almost triumphantly, the man grinned broadly and began talking excitedly, with gestures.

"He asks, can you guess how soon?"

"Well, if I had to guess, I'd say within a month."

The man was ecstatic. Papa, sensing this was the time for more celebrating, handed a full glass to the butcher and another to me. The other men filled their own. We tossed them off neat. The man reached for a package he had placed beside his chair. Turning, he extended it to me, uttering two words.

"Eat well," Renee translated. She thanked the man and I added "Merci." At the door, the butcher pumped my hand and then stepped jauntily up the street toward his shop. He probably brought the meat personally to make sure he wasn't being conned. He seemed satisfied when he left.

"He told us that he saw you in the parachute yesterday, near where you landed. He said four others were captured. Another officer was taken away in a truck," Renee said.

"He saw only four?"

"He saw only you and the other officer. But others said there were four."

I wondered what happened to my other crewmembers. We rejoined the others; I took a seat in a big leather chair. Antoine sat at my left with the cognac on a small table between us. The boy sat at my feet, looking and listening, not missing a word. The woman took the meat into the kitchen.

Grandma came back and joined us, her scarf and shawl removed to reveal long hair hanging loosely. Antoine poured another cognac and I decided it better be my last. I sipped it this time. When he asked if I wanted more, I said no, making a circling motion with my finger by my head. He laughed, recognizing the gesture.

The two girls came back to set the dining room table, and we took our seats there. They brought a tureen of thick vegetable soup. When that was gone, they brought the butcher's meat—cold, thinly sliced roast pork—as well as fried potatoes, carrots in a savory sauce, coffee, and some good red wine. I cleaned my plate hungrily. I thanked them for the meal and complimented Renee.

"We are as happy as you are. Before you came, we were just going to have soup, but then we thought the butcher might have some unrationed meat. Do you have rationing in America, too?"

"Yes," I said. "Everything is rationed."

I drank the last of the coffee and smoked a cigarette as the girls cleared the table. Renee grew pensive and asked where I intended to go. I told her I was heading to Spain, but I needed a map. I thought I'd try to learn as much from her as I could. It might be a while before I met someone else who could speak English.

"I think I'll have a better chance getting to Spain than to Switzerland. I'll leave soon; I don't want to place you in further jeopardy. If you have a map, I'll start right away. I didn't see much German traffic along the road."

"It is a great distance and a very unsafe journey for you with all the Germans," she said.

"Yes, but I was told not to stay very long with anyone until I reached the Underground, that they would try to get us out."

Her eyes lit up.

"Do you know anyone in the Underground?" I asked.

"Perhaps. Let us think about it. What else did they say?"

"To avoid Paris at all costs."

"Where? Paris?" She looked puzzled. "I don't know Paris."

"Paris. You know—your capital city."

"Oh," she laughed. "I can't pronounce it that way, even in English. I always think of it in French -- Paree!"

As she spoke, I remembered the old World War I song, "How You Gonna Get 'em Back On the Farm, After They've Seen Paree?"

"How far are we from Paris? I asked.

"Not far. Just a few miles downriver."

We began discussing a route. She said the hardest part would be crossing bridges. Most were guarded by Germans. It would be best, she said, to contact the Underground and get forged papers.

"We are almost a suburb of Paris," she said. "I'll see if we can get in touch with someone. There are those we think are in the Underground, but we do not know for sure." She went to the bookcase for a map, which she unfolded on the table. Looking it over, my guess of 500 miles seemed pretty close.

I decided to start by heading southwest. Renee suggested I go toward Paris and cross the Seine at the first unguarded bridge in the city. She showed me where it was. When the girls came back into the room, she told them I was leaving. Jeanne kissed me goodbye. Then Andre put his hands on my shoulders and gave me the three kisses on the cheek.

"Au revoir," he said gruffly.

They started back to their apartment. Renee made the boy stay in the house while she and Antoine talked. They knew a family who might help me with Underground contacts. Renee was going to ride ahead of me on her bicycle. She'd establish contact then give me a signal.

On their advice, I left the overalls there. I also removed the khaki tie, leaving my shirt open at the neck. As I put on the old coat, Yvonne came from the kitchen and gave me a goodbye kiss. Antoine was next, and gave me the hug and three kisses which I returned as Renee told me that was the thing to do. Even grandma gave me a kiss and a quiet word Renee said meant "until later."

They lined up to bid farewell to a stranger, a man from an Army they knew existed, but hadn't yet seen. They knew we hated the Germans, too, and that was good enough for them. We had a common enemy and they were happy to assist anyone fighting this foe. And, besides, they now knew the invasion was in the works. Saying goodbye, I felt a little sentimental. They were doing all they could to help me, risking their own lives. I'd known them only a few hours, but it seemed like forever.

Antoine stood on the porch and shooed the other four back inside as I followed Renee down the walk. As she mounted her bicycle, I waved back to the others. She was pedaling slowly a hundred yards ahead. I kept a brisk pace, feeling exuberant. I was already in my second day of evasion, I'd been well fed, bathed and was clean-shaven. I had a map and a chance at establishing an Underground contact. I remembered the RAF briefing officer. He was right: the garage certainly was the best place to ask for assistance.

I soon realized that I'd downed a lot of cognac. I wasn't drunk, but glad I stopped when I did. Just get through the day, I thought. I felt confident that most French people would help me, and the morning's tenseness gave way to a "what the hell," attitude. The sky was clear blue. This was going to be a good day. The farther I walked, the fewer homes I saw, and more vacant lots. The homes were older and a little run down. Renee passed an intersection ahead, then circled back to stop when a young couple riding a bicycle called to her.

Two men and a boy came out of a driveway and turned down the sidewalk toward me. As they neared, one of the men said "Bon jour." I nodded, smiling, and walked on. I could see Renee watching that exchange nervously from her vantage point ahead.

A gleaming German staff car, a big convertible sedan, came down the street, turning at the corner where Renee was standing. Two officers rode in the back, side by side, their elegant uniforms loaded with medals. One of them wore a sash diagonally across his chest. They were engaged in animated conversation and paid no attention to me or anyone else.

Ahead, the young couple moved up the hill slowly, the boy pushing the bike with the girl walking alongside. As I joined Renee, she spoke softly.

"These are friends of my daughter. They know someone with Underground contacts who will help you. It is luck to meet them, they are better for help than the people I was taking you to."

"What do you want me to do?" I asked.

"Just follow them up the street. About three blocks. There are other people who speak English and will help you."

"Listen. I want to thank you for everything. I hope we can meet again."

"Perhaps. Good luck, Henri."

"Thanks. For you, too." She gave a little smile and pedaled away. I walked up the hill toward the couple waiting at the edge of the road. When I reached them, the young man had a question.

"Papier?"

"No. No papier." He seemed reluctant to say more, but finally said, "Follow."

I nodded and walked behind them as they rode up the hill. Gradually, they gained distance on me and as they neared the top, they moved faster. When I reached the top, I saw them at least two hundred yards ahead. They kept on for another block or so where they parted, the girl continuing on as the young man leaned his bicycle against a building and disappeared inside.

I had to trust his judgment. I kept a steady pace, still slouching. I walked slower as I neared the building he'd entered, hoping to delay my arrival until I had some sign from him. Just then, he reappeared, and went to his bicycle. He rode over to me and stopped.

"That café. Go inside," he said. "A man will help."

I walked on at a normal pace. When I came abreast of the building, I saw a sign on the window in faded, but still legible letters: "Café-Vin." The entrance was on the corner at a 45-degree angle to the street. Three steps led up to a massive set of double doors with wrought iron handles of matching size. As I reached for the handle, the door burst open forcefully, the bulky figure of a stocky man in a black uniform filling the doorway. He seemed as surprised as I was, so I stood back, gave a little motion with my hand as if to say "after you," and he muttered a quiet "pardonnez-moi" as he passed.

The piping on his uniform was silver and red, but it didn't look like any German uniform I knew of or had ever seen, but just seeing him there really shook me up. The man was perspiring heavily, red-faced and puffing. He stopped to mop his brow with a handkerchief as three more uniformed men followed him through the door into the street. They walked across the street and climbed into a parked sedan. As they drove away, I grasped the handle again, opened the door, and went in.

A man stood to one side. He was square-jawed, in the mid-50s, wearing a black beret in stark contrast with the neatly combed silver-grey hair visible beneath. He wore a white pullover shirt, dark pants, and black sandals. He was handsome enough to be a movie star. He closed and locked the door behind me, then turned with his hand extended and said, "Well, well. So, you're an American, eh? Put her there."

We shook hands vigorously, like long lost friends, his hand on my shoulder. He was smiling, showing straight white teeth. I instinctively liked the man and I was smiling, too. He jerked a thumb over his shoulder toward the bar, "Let's go in the back where we can talk." He walked around the corner of the big mahogany bar, and through a door leading to the kitchen. He motioned me to a chair.

"Come in, sit down. It's only 1:00 and we're closed until 4:30."

I was flabbergasted. His English was as American as mine, slang where it was supposed to be used, and his casual greeting, under the circumstances, amazed me.

"By the way," he asked, "What's your name?"

"Woodrum. Lieutenant Henry Woodrum."

"Woodrum?"

"Yeah, with rum on the end."

He turned as a woman came in from the backyard carrying a bundle of clothes from the line.

"Maria," he said, "I want you to meet an American pilot. His name is Henri."

We shook hands and exchanged hellos. She seemed several years younger than the man. Her brunette hair was free of gray, and her face almost unlined. She was still slim, and I thought she must have been a beauty at 25, especially after I got a look at her beautiful smile.

"Your English -- it's so good. Are you American?"

"No," he laughed. "We are Basque, but we spent a lot of time in New York."

"That explains it. I've met three people who speak English. The young man who brought me here, a kid I met last night, and the woman this morning who speaks English as they do in London. But hearing you talk like an American was a big surprise."

"Well, we're glad you found us. Where are you from?"

"Northern California. Town called Redding. Two hundred and fifty miles north of San Francisco. By the way, what's your name?"

"Oh! Sorry about that. Carlos. Carlos Filipotto." He paused, then said, "San Francisco, eh? That's a beautiful city. We worked there for a while, a month or two, I guess."

"What kind of work did you do?"

"I had a rumba band. Maria sang and took care of the books, you know? Mostly we stayed at the Waldorf-Astoria in New York."

I wanted to hear more, but Maria, obviously nervous, had her own questions.

"Were you shot down?"

Yes. Yesterday morning about 11:15."

"Oh, I remember. The parachutes came right over our yard. Where did you go" How did you get away from the Germans?"

I understood why she took care of the business; she was inspecting me closely, speculating that I might be a plant. I briefly told them how I hid in the bush, spent the night in the cellar, and how I ended up at their café.

"You have no papers?" she asked after I provided my account.

"No. But I have escape photos they took in England. We carry them on every mission. And my ID tags. I'll need photos for false papers when I get into the Underground, I suppose."

"Yes, you will."

"By the way, who were those men who came out the door as I was coming in? For a moment, I thought they were Germans."

"They are firemen. The first one was the local chief. They just attended the funeral of their friend who died fighting a fire three days ago after a bombing raid. They stopped here for a drink, and they all had one too many. I hope we don't have another fire now."

"I was wondering why Carlos was speaking English," Maria mused. "I heard him talking to you and I thought it must be the German girl."

"The German girl?"

"Yes. She's really Austrian but she was drafted into the German Army. She works in an underground assembly plant the Germans have near here. She can't speak French, but speaks English very well. She sometimes comes with one or two German soldiers and they all wait here for the Paris bus because the stop is just across the street. She orders for all of them and they have a drink or two while they wait. Sometimes she just stays here and talks with us."

I leaned back in the chair and began to relax. Carlos poured three glasses of DuBonnet. It tasted great. Maria caught my mood shift as I relaxed.

"You must be exhausted after spending the night in a bush and a dirty old cellar surrounded by Germans," she laughed. "That's a good one. Come with me and I'll take you to the extra bedroom upstairs where you can sleep."

I followed her to the second-floor bedroom. There were two windows in the room, one facing the backyard, the other onto the side street. Maria pulled the blackout shades, darkening the room nicely. "Sleep well, Henri. You seem very tired now."

She left and went back downstairs and I took off my clothes, hung them in the wardrobe, and crawled into bed. As tired as I was, I couldn't go to sleep immediately. I wondered and worried about my crew, and considered how lucky I was to have survived the first 24 hours as an evadee - not a captive!

When I awoke after having slept in a bed for the first time in two days, I stretched luxuriously, and for a moment, my back didn't hurt a bit. The sore spot on my left arm itched and stung, but that was all. I must be getting used to being on the lam.

The room was pitch black. I lifted the curtain and saw it was almost dark. I'd either slept around the clock to dawn Tuesday, or it was dusk on Monday. I dressed. Looking around, I noticed a bookcase crammed with books and a pile of magazines on the top shelf. I was surprised to see many of them were American magazines. Ladies Home Journal, Better Homes and Gardens, Good Housekeeping, and a few issues of the Saturday Evening Post.

Some of the books had English titles. The first one, old and worn, was Thackery. There was a Dickens, and Hemingway's "For Whom the Bells Toll." I'll have to read that while I'm here, I thought. It would be appropriate, living as an evadee in a bar in occupied France with Germans searching for me. Another thick book in English drew my attention. It turned out to be a novel of espionage featuring a U.S. Army Intelligence officer named Matthew Steel. The first few pages introduced the intrepid major, a nasty Nazi colonel, a British industrialist, and his beautiful daughter.

There was a soft tap on the door. When I opened it, Maria was there. "You slept so soundly we thought you might sleep through the night, but we heard you stirring around just now. Will you come downstairs and have something to eat with us?"

"I'm not really very hungry, Maria. I had a good meal about 11:00 this morning."

"That's all right. Eat what you can."

Carlos was waiting for us at the kitchen table, which was already set for three with a soup bowl and chunks of bread at each place, and a bottle of red wine in front of Carlos.

"Try some wine, Henri," he said, filling my glass. We clinked the rims as Maria placed a tureen of creamy, vegetable soup on the table and began ladling it into our bowls. It was delicious and I ate a full bowl.

"I'm glad you woke up," Carlos said. "We wanted you to eat something, and besides, we have some news."

"I hope its good news."

Carlos nodded, sopping up the last drops of soup with his bread. "We have a friend who works for the Red Cross. We always thought he was in the Underground, but didn't know for sure. He wasn't home when I went to see him today, but his wife said they can help you. First, they will get some papers for you, then turn you over to the Underground. He will come here tomorrow."

"That's great news, Carlos! I have the photos and my dog tags, but that's all. I'm glad they will help."

"She said the photos are the main thing. The Germans watch the photo shops."

Maria took away the soup bowls and brought a crisp lettuce salad with a zesty oil-and-vinegar dressing—the best I ever tasted. I ate every bite. She was probably beginning to wonder how much I ate when I was really hungry. I told her how good it was, and she smiled, but said nothing.

I realized they were probably serving a bigger meal than usual because of me and I hoped I wasn't using too much of their food supply. Then Maria brought each of us a plate of chicken served in a sauce, potatoes and carrots sautéed in wine and more bread. There was no way I could pass that up.

"Maria, I know I told you I wasn't hungry, but this food is delicious. I'm going to make myself a liar and eat."

They both ate more as I finished and sipped my wine. I asked about their life in New York.

"It's a long story," Carlos started. "From 1914 until 1918 I was in the Navy, on a cruiser in the South Atlantic. We often spent shore leave in Buenos Aires and I fell in love with the place. I was already a musician, and I learned all those South American tunes—you know, rumbas, tangos, and sambas. When I came back to France, Maria and I were married and went back to Buenos Aires where we stayed until 1927."

"By that time, I had my own band, rumbas were a craze in the United States, and someone came out from New York to hire us to play the big hotels. We spent most of our time at the Waldorf-Astoria. After our first engagement there, they wanted us back. Sometimes we'd tour other cities, but we always went back to the Waldorf. We made so much money— I hate to tell you how much—but I lost a lot of it in the 1929 crash."

"We still made good money until we left in 1934, but jazz was the big thing then. Swing, too."

"Oh, well," he sighed, "we always had a nice apartment, and were always having parties and enjoying ourselves. I'll show you some photographs from those days before you leave."

"I'd like to see them. I always wanted to play in a big band myself," I said.

"Is that so?" He looked up, interested. "What instrument do you play?"

"Tenor sax and clarinet."

"Oh -- swing, huh?"

"Yes," I laughed at the way he emphasized swing. "I've played in some pretty good bands, but nowhere like the Waldorf."

We talked about music, then Carlos changed the subject.

"How did they shoot you down, Henri?"

I told them the entire story. Carlos was especially interested in the barrages, because he'd seen them, and couldn't understand why more aircraft weren't shot down. He reacted violently when I mentioned the Germans shooting at me while I was in the chute, muttering a few choice cuss words I didn't know. I finished by saying I didn't know if we hit the bridge or not.

Neither of them said anything for a moment, then Carlos asked, "Did you say it was upstream from here?"

"Yes, it was. I think it was near St. Germain-en-Laye."

"Well, I think you got it. One section is in the river. It won't be used for a while, but the Germans already have slave labor gangs working on it."

"I'm glad it's down. There are a lot more down between here and Le Havre, too. They'll have to keep plenty of people busy to get them all repaired."

"Do you ever bomb the self-propelled bomb sites?" he asked.

"The things with ski-launching ramps? Yes, we have. We've destroyed a lot of them."

"Remember what we said about the underground plant near here? That's what they assemble."

"Self-propelled bombs? Hitler's secret weapon? Well, I'll be damned. I thought they assembled them at the sites. We call them "no-ball" targets," I told him. "Didn't you say the Austrian girl works there?"

"Yes, she works in administration, but she doesn't like the place and neither do the soldiers. But for them, it's a lot better than the Russian front. They still grumble a lot, though."

"What's their problem?"

"Most of them are homesick, just young guys. They are sick of the war and sick of Hitler. It's worse for their families at home than it is for them here. They seldom get bombed, but their relatives are bombed all the time. The morale is terrible."

"Germany has been taking a pounding lately, all right, and it'll get a lot worse.

Maria served coffee. "This isn't real coffee, Henri," she said apologetically. "Its ersatz made from grain, but it's better than nothing." I sipped the coffee and found she was right, but it wasn't bad for a substitute.

Carlos opened a cupboard, revealing a small radio receiver. He turned it on and as the tubes warmed up, tuned in the Yankee Doodle station of the American Armed Forces Network. They were announcing the results of 8th Air Force bombing in Germany and said the 9th hit marshalling yards in Northern France and "no-ball" targets in the Pas de Calais. I remembered recent missions flown against that area as I listened, for it was a heavily defended area now, not like it had been earlier. One of my good friends had been killed on a "no-ball" target in the Pas de Calais. A bombardier, he was the only one hit in that ship. Flak hit the side of his head, just beneath the rim of his steel helmet, killing him instantly.

We listened to the report in silence. When it was over, I asked Carlos how he thought the Underground would take me out.

"I have no idea. Perhaps through Spain," he said, and then added, "While you are here, you better stay upstairs when the bar is open tomorrow. There are some French people, not many, who might report you. We have no way of knowing who they are."

We talked for a while longer, then I went upstairs. I couldn't fall asleep immediately, so I just lay there, thinking about my chances for a successful evasion. The odds certainly seemed to have improved. I was ready to take it one day at a time now, more determined than ever to sweat it out.

## Chapter 5

# THE BAR AT CARRIERES-SUR-SEINE

I pulled open the blackout curtain, revealing streaky layers of stratus clouds forming a low, gray overcast. It had rained during the night, and now a light breeze blew the clouds lazily across the horizon. It was Tuesday, May 30, 1944, and I was nearing the 48-hour point in my evasion.

I stepped into my trousers, pulled on a T-shirt and patted barefooted into the bathroom to shave. Then I went back to the room and sat in a chair by the window, resuming the spy thriller.

Maria tapped on the door and I slipped on my boots to follow her downstairs. She hummed happily as she cooked breakfast. Even the erzats coffee tasted good. I chatted with Maria, then went to talk to Carlos while he was swamping out behind the bar. I saw a push broom leaning against the wall and little piles of sawdust sprinkled around the floor. I picked up the broom and began sweeping. The windows were shuttered, making it impossible for anyone outside to see into the bar.

"You don't have to do that," he said.

"I know, Carlos, but I want to do something."

When I finished, I sat at the bar, but a knock on the door sent me scurrying through the kitchen and upstairs to my room, nodding at Maria as I passed. I sat down to read some more. Throughout the morning, I heard vehicles in the street and peeked out to see German army trucks parked at the post office, diagonally across the street from the bar. German soldiers and a few French civilians were hauling bags and boxes inside.

While sitting there, I decided this might be a good time to cut back on my smoking. Tobacco was scarce, and I needed to get in better physical shape anyway.

Just after 1:00, a mid-30s model, 4-door Citroen sedan parked at the curb below my side window. An attractive woman stepped out onto the sidewalk, waiting for the driver. He came around, took her by the arm, and walked to the bar's corner entrance. He was a tall, husky fellow, carrying a briefcase in one hand and a tan raincoat slung over his shoulder. He wore a rumpled suit with a white shirt, tie, and black beret. Black-framed spectacles rested on his nose. A few minutes later, Maria came to my door.

"The bar is closed for the afternoon. Monsieur Claude is here to talk with you. Please come downstairs, Henri."

I followed her to the kitchen where the man and woman were sitting at the table drinking coffee. Carlos was leaning against the door. They looked up as I entered, and Carlos stepped forward to introduce me. We eyed each other speculatively as Carlos introduced the man simply as Claude, ignoring the woman. I knew Claude would ask a lot of questions and I hoped I could answer them.

"Lieutenant, it's nice to meet you. The rest of your crew were captured, so you are really lucky.'

"Are they all safe? I heard yesterday they saw only four other chutes."

"No, they misinformed you. All the others were captured."

I guess my relief showed because Claude smiled and said, "That's good news, eh?"

"It certainly is. I was worried about the missing man. Do you know where the Germans took them?"

"To an interrogation center in Paris. Now they will be taken first to Frankfurt and then to a camp."

"Do you know where I landed?"

"Yes, we know."

"Is that in Carrieres-sur-Seine, too?"

"Yes, it is. Now I must ask you some questions. First, do you have any papers?"

That had become an all too familiar query. "No, just my escape photos and my ID tags," I said.

"Good, let me have the photos."

We went upstairs and I gave the photos to Claude. He looked them over carefully, selecting the one he thought best, a full-face shot with my hair tousled.

"What is your squadron?"

"495th Bomb Squadron…344th Bomb Group."

He sat down in the chair and began to take notes, evidently ready to finish the interrogation right there.

"Now, what was your target?"

"A bridge across The Seine, near Saint Germain-en-Laye. I think part of the name was La Fite."

"Ah. Maison Laffitte. Good. That is near Saint Germain-en-Laye. Were any other aircraft shot down?"

"My deputy flight commander was hit further downriver. We only saw three chutes leave the aircraft. I was leading what was left of our flight, but I don't know the results of the bombing—we were bailing out of the aircraft when the bombs hit."

When he asked, I gave the name of my other crewmembers, beginning with Bud Morgan. Then he asked for my parents' names. I'd wondered if he'd ask that. "Henry C. and Edith E. Woodrum."

"His name is the same as yours? Is he alive?"

"No, he suffered a coronary June 12, 1937."

Claude wrote a lengthy note. Then, "And your mother?"

"She's living in Redding."

"Where is that, Lieutenant?"

"At the head of the Sacramento Valley, 250 miles north of San Francisco."

"And what is the number of your aircraft?"

"My call sign is Y-5-T."

"What kind of escorts did you have?"

"Spits."

"Spits?" He asked quizzically.

"Yes, British Spitfires, from Number 11 Group."

"Very well. Now, one last question. Was there anything unusual about your mission?"

Unusual, let's see … Yes, there was. We were a fill-in crew and I should have been starting a two-day pass." I thought a moment. "One more thing. We dropped a plywood bomb filled with propaganda leaflets. It was supposed to fall about 100 feet then come apart, spilling papers over a large area to be read by the French people."

Claude smiled as I spoke and stopped writing. "It worked. They scattered over a several-mile-long area and a lot of them did get to the people. Do you know what they said?"

"Not all of it. Just the part about the invasion. I had one, but got rid of it."

I told him about burying it in the vineyard when the search was going on.

"You thought you would be captured them?" he asked.

"Yes, I didn't see how they could miss, but they did."

"What made you think of picking up the paint bucket?"

"You know about that?" I grinned, surprised, and told him about our instructions to do the most obvious thing.

"The leaflets told the French people to unite," Claude continued. "They also said the Germans would delay air raid alarms for the public hoping more French people would be killed, to create hatred for the allies. They also said the invasion would come soon."

"The other people asked me how soon the invasion would happen. I said I guessed it would be within a month. Really, I think it will be sooner—maybe a couple of weeks."

"Two weeks! I hope you are right."

"I do too. Would that complicate my getting out?"

"It might. But there will be a lot of confusion so it might even help. We'll just have to wait and see."

"How will I be taken out; can you tell me?"

"No. Not until these facts are checked out and we are given instructions. Even I won't know until the last minute."

"I understand." I knew they wouldn't tell me anything until they confirmed I really was Lt. Henry C. Woodrum. All I could do now was wait.

"How long will it take to confirm the information?"

"Oh, at least a day or two."

He said it casually as if it didn't make much difference, but I knew a lot of things could go wrong. Maybe I was getting paranoid. A radio message would have to be transmitted, and it would be easy to get caught that way. Someone who had helped me might inadvertently say something leading to my capture. But regardless, there was nothing to do except sweat it out.

Claude began stuffing things back into his briefcase. When he stood up, he asked if there was anything else I wanted to know before he left. He told me to sit tight and do whatever the Filipottos asked. He'd instruct them and stay in contact.

When we reached the kitchen, there was another visitor, Jacques, the guy on the bike who steered me to the bar. Carlos didn't introduce the two men and I don't think it was an oversight. Claude acknowledged him with a nod, then turning to me said, "See you in a day or two" and left with the woman, who was never introduced to any of us. I wondered about that as they got into their car and drove away.

I went back upstairs and Jacques followed me into the room. He wanted to talk about the war, curious about what was happening.

"How come you shot down?"

"Cannon fire. Many, many cannons."

"I was in a raid by B-26."

"You were? Where?"

"Near Mantes-la-Jolie. Ten days ago." In a broken mixture of English and French, he told me that he and his wife were having a picnic and fishing near a bridge over the Seine near Mantes-la-Jolie. It was mid-afternoon and since they were in the country, they ignored the air raid alarms when they sounded. But aircraft flew right overhead since the bridge was the target.

The young couple ran up the grass-covered slope of the riverbank to hide. They weren't hit in the brief attack, though the concussion was terrible. His wife was pregnant, and when they returned home that evening, she miscarried. He was taking her home from the doctor when he met Renee and me yesterday.

He showed no sign or remorse as he described the events, but as I listened, I hoped I wasn't involved in that one. Thinking back, I remembered bombing Mantes-la-Jolie only once, the evening before I was shot down. I thought about the other bridges and marshalling yards, thinking how it was for the French to be bombed by their allies. This was the second bombing resulting in personal loss mentioned to me, the other was the fireman killed fighting a fire caused by an air raid.

"I bombed the bridge at Mantes-la-Jolie the night before last. No, let's see, it was Saturday evening, about six o'clock."

"We were there a week before that."

Jacques asked lots of questions, many American things puzzled him. First, he wanted to know if I knew any movie stars. I told him I'd met a few and he asked me to name them. When I mentioned Victor McLaughlin, he became excited, having seen and enjoyed "The Informer."

Then he wanted to know about gangsters, especially Al Capone. When I told him Capone used to do my laundry, he wanted details. I'd almost forgotten about it, but laughed as I remembered the story.

I was in Citizen's Military Training Corps, a summer training program for officer candidates. The first year I was stationed at the Presidio of Monterey and the second at Fort Funston. Our laundry was taken to the federal penitentiary at Alcatraz where Al Capone was an inmate working in the laundry.

Naturally, the GIs forgot the other cons and said Capone did their laundry. I told Jacques I didn't know anything about gangsters except what I saw in the movies.

When he left, I rested for a while and was ready to go when Carlos called me to join him for a drink in the bar after he closed for the afternoon. He put a bottle of DuBonnet on the bar and came around to sit on a stool alongside me.

"Carlos, how do the Germans treat the French people? We hear all kinds of stories in England and back in the States."

"Not too bad in a lot of ways. But if you are Jewish, or in the Underground, or if they even think you are, they come and get you, and before very long, you are dead."

"How do they do all this?"

"Every so often, they round-up people on the streets, and if they get anyone they think is Jewish or suspected of being in the Underground, they ship them off to slave labor camps and nobody ever hears of them again. Usually, they torture them for information and then kill them."

"If you and Maria are caught, will you be tortured?"

"Yes, but we don't know much so they'll probably kill us right away."

"I hope I don't stay here very long. Then we won't have to worry about anything like that happening."

"Never mind. I'm getting tired of this bullshit occupation anyway, and I'm glad to have the chance to do something. I owe the United States a lot. Maria and I both do," he said.

Suddenly, the main entrance to the bar opened and a hard-faced, young German soldier came in. Carlos had forgotten to lock the door. The German didn't even look at us before turning to close it. Carlos and I glanced at each other, startled, but had no time to react. Carlos gave me a little shrug while the German's back was turned, but when the guy started walking to the bar Carlos slid off the stool and faced him.

"Well, hello," he said. "How are you?"

"Gud." The German sat down at the bar four stools away from me. I sat with my glass held upright, frozen in front of my mouth. Just then, the door opened again.

A young blonde in a German Women's Army uniform came in, closing the door behind her. I drank some of the liquor, looking her over. She was slender and her uniform fit snugly, accenting a tiny waist. She was voluptuous and tall, maybe 5-foot-8. She had clear, ivory skin and a mass of flaxen hair piled high, swept up at the sides and tucked under the overseas cap pinned in place. The front of the cap was pulled over her forehead to one side, just above her right eye. I wondered if she was the English-speaking gal.

Her uniform was a light gray-green shirt and tie, a skirt of heavier material nearly the same color, ending just above her knee, and a light jacket she carried under her arm. Her uniform was spic and span, carefully pressed and tailored. On her lissome figure, even a military uniform looked good. She was a doll!

I was watching, a little tense, ready to jump the GI if he started anything. Carlos said hello to the girl in English, too. "Just a minute," he said. "I'll lock the door again. In fact, I thought it was locked. We are actually closed for another hour or so."

He gave me a blank look as he walked over to shut the door. When he came back, he took their orders and poured the drinks. They exchanged a few words, all in English. Then Carlos motioned to me and said, "By the way, my friend here also speaks a little English." They nodded to me and I nodded back while Carlos said, primarily for my benefit, "These two sometimes stop here while they wait for the bus to take them to Paris, but they don't speak French."

The man didn't look up but the girl flashed a brief smile.

"How goes everything?" Carlos asked the Germans.

"Too many bombings," grumbled the man, with a heavy accent. He wasn't any better at English than I was at French.

"Do you have pate'?" asked the girl.

"I'll see. We may have some." Carlos went to the kitchen.

The soldier poured himself another cognac. Carlos returned carrying a small plate with several thin slices of bread and a small bowl of pate' which he placed on the bar for the girl. She began spreading it on the bread.

The German finished his drink and asked how much he owed. He paid and left quickly, Carlos following to unlock the door to let him out—then locking it again.

The girl ate the pate' and sipped her wine. I nodded toward the kitchen to see if Carlos wanted me to go, he shook his head. After a bit, the girl turned toward me and asked, "Where did you learn English?"

Deciding I might as well be an expert, I said, "My father was a merchant. We lived in San Francisco for many years where I attended American schools."

"Oh, how wonderful. I hear San Francisco is beautiful."

"Yes, it is." Her English was very good, too. I wondered where she learned, so I asked.

"I studied it in school, but later I worked for an American firm in Vienna—before the war."

"Oh. Is Vienna your home? You're Austrian?"

"Yes, but I'm still in the German Army, serving in France!"

She said it emphatically, as if she really didn't like it, and I was surprised that she'd be so outspoken. We talked until she finished the pate'. Then she moved down the bar to the stool next to mine. As she perched herself there, I was thinking that nobody would ever believe me if I told them that on my third day of evasion, I passed the afternoon with a beautiful, blonde, female German soldier drinking aperitif in a small-town bar owned by two Basques who were formerly featured performers at the Waldorf. I wouldn't blame them. I didn't believe it myself.

I took a good look at her as she placed her jacket, which bore corporal's stripes, on the stool next to hers. Her skin was a little rosier than I thought at first, and her eyes were a bright, pale blue. She was a beauty and I wondered what the hell she was doing alone. She'd obviously been looking me over, too. She turned and said, "You are very fair for a Frenchman."

"Yes, I am," I said, "But you see, I'm only half French. My mother is American. Most of her ancestors were Scots, with a German branch somewhere along the way."

"Oh, I see. Did your father meet her in San Francisco?"

"Yes, he did."

"Are your parents here now?"

"My father is dead. My mother is home in San Francisco." She's getting too nosy, I thought, suddenly alarmed.

She leaned back, sighing. "It would be nice to be in San Francisco now. No war there. No German army to worry about." She paused. "People do what they want without worrying about war."

"Yes, that would be nice but they are at war, too. There's just no fighting there. But some day the war will be over."

"Perhaps, but it seems like it's gone on forever."

"You must miss Vienna."

"Oh, yes, I do. But it is bad there, too. Worse than here. All the bombings have made it very bad."

Carlos came over, leaning his forearms on the bar just opposite us. I'd forgotten all about him.

He seemed relaxed. "Do you want another glass before your bus comes?"

She looked at her watch. "Is it that late already? No, I think I better go."

She finished the wine, paid Carlos, slid off the stool, and picked up her jacket. She turned to face me. "I hope I see you again. My name is Lisa."

"I do too, Lisa. My name is Henri." I tried to imitate Carlos' pronunciation. She followed Carlos to the door, gave me a little wave as he unlocked it, then went out. Carlos quickly locked it.

"I have to be more careful. Those two weren't too bad, but we could get in trouble with others. Especially if they get drunk."

"I was ready to go to the kitchen when you introduced us. I almost passed out when you started speaking English with them, but then I remembered you talking about the German army girl. I suppose that's her? Boy, she's something."

Carlos looked me in the eye, put his hand on my shoulder, and said, "My boy, she really is." We laughed.

"I was wondering what you'd say when she asked where you learned English."

"That was sheer improvisation," I said.

"Well, you did very well. She didn't suspect a thing and I don't think it would have made any difference, anyhow."

"Maybe. She seems bitter about the Germans."

"Yes, she does. I've noticed before."

I pointed into the big room off the bar where I'd noticed a billiard table while sweeping the floors. "How about a game?"

Carlos looked at his watch and smiled. "Time for a short game."

The last time I played I was in aviation cadets but I managed a few good shots and enjoyed myself before Carlos said, "It's time to open again. You better go back upstairs."

We replaced our cues and I returned to my room. I lay on the bed reading the spy thriller. I could hear the bar come to life downstairs as people arrived. A little later an air raid alarm sounded, but I didn't hear anyone leave. After the bar closed, Maria served a bowl of soup so hearty it was all I could eat. I went back upstairs and resumed reading until I fell asleep. I decided I could get used to this new life as a non-combatant very easily.

# Chapter 6

# LISA

I wondered if my family knew I was missing. It's too soon, I decided. Perhaps by the end of the week. I remembered the first time I seriously considered the possibility of being shot down. Our early missions were milk runs, but there comes a day when you get the hell shot out of you and you think, "Whoa! Somebody could get hurt this way."

On my first three missions, no one was shot down, but on the fourth, two ships from another group were lost. During briefing the next day, I remembered that. We were going all out that day on an anniversary mission. Anything could happen.

Colonel Vance started the briefing by saying we'd be bombing the same target selected as the first B-26 target in Europe the year before when only two of the 12 ships returned. Now, every B-26 group in the 9th Air Force was going back, with at least 36 ships from each group, but with a new tactic. We'd fly at our usual medium altitude instead of the low-level run flown the first time.

Our target was the submarine base at Ijmuiden, Holland. The colonel, who wore the biggest set of eagles I ever saw, was a darned good commander and everybody liked him, but he wouldn't stand for any nonsense. If he thought we weren't lined up properly on the bomb run, he'd circle back to make a second run, the hell with the flak. That day he was all business, as usual.

"We are really going to hit the Huns, boys." He liked to use World War I terms like "Huns." Nearly everyone I knew called them Nazis or Krauts.

"Last year, we sent 12 ships to this target and most of them were shot down. Now we're going back. But today it's a max effort with every B-26 we can get off the ground taking part. We'll stay at our normal altitude and be on our bomb run before we even make enemy landfall. Our initial point is a spot over the sea about here." He tapped a place on the map about three miles off shore.

"At bombs away, we'll be right here. All we have to do is make one descending turn and come back across the channel. I'm going as pilot on the lead ship. I can tell you that there'll be more B-26s in the air than you've ever seen in your life. Now, let's get on with the briefing."

The operations office took over and everything looked good except the weather forecast predicting heavy cloud cover by our expected time of return. Somebody asked him if they were sure the targets had only fifty guns. He said "most likely." It occurred to me they might be wrong.

What surprised me was that for our group, getting there turned out to be almost as easy as they promised it would be. I could see the target all the way in since we were in the middle of the whole 9th Air Force line of attacking groups. As each group bombed, the sky over the target grew blacker and blacker with bursting flak.

But as we turned after bombs away, we took a hit somewhere in the left wing. We felt the jolt, then saw the left aileron fluttering like mad. I decreased air speed across the channel, unable to stay in formation at the reduced speed. Gaggles of B-26s milled around under the overcast, so when I saw aircraft from the 386th on their final approach at Great Dunmow, I eased in with them and landed there, not wanting to chance maneuvering in bad weather at low altitude with an aileron that might come off at any moment.

All the debriefing teams were busy with their own crews, but while we waited, a nearby colonel approached me. His name was Maitland.

"What group are you from, Lieutenant?"

"The 344th at Stansted, sir. Had some damage so we landed here."

"What's the trouble?"

"The left ailerons loose, hit just after bombs away."

When he learned the officers conducting the debriefing were all busy, he said he'd debrief us himself. I kept going over the possibilities and finally, it clicked. A lieutenant of the same name made the first flight from Oakland to Hawaii—Wheeler Field—just a month or so after Lindberg's flight in 1927. I tried to recall the fuzzy details. A flight from a continent to a tiny island in the middle of an ocean is much more difficult than a flight in the other direction.

When he finished de-briefing, the colonel made sure our aircraft was being repaired. I approached him just as he prepared to leave. "Colonel, were you the pilot of the Fokker tri-motor which flew the first Oakland-to-Hawaii flight?"

He stopped and turned back, smiling broadly. "I thought that flight was forgotten a long time ago. Yes, I made that flight."

I told him I lived in Northern California and read about it. I asked him about his radio problem. He said it was one of the first uses of a beamed radio signal, but because his receiver failed, the system was useless. In finding a small island in the middle of an ocean, the navigational margin of error was substantial, but his navigator got him in without the radio. The flight lasted over twenty-five hours.

"Oakland was really a busy place then, you know," he said. "Kingsford-Smith took off from there, too. We chose Oakland because of its long runways. With our take-off weight, that was important."

Now, I wondered how Maitland felt when he realized his radio was useless and he'd passed the point of no return, wondering if they could ever find the island. He needed luck, and it reminded me that I too needed plenty of good fortune.

That was on my mind when Carlos gave me some alarming news.

A man came to the bar, he said, who knew I was there. Someone had talked. Carlos trusted this man, and was sure he'd keep the secret, but he worried someone else might soon find out. He said Claude didn't trust Jacques.

Carlos woke me early the next morning, poured me a cup of coffee and led me to an old shed in the backyard. It was much cleaner than the one I stayed in the first night, but still dismal. "Oh, well, you can't win 'em all," I said to myself.

"Don't say anything or go outside during the day," Carlos warned. "It will be as if you were never here. There's an old toilet through that door."

After he left, I took stock of the place. Garden tools, some broken furniture, cobwebs, old American magazines. As I expected, the toilet was an old one-holer. The next fifteen hours or so were frustrating. I looked out every time I heard a German truck roll into the post office across the street, apprehensive at what might happen next. But after the first hour or so, I just played the old waiting game, leafing through the magazines.

About noon, Carlos brought me a bowl of soup, hidden in the bottom of an old bucket, covered tightly with a cloth. It was midnight before I was allowed into the kitchen again. They told me there were no signs of trouble and I could sleep inside. While I ate, Maria mentioned with a grin that Lisa had returned that day and asked about me. I didn't know if that was good or bad. After dinner, I went upstairs, bathed, and drifted off to sleep.

Carlos took me back to the shed about 5:30 the next morning. This time a light rain was falling. It was even more boring that day and the time dragged minute by minute. When he closed the bar after lunch, Carlos came to my hiding place and told me I could go back to my room. When I went inside, Claude was there.

"Hello, lieutenant. Your notes have been verified. We have news. You will probably leave tomorrow or the next day."

"That's great," I said with obvious relief.

"We will come for you in a car. Your papers will be ready, but we don't know yet what your new name will be. It just depends. When we travel, you will ride in the back seat of the car I drove the other day. The girl who came with me then will be with us. Her name is Colette."

"You must not speak when anyone else is near. Never! When we are in the car by ourselves, you may talk. I don't think we will run into any Germans, but if we do, remember—be quiet!"

"I'll remember," I made a mental note to watch my tongue.

As Maria headed upstairs, Carlos and I went into the bar for an aperitif. He made sure the door was locked before we sat down. He made little circles on the bar with his glass between sips, saying nothing, wistfully swirling the wine in his glass with each twirl.

"You know, Henri," he mused, "I think Lisa has the hots for you."

I laughed; I hadn't heard that expression for a long time.

"No, I mean it," Carlos insisted. "When she came back, she wasn't on her way to Paris. She came to see you. She said she wanted to speak English." He paused, then added slyly, "But I speak English."

"She's a beautiful woman, Carlos, but after all, she's in the German army. There's too many things that can go wrong."

"Yes, that's true, but listen, there are plenty of French women going out with German soldiers. There is a club in Paris called the Scheherazade that is packed every night. Mostly German officers with French women. And there is plenty of collaboration with the Germans in other ways. I don't think we have to worry. She's not interested in telling anyone else who you are, even if she knew."

"You think she'll come back?"

"She said she would. Tell you what—if she's alone I'll let her in, and we'll stay closed until the usual time, but if there is anyone with her, I'll say we are closed until this evening."

I looked at Carlos suspiciously. "You're fixing me up, aren't you?"

"Hell yes." He laughed, his eyes twinkling merrily.

I sipped the chilled aperitif, then poured another glass and went into the billiard room. Along the outside wall was a long booth with an upholstered seat with room for a number of people to sit. There was a low table in front of it, coffee-table height. All of the windows in the room were shuttered.

It occurred to me that as a "Frenchman" I didn't have a full name— just Henri. I had to invent one. I said a few just to see how they sounded, but none were any good. Then I remembered Charles Boyer.

I went back to the bar and sat with Carlos. I was still on the second aperitif when someone knocked lightly on the door. Carlos peeked through the blinds into the entry.

"It's her," he called softly. "She's alone."

He unlatched the bolt, opened the door for Lisa, and then locked it immediately. She waited, facing Carlos, and they walked together back to the bar. She was smiling as she approached, as tall and gorgeous as I remembered.

"Hello, Henri. I'm glad to see you again."

She pronounced my name in French and I liked the sound of it. I returned the greeting and poured an aperitif for her, not asking if she wanted one. She watched me across the rim of her glass as we sipped. Carlos went behind the bar and paused facing us. He set a bowl full of ice on the bar. Glancing first at Lisa, then me and then back to Lisa, he said, "I locked up since we're closed until 4:30. I'm going upstairs for a nap."

He put the back of his hand over his mouth and yawned. "You can go into the billiard room if you want. There won't be anybody here, anyhow." Lisa said nothing, but slid off her stool and sauntered into the billiard room, taking her drink. I picked up the bowl of ice, the bottle, and my drink, and followed closely.

She chose a seat in the booth, placed her glass on the table and removed her service jacket. As I was about to slide the doors shut behind us, someone pounded on the front door. I saw Carlos run from the kitchen, around the bar and to the front door where he peeked out once again. "Just stay there," he called to me. "It's the firemen again."

I was really pissed.

I sat alongside Lisa. "It seems we have unexpected patrons from the local fire department whom Carlos must serve," I said. She made a disgusted face as I spoke, then shrugged.

"That's too bad. I was hoping we could forget the war for a while."

"I was too, Lisa," I replied, meaning every word of it. "But they're interested only in drinking. Maybe they won't come in here."

"Perhaps not." She emphasized the perhaps.

"Just in case though," I said, and leaned forward, put my arm around her and drew her close, tilting her face upward to kiss. We parted for a moment. She raised a hand to my face before we kissed again. As she responded, I put both arms around her and tasted her lips hungrily. As the laughter in the other room grew louder, we drew apart. Those pale blue eyes locked with mine as the crinkle of a smile curled at her lips.

"Perhaps we should hope for a fire," she whispered.

There was a touch of red in her cheeks, her long, straw blonde hair piled high, the cap still in place, pulled forward as it had been the first time I saw her. I visualized how she would look without the cap, her hair falling full length. I wanted to remove those pins myself.

I leaned forward and she met me as we kissed again, gently, until we heard someone fumble with the sliding doors. A fireman entered the room. He glanced at us, scowling as he caught sight of the German uniform, then picked up a cue stick and tried a few shots, glancing up occasionally, with a grin flickering on his face. Lisa was unperturbed. She sipped her drink and I watched her, thinking that she looked more beautiful than ever.

"Lisa, how long is your hair?"

She giggled, grinning at me, then stood. "Down to here," she said, her fingers brushing a point on her lower hip.

"I'm glad the German Army doesn't make you cut it short like some of the men."

"I am, too. Someday, maybe I'll show you," she said, "But not now." She sat down as another fireman came in, picked up a cue, and racked up the balls for a game.

"Tell me about San Francisco," Lisa said.

I didn't feel like talking just then, especially about geography, but under the circumstances, I thought I better.

"Well, it's located on a peninsula and has two big bridges—the Golden Gate and the Bay Bridge. It's not a large city, only about 650,000, but people from all over the world have settled there. You see them on the streets. And restaurants serve almost any kind of food you can imagine, from all over, you can eat about any kind you want. It has the most beautiful, well-kept Victorian homes of any place I've ever seen. The city is built on hills and has tremendous views of the waterfront and the whole bay. Do I sound like a travel log film?"

She laughed. "What was your favorite restaurant?"

"That's easy. It's a place called St. Juliens's. It's an Italian restaurant, but I've heard that many of the dishes are as much French as Italian, maybe from the south of France, I'm not sure. But the food is fantastic. They have specialties of the house that they display in a showcase in the middle of the foyer as you enter—20 or 30 different cuts of meat or fish, or whatever."

"It sounds wonderful. Where is your mother now?"

"Sacramento. It's the capital of the state, about 100 miles east of San Francisco, in the valley."

"You know, you seem more like an American than a Frenchman."

I began to think maybe I'd gone too far, reminding myself that this gal was still an enemy soldier.

"Well, I guess I am," I said after a moment. "After all, I've lived there most of my life. French is new to me and my French is very bad. Everybody laughs when I try to speak the language."

"Yes," she said, "I guess that's it. But I wish it was your father who is American instead of your mother, then you would be American instead of French."

"Well, I can go back anytime I want, once the war is over."

"Will you do that?"

"Yes, Lisa," I said, looking her right in the eye. "I'm going back just as soon as I can get there." I could be truthful about that, anyway.

"That would be wonderful. I'd like to meet you there after the war and have you show me your San Francisco."

"It would be a pleasure. I'd like to show you the City."

We sat silently, sipping our drinks as the two firemen finished their game and stowed their cues in the wall rack. When they went back to the bar, we could hear them talking to the others, followed by a raucous laugh from the group. I could imagine what they were saying.

"Will you be here long, Henri?"

"No, I don't think so. Maybe only a few days. I don't know right now."

"Well, if you do, the bartender will know, won't he?"

"Carlos? Yes, I'll let him know."

"Good. I will ask him then. Where will you go?"

"The south of France. It's better for me there, on a farm where I'll work this summer." Actually, I hoped I'd be in Spain.

"I will be going," she said. "This is no good here, now."

"I'm sorry about those firemen."

"I am too," she said, standing. I helped her into her jacket. She straightened her cap and tightened her tie.

"You're the best looking corporal I've ever seen," I said.

She laughed and we kissed goodbye. She squeezed my hand and we walked to the sliding doors. As she stepped across the bar, the firemen turned, watching her as I moved to the doorway into the kitchen. When Lisa reached the main door, she turned to give me a little nod.

As she walked out the door, I heard one of the firemen say emphatically, "Formidable!" No kidding.

In my room, I lay on the bed, hands clasped behind my head, staring at the ceiling and thinking about the strange circumstances that had brought us together—and the screwed up events that kept us apart. For an instant, it had been just the two of us, alone, and though it was strange for me to think about a German corporal with anything but hatred, Lisa made it easy. She avoided asking questions I know she wondered about and I guess she knew they were questions better left unasked.

I heard the firemen leave as other people arrived. It was already opening time, and the usual quiet but jovial bar noise filtered up to me from the room below. I tried reading but couldn't concentrate; Lisa was on my mind.

After the bar closed, another delicious meal was served. "You have to keep your strength up," Maria said.

"He almost needed more of it today," Carlos noted, grinning.

Jacques came to the bar around 8:00 and spent two hours talking to me, asking all sorts of questions about the States. When it was time for him to leave, I wanted to give him a souvenir as a token of my thanks for his help. I chose my silver ID bracelet; it was too much of a giveaway for me to wear anyway.

Jacques looked at it in his hand for a moment, not really believing I'd part with it, but overjoyed that I did. He turned it over.

"Argent?"

"Yes, silver. From Mexico."

"D'accord! Merci, merci, Henri." He went downstairs beaming and we said goodbye in the bar. I went back into the kitchen with Carlos and listened to the war news.

Finally, I went upstairs and read my spy thriller, subconsciously wondering when Claude would come for me, counting the days again, I decided that I had done well so far. I was near the end of a successful evasion. Things were looking up.

# Chapter 7

# LEAVING CARRIERES-SUR-SEINE

Maria brought me a cup of steaming coffee while I was still in bed.

"Gee, Maria, that's real service," I smiled.

"I want you to be comfortable. This may be your last morning with us."

She gave me extra underwear, socks, and a more detailed map. I drank the coffee as I shaved, noticing that the cut on my jaw was healing nicely. I dressed, then placed the new beret Claude had brought me on top of my head. I pushed it back a little, French-style.

Downstairs, Carlos looked me over carefully.

"Your beret is wrong," he declared. "You don't look right that way, you must wear it like this."

Carlos put his on. "This is the Fascist way, but it's the way I learned." He pulled the cap down on the right side of his head, then pinched the front between two fingers and pulled it forward, toward his right eye, forming a little brim. It looked pretty jaunty.

"It is natural to wear it like this," he said.

I put on the beret, pulled it to one side, and then pulled the front forward and slightly down over my right eye. "Like this?"

"Pull it down just a little more in front."

I followed his instructions. I turned sideways, looking in the barroom mirror, pivoting right and left. It definitely looked better.

"That's not bad. Here, let me help you." Carlos peaked it a little more, pulling it further down over my eye. Then he stood back for a better look.

"There, that's the way you want it. It looks natural, as if you've been wearing berets all your life."

I took a good look, took it off and put it back on. After a few tries, I was doing it right every time. It looked kind of jazzy, I thought, and thanked Carlos for showing me.

"Hell, you look like a regular Fascist now," he grinned.

I went into the kitchen and showed Maria. "How do I look?"

"Right out of the revolution," she said. She was talking about the Spanish revolution.

I left it on while we ate breakfast, a delicious omelet with mushrooms, and a little ham. The coffee was excellent; I noticed the difference right away.

"This isn't erzats."

Maria laughed. "No, it isn't. This is a celebration so we broke out a can of Maxwell House we saved. We won't open the last can until the occupation is over. I hope it's still good."

"This is, and it won't be much longer before you open the other can," I said.

We ate silently, knowing it was our last meal together. I was anxious to move on, but also sorry to leave this wonderful couple. Still, I know they'd be relieved when I left, realizing the great danger they were in while I lived here.

Maria handed me some new clothes Claude had brought earlier. When I dressed, I noticed how much the shirt, trousers and coat resembled the outfit in my photograph.

"How do I look?" I asked, downstairs again.

"A little better than a bum, like you did before," joked Carlos.

"Well, I guess this is what they want."

Carlos stood and lifted a box from the top of the cabinet.

"I found these last night," he said. "Old publicity shots from the Waldorf."

There were perhaps 25 photos, some of the entire group, some of Carlos and Maria together. Others showed band members in the background as Carlos played guitar or Maria sang.

I was right guessing that Maria was a beauty at 25. And Carlos looked like a regular Romeo. In every photo, he was looking brazenly into the camera; his head tilted jauntily, a wide smile revealing perfect white teeth.

While looking at the photos we heard a car pull up to the curb outside. Maria left, then returned with Claude and Colette.

Carlos and Maria gave me quick hugs and kisses, and then I was suddenly on the sidewalk, with a small case of extra clothes clutched in one hand. I slid into the backseat and waved.

The Filipottos smiled and waved back as Claude started down the hill to the intersection.

We made a left turn and once again I was traveling over an unfamiliar road, on another leg of my evasion from occupied France. Nearing the river, I saw the scars of bombings at a couple of bridges, and I hoped one of them was one we bombed. A mile or so further up river, Claude called over his shoulder, as if reading my mind, "There's your target, lieutenant."

A span of the bridge was badly damaged, partially in the river. A work gang was swarmed over it.

"It looks like we did a good job," I said. "Are we headed toward Paris now?"

"Yes, we are, then we are going on to Versailles."

"Is it far?"

"Not very far. And we are not apt to meet any Germans."

The girl turned to me with instructions. "When we reach Versailles, you will meet an official. He is the police chief. I work with him. I work with Claude, too, but several days each week I work at the Gendarmerie. You will stay in an apartment in Versailles for several days, perhaps two weeks. We will stop once and have your papers verified before taking you there. Then someone will come and take you to a place in the country. You will not see Claude or me again. There are other contacts. Your next contact will be an Englishman."

She said it all matter-of-factly and I decided she was the actual Underground contact, not Claude.

"Well, Colette, you know my real name, so tell me what you want me to do and I'll do it. I can't get out without your help."

"Yes, we know. By the way, you have done very well so far. Who showed you how to wear the beret? Carlos?"

"Yes."

"It looks good. Not exactly the way we may have instructed, but good. You will pass. Just keep on doing as you have so far and you will get out easily."

God, I hoped so.

We neared a city and crossed the river. Colette said we were on the outskirts of Paris. There were a few people in the streets and fairly heavy barge traffic on the river. Homes faced the sidewalks, newer homes than I'd seen in Carrieres-sur-Seine. German trucks were on the bridge as we crossed. We left the city quickly and came to an area of open fields. Some were plowed; others with field crops ready for harvest.

"In a little while, we will see Germans," Colette said. "They will be marching and a German officer will review them. There will be no trouble but remember, sit quietly and say nothing."

I wondered how they knew we were going to meet Germans.

It was misty, with stratus clouds moving in, casting heavy shadows on the well-worn rutted road which soon dead-ended into another macadam road. As we approached the intersection, Claude slowed as German soldiers walked slowly into the street; their arms thrust forward, palms out, halting traffic. We slowed to a stop, drawing abreast of a sleek, gray touring car. A German officer sat in the rear seat of the open sedan. The vehicle was pulled completely off the highway, ten feet from the side of our car. I turned my head to look at the man in the backseat.

Hollywood couldn't have cast a more perfect Nazi villain. Eric von Stroheim had nothing on this guy. Sitting ram-rod straight with a monacle screwed tightly into his right eye, he clutched a riding crop in his right hand, its tip pointing toward his right ear. He flicked it constantly from side-to-side, like a nervous tic.

His gray tunic ended in a tight monkey-suit collar with red and gold patches and a colorful medal hanging from just below the collar. His chest was a blaze of other medals. A red, gold, and silver striped sash was fitted across his tunic, and his cap set precisely on his head. His closely shaved skull was visible below the back of his cap, and the brim was angled down over his eyes, almost hiding the monocle.

On the side of his face nearest me, a pink, jagged scar curved from his temple and along his jaw to the corner of his mouth, long and hook-shaped. He stared straight ahead, utterly alone and aloof, ignoring the little French car parked alongside his glittering vehicle.

It was my first real chance to study a German commander close up. His head began to turn slowly toward me, and I noticed that his eyes were on Colette before they flicked to me. He stared into my eyes. I was smoking a cigarette which I held in the right corner of my mouth. I stared back and continued to puff, letting the smoke curl up and away, never blinking; as careful as he was not to show emotion.

Finally, he gave a tight little smile, the scar adding a sardonic touch, then actually chuckled before resuming his former stance.

A military band drew near. They were a cruddy-looking bunch. As a former member of the First Regimental Band, United States Infantry, I knew exactly what my band leaders would do if commanding a group like this. Our first sergeant would clean us up first, then issue orders for group rehearsal: four hours in the morning and again in the afternoon. And if the first sergeant was Boyd White Eagle, my first sergeant in that outfit, it would have been done quickly.

Hell, Eagle would have us on KP for a month if we looked like that.

But if the band was a sorry bunch, the troops marching along behind them were worse. They were a rag-tag lot in dirty uniforms that looked as if they were never meant to fit the men wearing them. Their Mausers pointed at all angles as they approached to pass in review. The scar-faced officer stood at attention in the back of the touring car like a robot, waiting indolently until the officers and the men in the first unit were saluting before he finally extended his right arm in the Nazi salute.

After standing erect for a minute or two, he sat down, a look of consternation on his face. He must be wondering why his superiors were punishing him by placing him in command of such a unit. When the last troops were past, he nodded to his driver who started the big automobile, and turned onto the road to Paris.

"What did you think of the review?" Claude asked at last.

"Lousy. Very, very bad."

They both laughed. "They are bad. They are new conscripts from Austria and a few other places. They are just glad they are not on the Russian front."

"I'll bet the officer is happiest of all not to be there."

They laughed again. "Yes, he's very glad. He is the commandant of Versailles. We are almost there now."

We passed a wide entrance to a cobblestone parking area. In the distance, I saw the elaborate façade of a building, which I recognized from history books as the Palace. Claude turned onto a large boulevard for several blocks before making a U-turn and stopping in front of a building.

"We get out here, it is the Gendarmerie," said Colette.

I waited with her on the sidewalk until Claude came around and we all went inside. We crossed a cobblestone courtyard into an office area. A gendarme nodded to Colette, then opened a massive door. Inside, they introduced me to a man they called Chief. He shook hands and said, "Lieutenant Woodrum, you are a very lucky man. I'm glad to meet you."

Collette gave him some papers which he signed before handing them to me.

"You can sign them when you have time. We must make it look like it was signed some time ago." He was a big, stocky man, with bushy eyebrows and a firm handshake.

Back in the hall, Colette said goodbye in French and kept on walking. Claude and I went back to the car. The street wasn't crowded. We headed back toward the Palace, and then turned onto the next main boulevard.

"You will live on this street," he said.

It was the Rue des Chantiers. I studied it closely as we drove. He stopped in front of a five-or-six-story apartment building at 41 or 44 Rue des Chantiers. It was difficult to read the last faded number. We entered through the main door and climbed the stairs to the top floor. Claude was puffing by the time we reached it, but I was in better shape and hardly noticed the climb.

He tapped on a door which immediately flew open. A man on the other side peered at us intensely. Past the man, a woman stood near an upholstered chair, also peeking at me. She pulled a chair away from a table and motioned for me to sit.

Claude spoke rapidly in French, answering questions the couple fired at him. Then he turned to me.

"Mr. and Mrs. Brenner, Lieutenant Woodrum."

We all shook hands. Then Claude gave me some last-minute instructions.

"You will stay in this apartment. Do not leave for any reason. Do exactly as you are told. Try to learn some French. And don't get frustrated. This may take time, but don't worry. Remember, as long as you are here, everything is okay. I will not return, but you will be contacted by the Englishman sometime soon. Do not worry. Okay?"

"Yes. That's fine with me," I said.

"The Brenners speak no English but they have a dictionary. It will come in handy. Any other questions?"

"No. Everything is clear."

"Well, goodbye and good luck."

He gave me a pat on the back and was gone.

The Brenners stood looking at me. They looked to be in their late-40s. His thinning black hair, flecked with gray, was parted from left to right over a small bald spot. He looked tired and underweight. He wore a tan, short-sleeved shirt with an open collar and dark brown trousers held up with a black leather belt much too large for his slim frame.

His wife was about the same height. Her dark brown hair, also graying, was pinned in a bun at the back of her head. She seemed like a direct, independent woman. She nudged her husband and he immediately walked to the sideboard and removed a bottle and two glasses which he placed on the table.

His confidence seemed to grow as he poured the cognac and handed one to me. We clinked our glasses.

"Bonne chance," he said.

We tossed them off and he refilled them immediately.

I made the toast "A la victoire!" We clicked the rims again and drank the smooth liquor. I began to relax in my new Resistance hiding place. With papers, I felt much more like an authentic evadee.

The woman approached me and pointed a finger to her chest, "Henriette."

Following suit, I pointed a thumb toward myself, "Henri."

She indicated her husband. "Charles," then made eating motions with her hands. "Avez vous mange?"

"Oui, mange a huit heure."

Henriette nodded and went to the kitchen. I could hear her banging pans. She came back with a cup of fine-tasting tea. As I sipped, they asked questions. For the first time, I found myself with a dictionary, and people who didn't understand English. They asked two-word questions.

"What city?"

"San Francisco.'

"What aircraft?"

"B-vingt-six."

It was pleasant in this house, but different from the other two I'd visited. I was used to musicians. Musicians and bars are the same the world over. I felt at home with the Filipottos, but of course, they spoke my language fluently. I understood the people at the garage, too. But this was somehow different.

We continued the broken question-answers.

"Combien de sorties?"

"Thirty-five." I raised three fingers on one hand, all five on the other. I peeled off my coat and Henriette, the good housekeeper, pounced to hang it in the closet.

"Encore?" she asked, holding up my teacup. I nodded.

While she was gone, Charles searched the dictionary for words. He wrote: "Me work in railroad." He scanned the book again and continued. "Work at 2:00."

I took out my watch. It was 1:00. Now it was my turn at the dictionary. I penned: "What kind of work?"

He found the word, pointed his finger to it, and held the book for me to see: "Stationmaster."

A short while later my new hosts guided me to a spare bedroom. I set my suitcase on the floor then reached for my papers and handed them to Charles.

Aviation Cadet Henry Woodrum, 1943.

Photo of my aircraft, The Shopworn Angel, Y5J. Because
it had been damaged in a crash landing by another pilot,
I was flying another aircraft the day I was shot down.

Crew working on the Shopworn Angel.

The Shopworn Angel after wheels up landing
after a mission flown by another pilot.

Another view of the Shopworn Angel after the
wheels up landing. It did fly again.

495TH BOMBARDMENT SQUADRON (M) AAF
344th Bombardment Group (M) AAF

APO 140, U.S. Army
26 June 1944.

Mrs H. C. Woodrum,
1523 Chestnut Street,
Redding, California.

My dear Mrs Woodrum:

During the time which this Squadron has carried out combat missions against the enemy, it has had many difficult assignments. Your son, Henry, did his share and more to see that our job was done effectively. He has served his country with honor and courage. Henry has flown Thirty three combat missions and has earned the Air Medal with Four Oak Leaf Clusters and One Silver Oak Leaf Cluster. That is official recognition of what he has done. I know he was a fine Pilot and always trying his best.

There are not many facts I can pass on to you. The incident occured during a combat mission over the Continent of Europe. The plane in which your son was serving was struck by anti-aircraft fire. The damage was severe to an extent it was impossible for the plane to continue with the formation. Nothing further has been learned of the aircraft or crew since that time.

Official directives require that I give positive identification, as to conform to regulations, I quote, " 1st Lieutenant Henry C. Woodrum, O-742102, is Missing in Action". I extend to you my deepest sympathy for the sorrow and suspense I know you must feel.

Very truly yours,

JENS A. NORGAARD,
Lt. Colonel, Air Corps,
Commanding.

Letter sent to my family notifying them I was missing in action.

Clair Engle
2D DISTRICT CALIFORNIA

HOME ADDRESS
RED BLUFF, CALIFORNIA

OFFICE ADDRESS
123 HOUSE OFFICE BUILDING

# Congress of the United States
## House of Representatives
### Washington, D. C.

COMMITTEES.
MINES AND MINING
PUBLIC LANDS
ROADS
WAR CLAIMS
WORLD WAR VETERANS'
LEGISLATION

June 19, 1944

Mrs. H. C. Woodrum
Redding, California

Dear Mrs. Woodrum:

The War Department has informed me that your son, Lt. Henry
Woodrum, has been listed as missing in action over France.

While the news is cause for great concern, it may be
tempered with the knowledge that our fighting men listed as
missing oftentimes ultimately return to their bases, or are
held as prisoners of war.

If Lt. Woodrum has been captured by the enemy, the word
probably will be conveyed to you through the War Department
or the International Red Cross, although it undoubtedly will
take considerable time.

If it turns out that despite the hopes of all of us your
son has indeed given his life for his country, I beg that
you and your family accept my heartfelt sympathy.

Very sincerely yours,

CE:nb                    CLAIR ENGLE M.C.

Letter to my family from Congressman Clair Engel.

# Chapter 8

# VERSAILLES

The buzz of aircraft engines shook me from my sleep and I rose to look out the window. About a mile east, a formation of six ME-109s was circling for a landing. Soon, an HE-111K followed the fighters.

I went into the living room, where I could see the street below in the other direction. Henriette was in the kitchen, but Charles was gone. I went back to my bedroom where the vantage point was great. Across the street, I noticed two hefty German trucks backed-up to a warehouse loading dock. Several large sliding doors to the inside were closed except for one, yawning partially open. A German soldier wheeled a crate-laden dolly across the dock to the back of a truck.

Houses, apartments, and small shops occupied the rest of the street. Across from our apartment was a four-foot-high picket fence enclosing a park with a wide expanse of manicured lawns, shrubs, and bushy shade trees. The trees obscured what appeared to be the base of a statue.

I felt strange wearing a white shirt after four years of military uniforms. I rolled back the cuffs and felt more comfortable. My new trousers, pleated at the waist, felt light and flimsy compared to my military issue.

Looking across the city to the west, I could see that most of the apartments had small balconies cluttered with large rectangular boxes. I noticed with growing curiosity, the same kind of boxes on our balcony.

Henriette soon ended the mystery. She reached down and raised a corner of the heavy burlap, revealing a chicken-wire pen holding several rabbits. There was a second rabbit pen and two others with chickens. Dinner!

Across the city in the direction of the Palace, I saw clumps of forest. Past that, a small, densely forested hill. Behind our building I could just make out the slope of another small hill, its carefully trimmed lawns dotted with white crosses. Henriette flipped through our dictionary and I learned it was a World War I cemetery.

She fetched my identity card and sat scrutinizing it at the dining room table. She looked up, pointed at me, and said, "Vous vous appelez Albert, pas, Henri?" She shook her head.

I was no longer Henri, she was saying. From now on, I was someone named Albert. I had to get used to the new name. Claude or Colette had probably filled in the vital statistics -the information was listed in obviously European handwriting. Only my signature was missing. My namesake was a real person who had died a few weeks before in a bombing raid. Now I was Albert.

Henriette handed me a pen and ink to practice writing the name before actually putting my signature on the identity card. I tried copying a sample Henriette provided, writing the initial "A" with a flare, then scribbling the last name in tiny letters run together. Regardless of my efforts, my signature seemed out of place with the handwritten data.

The ID listed my nationality as French, born September 29, 1902. Well, I'll be damned. I'm 42 years old! It also said I was a merchant, one meter 80 centimeters tall, blond with blue eyes and an oval face. Skin color was "blanc," and my address was 18 Rue des Chantiers, Versailles.

Henriette gave me her card for comparison and I felt better after seeing it. Except for the newness of the paper, mine wasn't much different. I remembered the chief saying we had to make it look older. My food ration card looked authentic as it had also belonged to the person whose identity I'd acquired. I checked the date and noticed a three-month gap since food was issued against the card.

"Albert?"

I didn't realize Henriette was addressing me until I saw her watching me intently. She smiled and tried again.

"Albert. Voulez-vous ecouter la radio?"

I guessed what she meant, but looked up "ecouter" anyway. It meant "listen."

Henriette switched on the radio. It was pre-set to the local French station. She held up a finger. "Un instant" she said, turning the dial. The BBC was playing chamber music that we enjoyed until the announcer gave a brief news report. Henriette said "encore" and turned the dial again, to the Yankee Doodle Network, where an American announcer was giving the news.

The 8th was hitting Berlin and Hamburg while the mediums hit airfields and "other selected targets" - probably bridges or no-ball targets - in France. The RAF had bombed the Rhur the night before. Next came a string of Glenn Miller hits. For the next hour I switched from BBC to Yankee Doodle, enjoying both. The British gave the news at dictation speed and included news of the war in the Far East, which also interested me. Yankee Doodle offered stateside news along with some good music.

When I tired of hearing the same news repeated, I turned the set off and Henriette opened her dictionary, teaching me a few words, listening to me struggle with French pronunciation. I was surprised how, by changing the pronunciation of some English words, Henriette could understand me. "Direction," for example. Other words were French to begin with - café, garage, restaurant, bouquet. I hunted through the book and when I came to a word I thought was similar, said it the way I thought it might sound in French. Henriette repeated it properly if she understood. I tested many English words that way. I tried "evasion," my top priority, phonetically: E-vay-zhe-one. She understood.

After a half-hour or so, I tried putting sentences together and discovered that we could hold short conversations without thumbing through the dictionary. Then she tried another method.

Holding up a fork, Henriette said the French word for "fork" and I mimicked her the best I could. By the end of an hour, I'd learned words for eat, sleep, knife, fork, room, wait, here, name, age, head, hand, hot, cold, right, left, north, south, east, west, and valuable phrases like "What time is it?" I suppose I was learning French as a parrot learns to talk.

I found my map and began figuring in detail which route I'd follow if forced to leave alone. When Henriette saw the map, she pointed to Calais, and asked, "Bombe?"

"Oui." I nodded. "Oui. Deux fois."

She pointed to Boulogne-sur-Mer, Again I nodded. "Oui, un fois." Then she pointed to Lille.

"Oui, un fois, aussi."

"Bon. Bon, Albert."

"Porquoi Lille?" I asked."

"J'ai ete faite prisonniere la bas pendant la Premiere Guerre Mondiale."

She'd been a prisoner there in World War One. I was curious and reminded myself to ask more about that later.

Henriette asked me about bombing other cities. Finally, she asked where I was shot down. I told her about the bridge near Saint Germain-en-Laye, and that I landed in Carrieres sur Seine.

I wanted to know about the airdrome in Villacoublay, a target I knew about from friends in the 8th Air Force.

"Beaucoup avion en Villacoublay?" I asked.

"Oui, beaucoup, beaucoup," she replied.

Then I asked, "Quelle direction Paris?"

She led me to the front bedroom and pointed out the window. "Tour 'Eiffel."

Sure enough. I could see its spire six miles or so away, roof tops and trees sandwiched in between, but there it was. I was glad to have another well-known landmark. The Palace in Versailles was good, the Eiffel Tower seemed better. I browsed some more through the dictionary, then searched the little bookcase for books in English. I found one—Charles Dickens' "A Tale of Two Cities." I decided to read it again and took it back to my bedroom where I could sit by the window.

Later, a six-ship squadron of FW-190s took off and headed northwest. I heard faint air-raid sirens from the northwest and I wondered if somebody was after Seine River bridges again.

At dusk Charles returned and asked me to join him in the parlor for a cognac while Henriette finished cooking dinner. I tested some of my new words. He understood most, though I knew my pronunciation was awful. By using the dictionary, we were able to converse.

After dinner, we listened to the radio, first the German-controlled French station, though Charles said it was worthless, and filled with lies, then to Yankee Doodle.

I slept late the next day, Sunday, June 4. It was the latest I'd slept since being shot down. When finally I rose, the Brenners joined me for coffee and were surprised when I told them I seldom ate breakfast.

I listened to the radio most of the day, hearing about raids into Germany by the 8th and the RAF with the 9th hitting airfields and other targets in northern France. There was no mention of bridges along the Seine. I guessed they were all down by now. Best of all, there was an encouraging, but unconfirmed report saying the Allies were entering Rome.

After lunch, we were visited by a friend of the Brenners, Madame Blanche, a bookkeeper with some French government agency. She was a pleasant woman in her late 40s with a quiet air of assurance. She spoke English quite well, and welcomed the chance to use it in conversation.

She told me that in her early 20s, she married a young English teacher. A Socialist, he was killed in a riot during the 1930s. She never remarried, and said she fully intended to remain single. In the meantime, she'd become an active member of the Underground. She offered to provide all the tobacco I wanted while there. She traveled from Versailles to Paris twice a week. Her contact there got Turkish cigarettes from a relative who worked in the Hotel Meurice, which had been taken over by the Germans after their occupation.

She was a courier for the Underground, and one group she worked with included teenage boys equipped with bicycles and small, radio transmitters. They'd ride to the countryside, set the bike on a stand, engage a small generator with its rotor shaft pressed against the wheel of the bike, and transmit. It required two people—one to pedal the bike on the stand, the other to transmit the message. For an antenna, they simply tossed the weighted end of a wire into the nearest tree, and reeled it back in again before riding away. There were several such teams, she said. Since they were so mobile, it was hard for the Germans to locate them even with direction-finding equipment. Their transmissions were always short, coded messages on pre-arranged, crystal-controlled frequencies monitored around the clock in England. She related all this very matter-of-factly, but she was certainly an unlikely-looking spy!

She said she'd bring some books for me next time. She also said the English agent Claude had mentioned would arrive in a day or two.

I spent the afternoon in the bedroom reading, checking each aircraft as it entered the pattern for a landing at Villacoublay and watching take-offs. Several Panzer tanks and about a dozen trucks loaded with troops came clanking down Rue des Chantiers from the airport. They stopped about 50 yards up the street and I got a good look. The soldiers lined up, passing large cartons, to each truck and tank.

After receiving its quota, each vehicle rumbled away toward the center of Versailles. I noticed that about 10 percent of the soldiers wore black uniforms with knee-high, gleaming black boots. They had peaked caps and swastika armbands, the red, white, and black bands in bold contrast with the uniforms.

When I asked the Brenners, they said only a small number of Germans were actually Nazi's, the rest were regular Army. I'd heard about Storm Troopers and brown shirts, but this was the first time I saw them up close. Charles said "SSers" were mean, politically-oriented Nazis. Later, I learned they were the politically oriented Imperial guard of the Nationalist Socialist Party. I'd assumed most Germans were Nazis.

When I looked up from my book again, I saw another HE-111 fly a long downwind leg, then turn left, ready to land. Something seemed different. Not until its turn to base was almost complete, did I realize it had a tail gun turret. Unheard of for an HE-111. About a half hour later, it - or another one just like it -took off heading northeast. I got a good look at it this time. I knew any pilot making a quartering approach from the rear of this machine was in for a deadly surprise. I made a note of its markings and decided to pass this information to Madame Blanche when she returned. Then if somebody thought it worth sending a message about, they could do so. I told the Brenners and they said they'd ask Madame Blanche to return the next day.

While waiting for dinner, Charles told me he'd been with the railroad all his working years and was now the stationmaster. It wasn't the largest railyard in the area, but even so, the Germans had troops positioned there to supervise French workers. Many of the materials sent to Brest left from that yard. For the last three weeks, German shipments, including tanks, had increased. That confirmed what I knew about the growing shipments of anti-aircraft guns. The Krauts were being especially watchful for sabotage, he said.

After a good chicken-and-dumpling dinner, we listened to the Yankee Doodle network. When Charles broke out the cognac, I tried my new vocabulary. I held up my glass. "Un grille."

They looked at me, puzzled, and asked "Un grille?"

"Oui, un grille. Aujourd'hui est un semaine de evasion!"

It was my bold attempt at toasting a week of evasion. When at last they understood, they laughed. Henriette raised her glass and we clinked rims. "Oui, tres bien!" she said. As twilight fell, we sipped our drinks. My good luck had continued during that week. But I did kind of miss that bar in Carrieres-sur-Seine.

The next day, June 5, I read, studied my dictionary, and worked on Henriette's latest brainstorm. Since my French was still bad, she suggested I learn deaf-mute sign language. She kept after me until I learned several signs and performed them reasonably well.

Henriette was an intense, surprising woman. She ran a catering business before the war with a dozen employees, booking all sorts of social events from small parties to large weddings. She promised to make something for me to demonstrate her ability as a pastry chef.

She and Charles noticed immediately that I used my knife and fork differently than Europeans. I held my fork in my left hand with the knife in the right to cut meat, then I switched the fork to my right hand to eat, with my left hand in my lap. Europeans keep their fork in their left hand throughout the meal, holding it upside down compared to my way.

I practiced eating their way, thinking how my table manners could betray me. It was awkward at first, but I soon caught on.

When Madame Blanche visited, I had a chance to ask all the unanswered questions between me and the Brenners. That's how I learned that the Brenners were Jehovah's Witnesses.

I once worked for people of that faith in the States and knew a little about it. An attempt to convert me failed despite lengthy discussions. I chuckled to myself that if Henriette could speak English, she'd be trying to convert me too.

Madame Blanche came that day bearing gifts: two books and new underwear for "Albert." I asked where she got them. Henriette said something in French that sounded like "machine wire." It was a slang expression and Madame Blanche didn't know the English equivalent. Finally, we came up with "Marche noir," or black market!

She stayed for dinner and afterward translated BBC news for the Brenners. When I switched to Yankee Doodle, it was confirmed that Rome had been taken by the Allies with little damage except to railyards. We toasted the victory.

Late that afternoon, while I was reading one of the new books, the HE-11 returned. I told Madame Blanche about it and said that it seemed to arrive everyday about the same time. She listened closely. When I told her about the HE-111s rear guns, she said she'd report it immediately, pleased that she would originate something of value herself.

I fell asleep easily that night, but woke around 4:00 in the morning. I lit a cigarette and tried to read but couldn't get interested. Finally, I got up, went to the parlor, and gazed across the rooftops toward the woods. It was quite dark, there were no city lights, and clouds overhead shrouded the moonlight. Only the largest buildings nearby were visible. The streets were empty. It was as if time hung suspended in a misty, surrealistic world. I couldn't believe it could be so quiet in the middle of a war.

I wondered how things would turn out for me, wishing I could control my own destiny. I was jittery, this sitting around was getting to me. I went back to bed and finally slept.

I was jarred awake by a woman's voice shouting "Albert! Albert!" I sat up, ready to jump to my feet. Henriette was standing just inside my door, motioning, clapping her hands, then motioning again. She was even hopping up and down, unable to contain her excitement.

"Albert! C'est le Debarquement!"

I understood her words, and their meaning hit me like a tidal wave. The invasion was underway!

I followed Henriette to the parlor. The radio was turned on full volume. The booming voice in French was from the BBC in London. Henriette anxiously wrung her hands as she listened. The announcer, his voice full and deep, was trying to suppress his own excitement.

"Henriette, ou est le Debarquement?" I asked.

"En Normandie! En Normandie! Dans le Pas-de-Calais."

The report ended and the station's music resumed. I switched to Yankee Doodle just in time to hear: "…word that it was a full-scale invasion, not just a show of force or a diversionary raid came with the announcement from Supreme Headquarters, Allied Expeditionary Force, that the Allies did indeed launch a dawn invasion on at least three beachheads. That announcement has just been released."

The American announcer continued: "The report stated that paratroopers were dropped during the late hours of the night followed by dawn attacks by bombers of the 9th Air Force and P-47s which dive-bombed German position just inland. RAF bombers were out as well as fighters flying sweeps of the area. There is a report that even B-17s joined in the attack. It also stated that a number of capital vessels of the navies of the United States and Great Britain have shelled the area from the beachhead inland. Some positions further inland have already been secured by our paratroopers."

"Albert. What are they saying?" Henriette asked eagerly.

I told her a landing was underway by a great many soldiers, at several places along the coast of Normandy and that many ships and bombers were participating. Then I turned back to the radio.

One report came a few minutes later that I couldn't believe. It said there were more than 500 warships and nearly 5,000 other vessels involved in the invasion.

God Almighty. I couldn't fathom an invasion force that large, although I'd seen the south coast ports jammed with vessels for weeks.

Over and over the news of the initial attacks was repeated. Every so often something new was added. One thing was sure, the 9th Air Force had been in the forefront, bombing inland German positions. I knew the 344th was in there. If I'd only lasted 10 more days, I'd be with them. That thought stayed with me.

Within hours of the initial news, it was reported that 50,000 soldiers were already on the beach and more were landing. I noticed there were no reports of opposition by German aircraft.

Then I realized that I'd heard no activity at all from Villacoublay. Later that morning, several flights of FW-190s flew in from the east to land. They were only on the ground a few minutes before taking off, heading west. Twenty minutes later a flight of P-47s came in low from the north, almost across Paris, straffing the airfield. German machine guns, 20mm cannons and 88s opened up on them, but the P-47s flew away undamaged, leaving towering columns of black smoke billowing over the airfield. Minutes later, some of the FW-190s returned but flew away again immediately.

We'd been bombing airfields throughout France for several months, but it was hard to believe the Luftwaffe wasn't putting up any resistance to the landing. I tried to recall the airfields our group had bombed in the last two weeks. Epernay, Cormeilles, Cambri-Epernay, and Chaartres—all since mid-May. That explained the absence of German fighters along with fighter sweeps. Allied air superiority had apparently been achieved!

Since Henriette didn't trust the French stations, we tuned in the BBC or Yankee Doodle most of the day. Armed with my trusty dictionary, I gave her short descriptions of the news.

Around four o'clock that afternoon, someone knocked at the door. I went to my bedroom and waited. I could hear a muffled conversation, after which Henriette called me into the parlor. It was Madame Blanche.

"The Englishman will arrive soon."

"Who is he?" I asked.

"The man I work for. He is the chief."

"Does he have anything to do with my getting out?"

"Yes."

If the chief was English, that probably meant he was a planted agent, perhaps sent here to organize a resistance group. Maybe he'll say they won't be able to get me out. Maybe things are getting too hot. I hadn't seen any unusual German activity, which was surprising. Maybe they thought this was a diversion rather than the full invasion, still thinking it would come further up the French coastline.

Henriette was beside herself. Of the French people I'd met so far, she hated the Germans the most. I later found out why.

Madame Blanche told me Henriette was born about 1900 in North France. As a girl of 17 or 18, she was forced to work for the Germans - the town she lived in had been overrun by the Kaiser's troops early in the war. She rebelled at something they did, and was imprisoned in a box the size of a telephone booth in the middle of winter wearing only a light dress. She was barefooted, with nothing to keep her from freezing. She was nearly dead when finally aided by two kind German soldiers; the only two she ever thought were good. It took her a long time to recover after the war and begin her life over again.

It was easy to visualize Henriette as an activist or a saboteur and I imagined that whatever she did in retaliation really fouled things up for her captors. Impetuous, haughty, intelligent, self-assured - she must have been a handful. Henriette talked endlessly even though she knew I didn't understand much of what she said, especially when she became excited and talked too fast for me. During those bursts of excitement, she used gestures I grew to love; they said everything, accented by a toss of the head and a choice explicative. I sensed that she worried about me. She thought I wasn't satisfied - that not enough was being done to get me out of France. And she was right. I didn't want to wait much longer, but there was nothing else I could do.

# Chapter 9

# D-DAY AND THE DOGFIGHT

Late that afternoon, there was a light tap on the door and I did the usual bedroom dash while Henriette answered it. She called me back to the living room and introduced a dapper-looking man in a business suit, holding his hat. He walked toward me; hand outstretched.

"Well, well, Lt. Woodrum, have you heard the good news?" he asked, shaking my hand.

"Yes, we've been listening to the invasion news all day. It's really wonderful."

"I'm Metcalf, by the way, Lieutenant. I've been meaning to get by sooner but it's been impossible. Today should be one of celebration between allies, so I thought I'd come introduce myself."

"I'm glad you did. I have a lot of questions."

"Yes, I'm sure you have. Are they treating you well?"

"Oh, yes. The hospitality couldn't be better."

"That's good. We try to get extra rations for those who take care of downed flyers and are usually able to, but now, with the invasion, it may become more difficult - but we'll manage."

"I certainly appreciate everyone's help."

"We intend to get you out," Metcalf continued. "We hope to fly you out and I think we'll now have a greater need for new people so it may be sooner than we might have expected."

"It sounds as if you've been here for some time."

"Yes, I have, since 1922, actually." He smiled at the look of surprise on my face.

"I've been home often. I'll tell you about it tomorrow when we have more time. I want to pick you up about four in the afternoon and take you to my home for dinner." I was surprised that he wanted me to move about so freely, but I welcomed the invitation.

Henriette asked Metcalf a question, and he nodded "Oui, merci," then turned to me. "I suppose you'd like tea also, lieutenant?"

"Yes, I would."

"The invasion news is splendid," he said. "They've apparently established three beachheads along the Normandy coast. It seems Carentan will be the key point in the attack and the sooner we take it the better. They are continuing to land more troops and have made some penetrations, but the resistance is fierce in some places where they didn't expect much of a fight. Caen is also a key, it seems."

"What I couldn't believe was the number of warships involved," I said. "One report said there were over 500 taking part."

"Yes, the BBC said that also. There haven't been any air attacks, either. I heard one report which said only one ME-109 flew over the invasion ships all day. That's hard to believe."

"It is," I agreed. "I just counted the airfields bombed by our group the two weeks before I was shot down. There were four total, and we hit others in April. Lately, we concentrated on bridges over the Seine. Now I know why."

"Isolation of the battlefield, I suppose."

"That's it, I guess."

Henriette brought us a pot of tea, a bowl of sugar and a small pitcher of milk. As we served ourselves, she stood, her eyes darting from me to Metcalf, wondering what we were saying. Occasionally, Metcalf would speak quickly in French to keep her in the conversation.

"Lieutenant, we'll get you out as quickly as possible. You will be taken to a place not far away from a field where you'll be picked up by a Lysander or a Dakota some night and returned to England. We've made quite a few night pick-ups and have been very successful. But that may change because Jerry is sure to change his tactics and may take action to stop such flights."

"I wondered how the invasion might affect evasion plans."

"Yes, I'm sure it's natural to feel that way. I'm glad I could relieve any fears you may have had about that."

Metcalf shook hands and left, saying he'd return the next afternoon. Instead, he was back an hour later. Taking me by the arm, he decided we should celebrate on the actual day of invasion. I carefully wore my beret the way Carlos had shown me and slouched a bit as I walked downstairs and across the sidewalk to the car.

We headed to Avenue de Saint Cloud, the main street, then north to a pleasant residential neighborhood where Metcalf pulled into the driveway of a house. The yard was shaded by weeping willows and poplars.

Inside, he introduced me to his wife and sister-in-law, then poured both of us a whiskey and soda. We toasted the success of the invasion. As we drank, he told me his story. He had come to France as a businessman, married a French girl, and although he maintained his British citizenship, he thought of himself as French. He was a captain in the Royal Artillery during World War I. He illustrated his story with pictures in a scrapbook. Although younger and thinner, with a slightly bushier black mustache than he sported now, he looked much the same. He was now 48, he said.

The Germans had placed him on parole when they occupied the country, leaving him alone as long as he checked in on schedule, twice monthly. He thought the check-ins would increase now. I was surprised they were so lenient with him. He said they wouldn't allow him to live in the coastal city that had been his home before the war, but forced him inland. He had chosen Versailles.

His wife spoke English fluently, but her sister, who understood nearly everything, hesitated to speak it. His wife was nervous about

Metcalf's Underground activities. She said I was the first English-speaking guest in their home in almost two years. She confided that each time her husband left the house, she wondered if he'd ever return. Now that the invasion was underway, she thought he'd be asked to do more at greater risk. It was possible that the Germans might place him under arrest, and she half-hoped they would. At least then he'd be safe.

Metcalf listened as she discussed the problems of having a husband in the resistance, smiling occasionally and shrugging off her fear with his motto, words to the effect of "Live Free Or Die!" He hated Nazism with a passion and wanted a personal role in ridding the world of it. He'd been contacted by the Underground just after the fall of France and had been active ever since.

We talked more after dinner, then Metcalf took me back to the Brenners, a half-hour before curfew. En route, he told me that he personally wrote the message about the HE-111 and asked me to let him know if I saw anything else of importance. His teams would respond quickly. At the apartment, he came upstairs to give the Brenners instruction to contact him if Madame Blanche wasn't available.

I drank cognac in the parlor with Charles and Henriette, telling them about Metcalf's house and family. They were surprised. They thought he'd been in France just a short time.

The next morning, I was stirred by the roar of aircraft engines. I sat up in bed as the high-pitched snarl built to a furious thunder, all from Villacoublay. I tumbled out of bed and sat at the window, watching formations of FW-190s swarm to land. It was just past dawn. The sky was streaked a rosy-gray along the eastern horizon, but clear overhead. When the planes landed, I watched for a few more minutes. Then I went back to bed.

But soon I was back at my window seat, beckoned again by the sound of engines. Suddenly, an ME-109 angled sharply upward from the tree-lined horizon at the airport. It had two diagonal red stripes from the front of the wing root to the outer trailing edge of the wings, and its entire engine nacelle was red. There was another large emblem on the side of the fuselage, just behind the cockpit. As it reached an altitude of perhaps 300 feet, the plane banked left. Watching it, I noticed another

ME-109 following close behind, then another and another, each of them starting left, climbing turns. The leader was at an altitude of at least 3,000 feet, forming an ever-enlarging corkscrew shaped spiral.

When the last ship was airborne and melted into the snarling swirl, the whole shebang seemed to collapse as the leader nosed his ship down, accelerating, and the others tagged along in a sort of indiscriminate mass, alongside, underneath, above, below, and behind. As the leader leveled off, the others simultaneously made the same turn, moving together like a swarm of bees. If even one ship had started a turn in any other direction there would have been a massive collision. Either there was no precision at all or the utmost precision possible, I couldn't tell which. Counting as fast as I could, I estimated there were at least 150 ME-109s and FW-190s in that group.

When they were out of sight, I went into the parlor and turned on the radio. Charles and I pinned a map on the wall and began plotting invasion battle lines with each new report. The news was still excellent that morning and our pins protruded a little further into France from the beach. The first bulletin reported the Germans still hadn't shown air strength over the invasion area. I wondered how long that would last, in view of my early-morning airport show. That many fighters could raise a lot of hell.

Henriette brought us some coffee and toast. I brought her up to date, editorializing that the news was good. Charles left for work, and a little later, Henriette said she had to leave for a while. I was to keep the radio very low and not answer the door.

My thoughts were on the German fighters, far and away the largest gathering I'd ever seen. Their action would have a major impact if they were able to penetrate air defenses over the beachhead. I listened to the radio repeat the news from the night before - some advances on the ground with sporadic resistance in some places and heavy resistance at others, and a few unexpected early gains with more allied troops landing every minute.

An hour and 15 minutes later, the German fighters returned.

The first came alone. Others soon followed - individually and in pairs. Some were damaged, their engines interrupted by silent pauses, trailing black smoke. After the first dozen or so planes landed, the red-nosed Messerschmidt came slanting in hurriedly from the west, in a long, descending straight-in approach. There was a sense of urgency about it: the pilot made no attempt to set up a normal landing pattern - just a long dive from the west right into the field. Before he touched down out of sight behind trees that obscured the actual landing, others flew in from the same direction, several trailing black smoke. Then another large group arrived, milling above the field while they determined their landing priority. Some were FW-190s, but most were ME-109s. I must have seen 100 fighters return. I counted 60 before I lost track when several large groups appeared. During the next 30 minutes, more straggled in, revving and jazzing their engines like kids in hot rods until the power kicked in and the motors took on their peculiar whining-roar in the final approach. The jazzing bit made me cringe. In a B-26, I wanted power all the way! By now, some 200 fighters had returned to Villacoublay, more than I'd seen leave. As the last of the huge flock straggled in, Henriette returned. We watched the crumpled remnants return to earth.

"What is happening, Albert?" she asked in French.

"Nothing good for the Germans."

"Tant mieux!"

When I watched them leave earlier, I was nervous, well aware of the damage they could inflict. But seeing them return so injured, I knew they'd been seriously mauled by Allied fighters flying cover over the beachhead or making fighter sweeps inland.

I decided the Germans must have diverted their fighters from all over France and Western Europe to Normandy. Certainly a lot of them had come to Villacoublay. They'd been caught napping the day before and I felt sure every fighter the Allies could spare was guarding the invasion area.

Considering all of the P-47s, P-51s and P-38s the 8th and 9th Air Forces used, in addition to the Spitfires and Hurricanes the RAF could put over France just across the channel from their bases, I realized the type of defensive umbrella the Germans must have encountered. I felt proud. If we could repel such a massive fighter strike so easily, we could surely maintain air superiority and the invasion landings could continue with likely success. Listening to the radio that day, I heard cryptic messages announced on BBC, giving coded instructions to Underground agents behind the lines. They were classics.

"Pierre, there is a red, red rose in the ice-box for you."

"The tomato is red when it is ripe."

"Tomorrow, I am going to camp."

"The little girl says, "This is too much for me!"

"Marcel, your interest is due on the 12th."

I imagined all sorts of people scurrying around, triggered by those messages. I wondered if they were all authentic or if some were intended merely to confuse the Germans.

That afternoon I watched the HE-111 arrive about the same time I'd seen it before, then take off again. Charles came home from work and said the train crews told him that railroads to the west were clogged with engines and rail cars strafed by the Allies. As we talked, we heard the first few fighters leave Villacoublay again. We went to my bedroom to watch the planes take off, not in formation, but in much smaller groups, heading to safer airfields in eastern France or Germany.

Charles and I updated our map after another radio session. Some advances had been made along the western edge of the front, but to the east, near Caen, the line was stuck in virtually the same spot as the day before.

The next few days blended together. I listened to the radio, read, and wondered in frustration what was happening with my evasion. Charles brought home valuable news from the train crews.

That's how I learned an American P-47 pilot had discovered a new way to kill Panzer tanks. He made a frontal attack on a Panzer column on an asphalt road. On the way in, he noticed his tracers hit the tank's armor without effect, but as he fired on the tanks near the end of the column, his tracers struck the road just in front of the tank, which then exploded. He tried it again, aiming at the macadam between the last tank's treads, realizing that his 50s were deflected by the road surface into the vulnerable belly of the tank. He had a field day until he ran out of ammunition, getting five by himself in the process. He spread the word, and as a result, a lot of Panzers were turned into burning hulks.

One evening after dinner, an air raid alarm sounded. We went onto the one balcony that had enough room for all of us to stand and heard flak open up just west of Versailles. We saw aircraft enter from the north. Searchlights blinked on, spearing bombers as they lined up to approach the target. Flak exploding near the first bombers illuminated them high in the sky, but soon they were gone. The searchlights blinked out, and the night sky was empty. Charles and Henriette guessed the target was an airfield at Dreux.

I awoke the next morning, yawning, knowing it was too early to get up. The head of my bed was against the east, outside wall of the building. I could hear street noises, then the far-off hum of straining aircraft engines mingled with a popping noise I recognized as 20-millimeter cannon. I lunged out of bed, taking the sheet with me in my rush and stared out the window. Incredulous, I saw, coming straight at me moving flat-out, an American P-51 Mustang. Trailing were five FW-190s like a swarm of bees, all taking pot-shots at that poor little Yankee boy.

The two-tone checkered nose and rudder of the Mustang were distinct. The fuselage was otherwise unpainted, except for what I learned later were invasion stripes and the usual Army Air Force insignia. The plane was bright, shiny aluminum. Its squadron designation, black letters painted on the side of the fuselage stood out clearly. In the instant it passed not fifty feet overhead, I noticed its bubble canopy, the first I'd ever seen.

I dashed to the parlor where I spotted the group again, but as they flew away from our building, they'd dipped lower so I was looking straight at them. They flashed out of sight. I turned from the window, realizing I was still wearing only my floppy shorts as Henriette came in from the kitchen, in her bathrobe. She looked at me, "Albert, le Americain a du se faire abattre?"

"Je pense que oui." I nodded slowly.

She turned away; sadness mirrored in her face. I went back to my room, pulled on pants and slippers, then started to the dining room, just as Henriette cried out.

"Albert! Albert, venez vite."

I jogged to the living room and onto the balcony. Although several minutes had passed since the planes disappeared, the battle had unexpectedly continued, but the tide had changed. Coming toward us on a course that would take them within 200 yards of our apartment at roof level, were the fighters. Leading the pack was a lonesome FW-190 frantically trying to escape the P-51 pilot who was hosing him relentlessly with .50-caliber slugs. Behind them were the other four Jerries, holding their fire because of the awkward position of the FW-190. Less than 300 yards separated the first ship from the last.

I was sweating for the American though, because the Jerry was playing it cozy - flying over the anti-aircraft battery in the little park across the street from our apartment. The Jerry wiggled his wings as the battery opened fire, but the Mustang did the same thing and the firing stopped. Just then, the law of averages caught up with the German plane. It exploded in an angry orange and black burst.

The Mustang ducked the debris, but he was again the hunted. More shots flew. He banked to the right, toward Villacoublay, still right on the deck. At the field, he started a strafing run and all the ack-ack on the ground opened up on him, even on the German fighters.

The three FW-190s nearest him broke left, toward Paris, trying to avoid their own flak, but one on the right broke free. Finishing his run, the Mustang spotted him and headed for the lone FW who had apparently lost sight of him, for within seconds the Yank was sitting on his tail taking pot-shots at the Luftwaffe again.

I saw the other three planes complete wider turns, some distance behind now, and although nothing had changed in the physical appearance, they no longer had the pouncing, snarl of the hunter.

I ran through the apartment to the other window. As the planes passed, the thunder of their engines rocketing over the roof was punctuated by short ammo-saving bursts of .50-caliber machine guns.

Scraping roof-tops, twisting and yawing, they crossed the city. At last, smoke trailed from the FW as it nosed into the landscape, self-destructing on impact west of the city.

The Yank racked the Mustang around in a steep chandelle, nearly reversing course. The first two 190s flashed past the wreck and pulled up also, but the third, tagging along behind erred, turning north, away from the Mustang. The American fired on the pigeon. Smoke trailed from the FW immediately and the Mustang turned again as the remaining enemy ships closed in. The distressed FW limped away, gushing smoke and flames until its airspeed dropped and it crashed in the woods north of the city, only a few miles from its base. Now only the three machines remained, but there was little distance between the American and the pursuing Krauts.

I glanced around and noticed that neighbors were clustered on all the other balconies and roof-tops. They gestured, reliving the combat, cheering silently and openly for the gutsy, lone American. A stocky man with a bushy, black handlebar mustache looked up from a lower balcony, raised a clenched fist, and shook it emphatically; glad to see Germans losing for a change.

I was overwhelmed by the pilot's fantastic maneuvers. Adrenalin flooded through me. I'd never been so proud of a countryman in my life, but I knew the guy would have a tough time from here on out; those last two weren't going to give him any breaks. On the other hand, I thought, the Jerries were nervous now, which might be in the Yank's favor.

They disappeared southwest of the city and for a few minutes, all was quiet, the roof-top crowd silent, watchful and waiting, frustrated not knowing what was happening. But suddenly, the three ships burst back over the horizon, the Mustang miraculously in the middle. They made a long pass over the city as the American slowly closed in to a range from which he couldn't miss, holding fire.

That FW pilot is really sweating, I thought, as the roof-top audience broke into a cheer. The Mustang had to be low on ammo by now, but the FW pilot couldn't outrun him, so when he saw his nemesis close the gap, the German pulled up frantically just as the 50s sounded a chattering burst. The FW's nose straight up, its prop windmilling to a stop, the ship stalled some 1200 feet above the ground and the luckless pilot bailed out, opening his chute immediately.

It was incredulous! The American narrowed the odds to one on one. Even! Unbelievable. What a dogfight! It seemed like an eternity, but it had all transpired in just minutes.

Off in the distance, I watched the two make another long, low arc. The American started a gradual swing to the west, but he wasn't about to leave the treetop altitude that had been his salvation.

The Jerry on his tail was further back, his guns silent as he waited to get a real pot-shot, just as the American had earlier. I wondered if he, too, was low on ammunition. The Mustang weaved from side to side as they disappeared. I was sure it was all over. The Jerry held the final card and was waiting to play it. Seconds later, a black mushroom of smoke surged upward. That was it. All over for the Yankee pilot.

"Damn, damn, damn" I cursed.

One hell of a good pilot had bought the farm. He gave it all he had, cutting insane odds to even terms before the end. I wondered what he'd been thinking, getting so many and having only the one guy left. Shit! What a way to go!

I knew that no American had ever shot down five in on day - not in Europe anyway. But to get four and then not even live to tell about it!

I checked my watch and noted the Mustang marking, making a silent promise to wave his flag for him when I got back, determined to make known the four victories and the circumstances.

The spectators on the roof-tops and balconies must have felt the same. They moved slowly, scowling, stretching, and disappeared inside. They felt an intense personal loss, much as I did, as if it had been their responsibility to cheer the pilot on to a final victory. A woman on a nearby balcony called to Henriette and they talked back and forth. The mustachioed man below poured a glass of cognac, raised it for all to see, then tossed it off in a salute. Others echoed his tribute, and then ducked back inside, leaving balconies to chickens and rabbits.

Henriette went into the kitchen and poured two glassed of cognac, waiting for me to join her. We clinked the rims and Henriette said, "Aux pilotes Americains."

Twenty minutes later Charles returned from his garden plot on the other side of town, bursting with glee.

"Did you see that American kill those Germans?" he asked.

"Yes, we saw," I said. "He got four out of five."

Charles looked quizzical. "Non, non, he got them all! I saw it. It was magnificent, especially the last!"

He said this in French slow enough for me to understand but, even so, I got the dictionary and sat with him at the table as he poured cognac for both of us.

"How do you know he got them all?" I persisted.

"I saw. Especially the second, third, and fifth. The last was very near me. I was working at the garden. The last one he did not even shoot - much. They came by so fast." He motioned to indicate how fast they'd passed.

"They are right on the ground. There is a little hill, you see." Charles formed airplanes with his hands. "They skimmed the ground. The American goes - zip, like that," he said, turning his head. "Around the hill and the German follows - but in a greater circle. Then as they start around a second time, the American slows – abruptly - its wheels come down, you know?

"The German turns in toward the American, now so much slower, and they are side by side for a moment but the German plane moves ahead trying to turn toward the American when the German loses control of his machine. The American's engine roars again and he fires once. Less than a kilometer from where I am standing, the German crashes in the woods. I jump up and down and wave my hoe and everybody does the same until the Germans come. I passed the wreck coming home on my bicycle. The American flew back to Normandy. I come on home, fast!"

I realized what the American must have done. He dropped his gear, flaps, and chopped the throttle, doing everything possible to slow suddenly, forcing the German to turn in, risking a stall himself to make the German stall. The German had no choice; he would have wound up in front of the Mustang anyway.

The dogfight was the topic of conversation for days. Metcalf told me later that even the German commander had seen some of it. And that made me feel a whole lot better.

# Chapter 10

# HENRIETTE AND THE BELGIAN

After the dogfight, everything else seemed uneventful by comparison. At least until June 11, the first time I met the little Belgian.

It began with a visit from Metcalf whom I'd come to like very much. He was an intelligent, fair-minded man working like hell to get me out. He took many risks for the Underground he'd probably never get credit for. After one of our afternoon meetings, he said he'd bring a man who wanted to interview me.

"Someone I haven't met before? Is he with the Underground?" I asked.

"Yes, this man does everything. He helps with our protection. That's all I can say. But he will ask many questions. Some of them may seem strange, but do your best to answer them."

"Strange - you mean political?"

He glanced at me sharply. "You are getting very perceptive. Yes, I imagine some of them will be political?"

"OK. Who is this man?"

"Let's call him The Belgian. I'll bring him over tomorrow."

"And you think I'll be leaving soon after that?"

"It won't be long."

They came around 4:00 in the afternoon. The Belgian was very small, only about five feet tall. He was solidly built, with piercing blue eyes that reminded me of a ferret. He grinned perpetually, whether angry or happy. I usually make quick judgements but I reserved my opinion of him, unwilling to accept my initial feeling to be wary of him.

Henriette disliked him immediately. He ignored their introduction, telling Metcalf she was not to remain with us for the interview. She almost asked him to leave then and there, but Metcalf interjected, asking Henriette to trust him. Reluctantly, she left the room, muttering to herself.

The Belgian ignored Henriette's outburst, eyeing me the entire time. He pulled up a chair and straddled it, his chin resting on the top rung of the back. He began with a softening-up technique I'd heard about in England.

"I have photos of your aircraft, two on the way down in flames, and one after it crashed. I'll have copies made for you."

I thought it was a phony offer but said thanks anyway.

"Think nothing of it, Lieutenant. You know that all of your crew are prisoners, don't you?"

"Yes, does anyone know if they are all right?"

"They were all well when they left Paris for Germany." He thought a moment. "The Germans have posters out in Carrieres-sur-Seine with a remarkable likeness of you. Someone in the crowd apparently gave them a good description."

"Well I'll be damned," I said. "It must really irk them to know I got away."

His eyes darted about the room. I was thinking about getting one of those posters for a souvenir.

"I have some important questions to ask," he said, his smile suddenly replaced by a frown as he stared at the floor deciding how to begin. Abruptly, he looked up, "Why are you in this war?"

I knew he meant the United States, not me personally, but the question bothered me since he was supposed to be on my side and should know the reason.

"To kill as many Germans and Japs as I can, if you want my personal reasons," I said, "and they are about the same if you want to know why my country is at war. We got the hell kicked out of us in a sneak attack after waiting too long to become involved, so now we are going all the way."

"It's interesting to hear you say you are in the war to kill personally. Why is that?"

"I was stationed in Hawaii on December 7, 1941. Does that answer your question?"

He looked puzzled, but when he heard my answer, his expression changed. The smile returned with a look of pleasure. "You don't like the Japanese at all, do you?"

"No, I certainly don't."

"Did you almost get killed that day?"

"The first damned bomb in Hawaii fell about 200 yards away from me. They came a lot closer after that and for over twenty minutes, in another place where they pinned me down, they took pot shots from a range of less than fifty feet. I lost a lot of friends out there. Since they didn't bother to declare war, yes, it made me mad as hell."

"But why does the United States fight the Germans?"

"Because they're taking over peaceful nations, disregarding treaties and overrunning Europe. Look what they do right here in France to anybody they capture from the Underground!"

"You don't really know that is true, do you." He didn't say it as a question.

"I've talked with a lot of knowledgeable people - that's good enough for me," I said.

"Lieutenant, don't kid me. Really, what territory will your country keep after the war?"

I finally got the drift. I'd heard a lot of stories about who ran the Underground, but this got me mad. I decided to answer, certain by now the Belgian was communist.

"Hell, we left Europe long ago for places like Florida, California, Colorado, the Plains States, the Gulf States - you name it. We didn't lose anything over here. We don't want it. All we want to do is kick the shit out of Hitler and go home."

"Do you think you'll be able to do that?"

"Who's going to stop us?"

The Belgian didn't say anything for a moment, just stared moodily, the smile gone.

"How about the Pacific?" he finally asked.

"Out there we'll keep whatever we damn please. They asked for it with that sneak attack so we'll keep what we need to oversee that area."

"You seem pretty sure of yourself."

"Yes," I grinned. "Guess I do."

"What makes you feel that way? Pearl Harbor happened two and a half years ago and the US has done nothing significant there yet."

"I disagree because we have. But we didn't start arming until then, either, and you know what's happening right now, just west of here, don't you? Don't worry; we'll get to Tokyo a lot sooner than you might think."

"Do you have a new weapon you expect to do all this with?"

"Sure. But you're an ally, you ought to know. We'll just bomb the hell out of every damned Japanese-held island."

"You have such planes?"

Everybody knew about the B-29, already in action. I began to tire of questions that didn't make much sense, so I asked a question.

"They say you know what's going on everywhere. How soon will I get out of here?"

"Soon. And you're right. I do know what's going on because I work in German Headquarters."

I believed him. He had guts; I bet he did work there. I looked him over carefully as he puffed his cigarette.

"Yes," he said. "They will torture me for a long time if they discover me. Do not say anything to Madame Brenner. She is mad enough at me already. She does not know what I do and I don't want her to know. I tell you this because they do not torture downed airmen no matter what you may have heard."

"When will I leave here? Do you know?"

"Within a week, I think. We'll let you know the day before very long." Whether or not the guy was a communist didn't make much difference. He was a double agent and, as far as I knew, was against the Germans, a communist working for the downfall of the Nazis. But his ultimate goal was to set up Europe for a Russian takeover. It was the same damned thing all over again, I thought.

The outcome of one war is frequently responsible for the beginning of the next. Hitler used the Versailles treaty as a rallying cry in Germany along with his tirade against the Jews, to make his pitch for Nazism and the master race. But when he took over Poland, France and England declared war. Now, Russia was set to grab it and whatever else they could get. If the Polish people hated anybody worse than the Germans, it was the Russians.

I was confident Metcalf was a communist, too. Is that why he remained in France since the twenties? I wondered.

"Will I be flown out or go through Spain?"

"We intend to fly you out but the invasion may change our plans."

"If anything does happen, shall I let Metcalf know?"

"Yes, that's right."

"Did the German commander really watch the dog fight?" I asked, smiling.

"He saw much of it. He saw the Focke-Wolf crash and its pilot bail out."

The Belgian stood and stuck out a hand, looking me squarely in the eye for a change.

"I think you are in earnest when you say the United States does not want anything in Europe."

"That's just my opinion. The only thing that would screw it up would be if somebody else tried to take it over as Hitler did. That would change a lot of things."

"I understand."

As I shook hands with Metcalf, the Belgian opened the door into the hall. Henriette stood there, a defiant look on her face. The Belgian bowed to her and made a long flowery speech in French, which had little effect on her attitude. Still smiling, he walked down the hall, calling softly over his shoulder, "She hates me!"

Henriette spoke to Metcalf, then he turned to me translating, "The Americans and the British have just linked-up. They now have a 70 mile long front established."

They departed, Henriette standing in the hall, mad as hell. She immediately steered me into the parlor where Madame Blanche sat waiting. Henriette asked questions for her to translate into English.

"What did he want?"

"Who?" I asked, teasing.

"The Belgian! The Belgian!"

"Oh! He wanted to know why the United States was fighting in Europe." I kept a straight face, certain of her questions.

"Why was he so impolite?"

"He was in a hurry."

"In a hurry. Humph. He could at least have been courteous to me in my own home. He actually ordered me out of the room - did you see that? In my own house. I don't trust him! I think he's a spy. I'm going to tell Mr. Metcalf not to bring him here again."

Several minutes passed before she calmed down to talk about the good news from Normandy. But when Charles came home, she started all over again about "Le petite Belge!"

I was obviously being controlled by a communist, and depending upon him to help get me out of occupied France. I'd been here 15 days and doing pretty well. I remembered fighter pilots, aces, getting out of France or Holland in a week. But things were different now. The invasion changed everything. I couldn't afford to slip up and get caught now. I didn't know what kind of treatment I'd get from the Germans at this point.

Charles and I listened to the radio, learning that the U.S. bombarded the Marianas. I grinned, thinking, "How about that, Le Belge? The Japs know for sure we're in the Pacific."

The next afternoon, about the time the fighters usually took off for the east, a flight of RAF Mosquitos bombed and strafed

Villacoublay. I was surprised to see Mosquitos in the afternoon but decided the invasion changed tactical needs. They left several fires and I wondered if they caught the fighters or the HE-111-K on the ground. I hoped Madame Blanche's message about the regularity of flight was the cause.

The next day, I heard some news from the Pacific I would have enjoyed telling the Belgian. A big American task force raided the island of Iwo Jima only 900 miles from Tokyo. That was a deep penetration into Japanese waters and probably a forerunner of things to come. There was some news for the Brenners too, because General De Gaulle visited parts of Normandy that day, the first time he set foot on French soil since 1940.

The Pacific news continued a few more days. U.S. forces landed on Saipan and B-29 Superfortresses from China hit Japanese cities in Kyushu. I really wanted to see Le Belge that day. I saw a few B-29s in the States on bases where I RON (remained overnight) and was aware of their range. If they bombed Japanese industrial plants regularly, the Japs would soon be in trouble.

On June 15th, Madame Blanche and Henriette completely surprised me with a birthday dinner. For wartime fare, it was fantastic. They went all out, even serving one of Henriette's favorite prewar desserts, a superb chocolate mousse. When I told her how good it was, she gave me one of those shrugs and said, "Ah, well, before the war, with the right ingredient . . ."

Metcalf joined us after dinner and we all drank cognac, for they clued him in on the celebration. He told me he was sorry about the political questions and I apologized for sounding off. He said he understood.

I asked him about any news; he said nothing startling had happened. But buzz bombs troubled him deeply. It was the ultimate panic weapon, falling all over London, killing innocent civilians.

"They've taken so much in London, and now this," he said.

Before Metcalf left, he urged me to take off on my own if a truckload of Germans made a fast stop in front of the apartment or if I saw unusual activity. I knew something bothered him to issue such a warning. I told him not to worry, that I'd take off if I thought it necessary.

The next day passed quietly. No aircraft used Villacoubly. Charles didn't go to work until 10:00. They told him to be there at that time and plan to work later than usual, but didn't say why.

In early afternoon, sitting by the window reading, I heard the rumble of tanks up the main street in the direction of the airfield. The rumbling grew louder. I put my book down and watched as they came into view at the far end of Rue des Chantiers. Their treads clanked over broken patches in the cobblestones.

As they neared our building, I realized there were a lot more of them than I first thought. The line reached all the way back to the low bluff near the airfield. Most of the crews wore black SS uniforms. The red armbands with white bordered black swastikas stood out boldly. They were hard-looking, well-disciplined soldiers, their eyes flicking from side to side as they trundled down the street, ready to blast away if necessary.

There was no comparing these guys and the troops the Commandant of Versailles reviewed the day I arrived here. These men were sharp, the best I'd seen. The steady rumble continued for some time. All the tanks seemed new and I wondered if they were manufactured in a nearby French factory.

When the last of the tanks passed, I'd counted more than 300 tanks and at least 3000 troops. Charles came home about 7:00 that night and told us all of the tanks were in the small nearby marshalling yard, ready to be loaded on rail cars for midnight shipment to the front.

I wondered if this was something to report to Metcalf, who must surely know. We talked it over and decided to let him know anyway. Henriette left the apartment to fetch someone. After she left, I wrote two notes. Each read: "300+ tanks leave Versailles RR yard tonight. Midnight latest."

Henriette returned with a young girl, about 13. Watching from my partially opened bedroom door, I saw them roll my message into a tiny square then slip it into the sweatband of the girl's beret. She left to take it to Madame Blanche. Later, Henriette said the girl was 11 years old. Charles left, and returned in 30 minutes, saying it was done. Now we just had to wait.

I went to sit by the window. The HE-111 came in as I sat there watching. At 8:15, Madame Blanche came to the apartment to tell us the message was transmitted a few minutes earlier. Then she stepped into the darkness to beat the curfew.

# Chapter 11

# THE BOMBING

I listened to the news, and went to bed just before eleven. Henriette and Charles had retired earlier. As I climbed into bed, I heard aircraft in the distance and as the sound of their engines grew louder, I realized the RAF was already approaching Versailles. They were coming from the northwest. Suddenly, the anti-aircraft battery in the park across the street which had fired at the Mustang a few days earlier, opened up; the sharp, unexpected boom of several cannons reverberated through the night, three quick bursts, then three more. Muzzle flashes lighted the room with each firing.

The Brenners joined me at the window. Henriette looked worried, but Charles was as stoical as ever. We went out on the balcony to watch the approach of the aircraft. Searchlight beams swung across the sky, sweeping through the darkness.

Anti-aircraft guns continued to fire as other batteries encircling the city joined in, their sound rising to a furious crescendo. I realized there were more guns nearby than I'd been aware of, and guessed that some of them were on tanks in the rail yard. The roar intensified as the aircraft drew nearer, and smaller caliber weapons, probably 20-millimeter guns, joined the 88s. Then we saw, ensnared in the crossed fingers of light, the lead bomber.

As it made a small turn to the right, flak exploded around the plane, scarring the darkness with crimson flashes. A flare burst above us, burning fiercely, hissing as it drifted down onto the city, lighting the area for the bombardiers. I could see neighbors on other balconies, watching the flashes of the anti-aircraft guns.

An eerie whistling broadened into a rushing sound as the night was further shattered by the detonation of the first bomb. It seemed to blow the sky apart. I recalled that the RAF flew a bomber stream - one after another - instead of flying formations. I wondered how long this would last.

The constant dissonance of cannons pounded around us, the clamor accented by what could only be those huge British blockbusters detonating nearby. The noise clawed relentlessly at the night. Surely, nothing could survive another horrendous, ear-splitting, mind-boggling blast. Then it came - worse than I could have imagined.

I reeled as if struck by a physical blow. Glancing toward the cemetery on the hill behind our building, I saw the earth erupt. The eerie light of flares illuminated a tree as it was torn from its roots and lifted, suspended momentarily into midair. The ground at its base swirled wickedly. The bombers continued to pound their target, until I wondered if this was the nosiest place in the world at that precise instant. My ears were ringing and my head ached. But there was no sanctuary, no shelters. Henriette and Charles went to their room, but I stayed on the balcony a little longer—long enough to hear a long shriek from above, louder than the others, growing closer, seemingly with a personal message to deliver. I couldn't do a damned thing. Hope and prayer appeared to be my only options. Take it standing up or lying down.

Choosing the latter strategy, I went to my bedroom and lay down, covering my head with a pillow. I screamed at the top of my lungs with the next explosion. Oddly enough, it seemed to help. The electricity in the city had been shut off early in the raid and now it was pitch black, except for the constant bomb blasts that lit up the sky as if it was high noon.

I tried to anticipate the detonation of each bomb, then shout. I kept yelling, sometimes guessing right, other times yelling just after the burst. Finally, I decided it was best to sit up and watch whatever happened. I sat in the darkness waiting for the detonations, which finally began to slow. I walked back to the parlor window and followed the searchlight's beams, spotting an occasional bomber penetrating the light to reach the target.

I hoped the bombs were destroying the tanks. Flames from the rail yard indicated they'd hit that target.

Every minute or so, another plane in the stream reached the bomb-release point, the interval between arrivals varying slightly, but not much. It started about eleven, and it was now almost 11:45 p.m. I thought it would never end.

Occasionally a bomb would fall short, rocking our building on its foundation. One fell just over the brow of the hill and I craned my neck to see the cemetery practically demolished. Trees were down and large chunks of lawn blown away. Bare spots appeared among the row of crosses, exposing craters in the earth. The dead from the last war were still being disturbed.

Henriette and Charles emerged from their bedroom to see if I was all right. Henriette was sobbing, and fearful. We tried to comfort her, but as long as bombs were falling, it was no use.

Frequently, as many as three planes would appear over the target simultaneously, and within seconds, several tons of bombs would come spinning down through the blackness, gigantic thudding WHAMS announcing their impact with earth. Dirt, rocks, and other debris struck the sides of our building sounding like a crowd of idiots throwing handfuls of rocks against the walls. After a while, that sound became so muffled, I could no longer hear it. I decided there were a lot of sounds I could no longer hear. I guessed I'd be partially deaf for a few days, at least.

I raised my watch and saw that it was midnight. Almost an hour of bombing. There couldn't possibly be any tanks left, I thought.

I stepped back from the window because flak and splinters were being hurled through the air as shrapnel. I sat down, grabbing a pillow and holding it over my head as I continued yelling. Soon I was hoarse as well as deaf.

Charles handed me a bottle of cognac, which I accepted gladly, taking a long pull and wondering why I hadn't thought of that myself.

The last bomber dropped its payload just after midnight. Finally, it was quiet again, except for the distant "beem-bom" sounds of fire engines. Searchlights blinked sporadically. Henriette returned to her bedroom, and Charles followed after we shared another cognac.

As I scanned the now empty sky over the rail yard, I wondered if this was the result of my message, or if someone else had gotten the word to Metcalf? The bombers must have wiped out their targets. I hoped so, because that made enduring the terror a little more bearable.

It was far and away the biggest bombing raid I ever experienced. Two hundred plane raids on London were bad, but I was never in the center of the bombing area there, if there was a center. The attack on Wheeler Field took place during the day, and that wasn't so bad, mostly dive bombers, not high-altitude stuff you couldn't see. This was the worst. I went to bed. Stretching out full length, I shut my eyes. The bed seemed to rock with bomb blasts and my eyes still throbbed from the flashes. My temples ached, and the painful pounding kept me awake for a long, long time. The headache was still there when I awoke, but I went to the kitchen anyway. Charles and Henriette were there. He'd been sent home because the yard was closed. Slave labor gangs and several battalions of German engineer troops were already there, cleaning up the wreckage.

Charles learned that none of the tanks escaped, and several crews, unable to reach shelter in time, were killed in the raid's early stages. Someone also told him that P-38s had flown over the city just after dawn. I knew photos were probably already on some British intelligence officer's desk along with a full report of the damage. They very likely knew when to expect the yard back in operation.

Three hundred tanks. I was glad to know they would never get to Normandy; they would have delayed the Allied advance a long time.

The rest of the day passed quietly. We listened to the news and heard only one mention of a raid on Versailles. It simply said that a small force of Lancasters had struck a marshaling yard. Heavy damage was reported.

Metcalf came by at four that afternoon while Charles was in the garden. He said Germans were scouring the city trying to learn which group had sent the information back to England. They were rounding up a lot of people and forcing them to talk. So far, they hadn't picked up any of his men. He said he'd try to get me out the next day. He had come personally to let me know how it would be done.

"Listen carefully. When it is time, there will be two gendarmes. You will leave as their prisoner, probably in handcuffs, and they may get rough with you," he said.

"They have to be realistic. Do not cry out in English when they do. You must say nothing to anyone once out of this room, even if spoken to directly by a German. Do not talk! Understand?"

"Yes."

"Good. I'll be back tomorrow with the gendarmes if I can. Otherwise, good luck."

He stood, spoke briefly with Henriette, then left. She was obviously worried and I think she believed they may have been betrayed, but she said nothing to me about it. Henriette told me she still didn't trust the Belge. She thought he would betray them to save himself, but she didn't know what I knew about him and all I could do was remain silent.

The next day passed slowly. Charles was already at work when I got up. Charles and Henriette had replaced my supply case with a small canvas one, almost like a musette bag. I packed my new, extra clothing, a razor, toothbrush, and an extra pair of socks. I was ready to go within a moment's notice.

I sat listening to the radio, wondering if they would come that day and where they would take me. I knew only that it would be a place in the country near an open field where an airplane could land safely at night.

I still hated the "hurry up and wait" stuff.

The delay gave me a chance to review my position. I felt confident that I'd really be able to evade. My hopes had been high all along, but now, if I could just reach the hideout in the woods and wait for the plane, I'd be on my way. I wondered how I'd ever be able to thank people like the Brenners and the Filipottos.

Yankee Doodle radio reported that more buzz bombs, as they were calling them, were falling on London. The BBC said some pilots were successful in flying formation with them, then nudging them out of control with a flip of their own wing tips so the buzz bombs would crash over open countryside before reaching London. That took a lot of guts, I thought, and a highly skilled pilot.

That afternoon, Metcalf returned with the Belgian. Henriette raised hell when they arrived, but Metcalf took her aside and had a long talk with her until she quieted. Apparently, she thought the Belgian was going to dump me. But they'd come to deliver a warning.

"Lieutenant, the raid has caused a lot of strife," the Belgian said. "The Germans are questioning everyone ever suspected of having worked with the Allies, no matter how small the connection. Things are disrupted to say the least. But tomorrow you go, regardless.

"The order has already been given and no matter what happens now, two gendarmes will arrive here about two o'clock tomorrow afternoon. Remember, do not talk. No one will visit you until then. When you get back, tell them we thought 300 tanks was worth the exposure."

"Very well, I will."

He smiled. "Also, see if you can get Madame Henriette to be quiet long enough for me to thank her, eh?"

I followed him into the hall and walked over to Henriette. I put my hands on her shoulders and, looking her in the eye, told her everything was all right, then I asked her to thank the Belgian and tell him goodbye.

She regarded me very seriously for a moment, then went to him and nodded, "Au revoir et merci."

The Belgian bowed, and said, "Au revoir, Madame."

We shook hands; they wished me good-luck, then left. I never saw either of them again.

I had trouble falling asleep that night, and awoke early the next morning, feeling something akin to those old mission jitters.

Charles was home and we listened to the radio and played hearts. The rest of the morning, I just sat. And waited. There was a bulletin on buzz bombs, reporting that bombing of the launch sites was a top priority.

While drinking our coffee after lunch, I told the Brenners I'd be leaving soon. Henriette was shocked to hear that I'd be handcuffed between two gendarmes. I told them in advance so they'd have plenty of time to make up a story to tell their neighbors. After I explained there was no safer place for me than in the hands of the police, Henriette saw the wisdom of the scheme and quit her fretting.

"There is no better way, Henriette, the Germans will not talk with a French prisoner," I told her.

The gendarmes arrived just before two o'clock. They were both tall and burly. They looked like authentic gendarmes. They briefed the Brenners with some additional information they could give the neighbors; they then placed me in handcuffs and leg irons. As we prepared to leave, one of the big men came close to me and muttered, "We go. No speak!"

As the other opened the door, the guy who had spoken English pushed me into the hall. They both began shouting at me, their voices sounding madder than hell. Both of them used billy clubs as they pushed me down the stairs, pounding on my back and shoulders. I got one quick glance of Henriette and Charles in the door. She held a hand to her face as she gasped, but Charles showed a sly grin, knowing these cops weren't really trying to kill me with their clubs.

But it must have been convincing because suddenly there was a babble of voices as doors opened up and down the halls on each floor as we went downstairs. People gathered to watch our progress, asking each other, "What happened? What did he do?"

On the sidewalk, each gendarme grabbed me by an arm and hustled me into the front seat of a car very similar to the one in which Claude had driven me to Versailles. I took one terrific wallop across the shoulders as I bent to get into the front seat, and half-turned toward the cop who hit me, snarling at him in protest. It wasn't hard to do because it hurt like hell. One of them jammed in alongside me, the other went around and got into the driver's seat.

We started down the street toward Villacoublay and after a couple of blocks, the guy on my right bent down and unlocked the leg irons. The gendarmes maintaining their stony silence.

I felt eager; happy to be on a new leg of my journey to freedom, feeling good just to be out of the apartment and seeing new country. From our direction, I guessed we would pass Villacoublay, which I was anxious to see up close.

I sat back against the seat, relaxing, fumbling with both hands and maneuvering the cuffs so I could get out a cigarette.

I placed it in the corner of my mouth, turned to the gendarme, and said, "Donnez-mois illuminer, s'il vous plait?"

The gendarme turned, looked at me, broke into a laugh, and gave me a light. I took a couple of drags and looked at the beautiful countryside, with an overpowering feeling of confidence. Hell, I thought, this is going to be a cinch.

# Chapter 12

# ROADBLOCK

At the end of the long boulevard, our car entered a stretch of highway where the tanks had rumbled into view a few days earlier. Soon we reached the trees that had blocked my view of landings at Villacoublay so many times. My first glimpse of the airport was a grassy tarmac with concrete ramps near a few large hangers. Gray and dingy, their walls and roofs showed the scars of many previous bombings and strafings. Around the perimeter of the field, 88-millimeter guns, ringed with sandbags, were manned and ready. In front of one hanger, I saw two JU-52s and further on, three or four ME-109s parked on a ramp. All was quiet.

As we continued, the driver turned south onto a secondary road. I decided the P-51 pilot must've flown directly over three 88-millimeter emplacements a couple of times on his turns away from the airport towards Versailles since they were at the edge of the tarmac almost in line with the apartment. My admiration for that pilot continued to grow. It took a lot of guts and some quick decisions to accomplish those moves.

We drove through woods that dotted the gently rolling countryside. Rows of tall poplars stood guard along the road. Cattle grazed in the fields. It felt good to be outside after being cooped up for so long.

Earlier, Metcalf said we'd be taking the back roads, and now I was glad. There were no other vehicles in sight. Once, as our car lugged while scaling a low rise, our driver cursed. Upon reaching the top, he paused to stoke the burner of the "gazogine" which consumed wood and used compressed gases to run the engine.

A few miles further, I saw a road sign with name "Corbeil." I asked the gendarme, in my fractured French, if that was where we were going. He answered maybe Provins, perhaps Melun, he didn't know. I wondered if he was telling the truth.

I thought, here I am, out in the middle of France with a couple of guys who have no idea where they're going. What a deal!

But my question was answered a few minutes later. As we approached an intersection just outside a tiny village, the gendarme pointed.

Ahead, just short of the intersection, a bicycle stood on its stand; a man squatted in back of it. He was fiddling with the value stem, but as he recognized our car, he hopped on the bike, kicked up the stand and pedaled down the left fork of the road toward Melun.

Not slowing perceptibly, our driver took the same route, passing without acknowledgement, the rider who was their signalman.

That's pretty neat, I thought. If you don't know where you're going you can't tell anybody if you get caught. I'd heard a lot about the ingenious means used by the underground to stay clear of the Germans but this was my first personal experience - aside from my leg irons and handcuffs, of course.

It was little use talking to these guys so I kept quiet. They were both understandably nervous: it was their ass if we were caught. They were sweating worse than I did on missions. They knew that if they were stopped, their chance of ever getting home to their families again was zilch.

As we continued, a few high-wheeled carts drawn by husky draft horses lumbered along dusty side roads, but there was no other traffic. Thirty minutes later, we entered a small village. Our driver parked at last in front of a small garage near an open courtyard with a white arrow painted on its gate. I wondered if that was another sign.

I was immediately led by a neatly dressed stranger in a hunting jacket, plus fours, and hiking boots, to a small café where I waited until another vehicle was readied and the route checked.

The café owner told me she'd been married to an American who had died almost a decade earlier. Answering all my questions in fluent English, she told me the stranger who brought me to her café was the chief of the local Resistance unit. She also told me the field where I was headed was further south, almost a day's drive away.

The stranger returned a while later and, speaking perfect English, introduced himself as Andre. I left with the same two gendarmes later that afternoon.

Leaving the village, we followed a narrow dirt road to a main highway. We crested a rise, and then started down a long incline bordered by thickets of trees. At the end of the stretch, vehicles appeared on both sides of the road.

Both gendarmes leaned forward, staring intently ahead until we identified them as German vehicles. Figures emerged as we drew closer, and we realized that we were approaching what we had been trying to avoid - a German roadblock.

My mouth was dry as we rolled slowly to the spot where we would place ourselves in enemy hands. I felt the old mission tenseness take root. The gendarme on my right snarled "Allemand! No talk." I turned to see him staring rigidly ahead, sweating profusely.

As if I had any intention of uttering a word! I scrutinized the German setup as we approached the check point. Heavy, air-cooled machine guns were tripod-mounted on either side of the road with two soldiers lounging near each. It was a well-chosen site for a checkpoint, because on both sides, a bank rose vertically almost five feet above the pavement. From their vantage point, the gunners could fire on any vehicle within the first hundred yards, but if anyone did manage to get farther than that, motorcycles with sidecars, staff cars, and several trucks stood ready at the edge of the forest.

Field telephones were set up on tables in the shade near the trucks. In the back of one of the trucks were several large reels of wire. Communications points and more guns were probably set up a half-mile in either direction. In my nervousness as we approached the checkpoint, I probably missed the one we'd already passed.

A non-com slouched in a folding canvas chair near the telephone table while two soldiers talked into handsets. He munched a sandwich and guzzled wine from a tall, green bottle, tilting it back to take long pulls as he basked in the warm sun.

The car ahead of us was a real clunker. Its driver either shut off the motor or it had stalled, but now that he was clear to proceed, it refused to start. A sneering corporal walked to the driver and shouted at him to get going. Then he stepped back, and continued shouting while banging on the top of the car with his fist. Finally, the car sputtered away.

I turned my attention to the corporal. He was a small, wire-thin man, not more than five-feet-two inches tall, wearing a forage cap from which long whisps of shaggy brown hair protruded. His uniform was far too large, and the jacket, which should have fit snugly, hung loose, especially at the collar. Bunches of cloth were gathered around his waist, leaving two big folds under his belt on either side.

He stood in the middle of the road for a moment staring at our driver's uniform, then stepped toward our truck as we eased into place and stopped. The little man leaned forward, peered into the cab, and uttered a single word.

"Papiers," he demanded, turning his head away again.

His neck was thrust forward from the tunic so that his head was way ahead of his shoulders, as if a race was being waged that his body would never win. His sharp nose protruded downward, and he had no eyebrows. His sunken eyes had dark circles underneath like a guy coming off a three-day drunk, and his face was very dirty. He was a scrawny little sad sack if I ever saw one.

Hitler's raving about the mighty Aryan superman flashed through my mind as I watched this ludicrous little man strut and pose, keenly aware of his importance.

I tried to show no expression, ready to look away or rub a hand across my eyes if he showed interest in me. I was nervous but determined not to do anything to reveal our scheme.

The corporal was armed. A bright, shiny machine pistol, fastened to a leather harness buckled around his body, rode smoothly at his side in such a way that he could easily raise the weapon with a flip of his hand and blaze away. I didn't doubt he was an excellent marksman.

The whole thing struck me as strangely comical, watching the corporal stare down the road while he waited for our driver to hand him the papers. I started one of my silent conversations with him:

You sure are a sorry little son-of-a-bitch, you little bastard, I thought. You're the poorest excuse for Superman I've ever seen, but as long as you've got that gun and all of this backup, we won't argue a bit. Just take our damned papers and let us go on our way.

I'd expected to be jumpy as hell, but I wasn't. When I was shot down, and assumed I'd be caught immediately, it wouldn't have made much difference to me. But now that my chances of walking out were looking so good, I sweated every move. I'd hate to see all my good fortune go down the drain if this measly wimp noticed anything out of the ordinary.

Nevertheless, I felt confident as our driver handed over our papers. The corporal flipped through the pages with a practiced waving motion. He barely glanced at them, and I doubt he read much. Then his eyes stopped flickering for a moment, and his face reflected a hint of interest as he flipped back a page to read carefully.

"Ahhh," he said. "Prisonnier, eh?"

"Oui," said our driver, looking at the dashboard.

The little corporal browsed some more. "Ahhh, execution!"

Then he gave a little tight-lipped grin, leaned over, and peered across our driver's chest to look at me. As I turned slightly toward him, his mouth opened in a wide smile, and I almost laughed aloud, because when he grinned, I saw that he was missing almost every other tooth, upper and lower, so that tooth met space and space met tooth. Unable to help myself as he continued to stare at me, grinning, I smiled back.

At that the corporal chuckled, perhaps glad to see someone worse off than himself, stood back, handed the papers to the driver, and with a wave of his hand muttered, "Passez."

The driver accelerated, shifting gears rapidly to get away from there. None of us spoke. Finally, we spotted three soldiers in the forest with their telephone and another machine gun. A quarter-mile further down the road it was still quiet in the cab and I admired how professional these two men were. They seemed as confident as authentic gendarmes.

A little further on, the truck slowed. The guy on my right lit a cigarette and handed it to the driver who took two, long hard drags before leaning back, relaxing, as he eased our truck down the road.

Then he lit a second cigarette and handed it to me. The driver turned and asked "pourquoi" and then formed an exaggerated smile. I couldn't answer in French and said I would explain later, with an interpreter, then added, "J'ai ponce une bon idée."

The driver didn't say anything for a moment, then half-turned to me, leaned over to look at his friend, and said, "Une bonne idée!" He then laughed, a big belly laugh and the other man joined him.

I chuckled, realizing what a sweat job it had really been for them. They probably thought it was crazy for a supposedly captured French murderer heading for execution to grin at a German corporal under those circumstances.

The driver slapped me on the leg. "Il n'y a pas a dire, vous etes un bon acteur!" The somber mood was broken. We continued down the road more relaxed, even after we later passed through a second, unexpected roadblock.

This one was manned by fewer German troops and they quickly passed us through. I didn't even look at the guy checking our papers, but sat there scowling at the dashboard.

The rest of the trip was a cinch. As we neared the outskirts of a small city, the gendarme on my right began removing my handcuffs and leg irons.

"Five minutes, we part," he said in French. "Change automobiles."

At the edge of town was a wide sweeping turn. A sedan was parked on the side of the road. Its hood was up and a small suitcase rested on the roof. Our driver slowed, pulled to the side of the road ahead of the other car and handed me a note in English.

It read, "Get into the other car. Say nothing."

I grabbed my canvas bag and got out. I walked to the other car and sat in the front passenger seat. The truck and the two gendarmes drove away as my new chauffeur slammed down the hood, and got into the car without a glance in my direction.

He was a skinny blond kid, about 19 years old I guessed, sporting a wisp of a mustache. We drove about three blocks, turned, drove another block, and nosed into a courtyard where he parked behind a large two-story stone house. A man sitting on the back porch waved us inside. I got out of the car and followed him. The kid waited outside.

We entered a kitchen where a woman motioned both of us to follow her. In the living room, a slender man in his late twenties eased himself up from an overstuffed chair and ambled around a big sofa to shake hands.

"Well, I see everything went all right," he said, grinning broadly.

"There were no problems, but we did go through two roadblocks," I answered.

"You did! My God, tell me about it," he said, his eyebrows shooting up in surprise. I described the first in detail. As he translated for the others, I could tell from their expressions that they hadn't expected the roadblocks either.

"You were lucky," he said when he finished translating. "Few in your situation get through roadblocks so easily."

"I guess I had good cover."

He nodded. "I'll have to get word back to Andre. By the way, I'm an American, too."

"Oh? Where are you from?" He didn't look American, more like a Cuban.

"Buenos Aires. I'm a South American," he laughed.

He introduced me to the others, it was their home.

"This is Leon Fournay, he is in the trucking business and it was his vehicle the gendarmes used to bring you here."

The middle-aged man bowed and shook hands with me. His wife, Emilie, made a little bow and took my hands in hers as she greeted me. The men sat down as Emilie poured coffee. I offered each of them a cigarette. They noticed immediately that the cigarettes were

Turkish and held them under their noses, sniffing the real tobacco appreciatively, asking how I got them. When I told them they came from some Germans living in the Hotel Meurice they laughed heartily about the black market.

I asked the South American his name, and how he happened to be in France during the war. "Oh. I'm sorry," he said. "My name is Juan. I was a student here when the war started and decided to stay. I couldn't take sides with the Germans and the French treated me so well I decided to help them any way I could."

"So you became a member of the Underground?" I asked. He nodded.

"Well, there is a lot of good news lately for you then."

"Yes, there is. We do whatever we can to disrupt things and Leon is very active transporting people. The Germans confiscate his trucks from time to time and force him to transport for them, but that gives us a good entre into all sorts of things. He hates the Germans with a passion."

I said I understand.

"Yes, well they are such bastards, you know," Juan said, spitting the words. "The American troops will recapture France before long and if they keep supplying us with arms we can help when the day comes."

"But politics in France must change," he added. "There are too many political parties so there's no way anyone can ever have a successful majority. How long do you think Roosevelt will be President?" he asked abruptly.

"That's hard to say," I replied, "There are a lot of Americans who don't like him, but he keeps getting re-elected. He's in his third term now."

Juan appeared surprised. "They must be crazy not to like him. He's a wonderful President."

I didn't want to talk politics. It was too risky. Fortunately, the blond teen-ager who drove me to the house came in just then with two young girls, brunette look-alikes. They were the Fourney's twin daughters.

Juan said he was leaving, but added that the twins spoke some English and would help with translating. He said he'd try to see me again in a day or two, before I left.

While Leon and I chatted, one of the twins came in and said "Come. Another place." I followed her across the courtyard to a concrete block building and up the stairs to a small two-room apartment on the second floor. There was a bed, two chairs, a dresser, table, and radio, with a separate lavatory and shower - all the comforts of home.

There was even an English novel on the dresser. I stayed there until evening when I was called to the main house for dinner.

The next day, I stayed upstairs. Emilie and her daughters brought me breakfast and lunch, but led me downstairs for the evening meal. Through the day, the girls visited my small room and peppered me with questions. They were nice kids with a tremendous curiosity about the United States.

After dinner, I remained downstairs for several hours talking about the war and answering more questions about the United States.

Leon was especially interested in the war in the Pacific and asked about the sneak attack on Oahu. It was after midnight when I finally returned to my room.

About noon the next day, Leon told me to bring my musette bag and meet him on the patio. As we stood there talking, a truck pulled in. Leon motioned me into the back and quickly climbed into the cab with the driver. They drove me to a small country village where I changed to an automobile which was, surprisingly, driven by the same Gendarmes who had taken me through the roadblocks.

Once more they slapped on the handcuffs. Leon wished me luck, and we departed.

We drove along a country lane, passing open fields, and croplands bordered by tall poplars interspersed with clumps of dense forests. As usual, the sky above was cloudy.

We passed through several villages, usually nothing more than a cluster of brick or stone homes, adjacent to barnyards. I noticed a few draft horses, but no tractors.

After a half hour or so, we turned onto a major road and soon entered a small city. While we were still in the residential area, the gendarmes parked at the curb and one of them escorted me to the entrance of a home. A woman opened the door and, without speaking, motioned me inside. The gendarme went back to the car and they drove away.

The woman had piercing black eyes. Long gray streaks showed in her black hair, pulled back tightly to lie flat, held in place with a clip in the back. There were wrinkles at the corners of her mouth and eyes but I didn't think she was much over forty. Her face was angular and she had a slim figure. Dressed in loose fitting, frayed old clothes, she could still be an attractive woman. But her piercing eyes were her most striking feature. She motioned me into a chair and went into the kitchen.

As she moved about in the kitchen, she kept up a steady dialog in French sprinkled with a few words of English. Some phrases were repeated from time to time with gestures used for emphasis. Her eyes flashed whenever she mentioned the Germans, tossing her head and fanning her cheek with her hand as she cursed the Krauts with furious venom in her voice. When she finished in the kitchen, she brought a bottle of wine and two glasses, which she filled, handing me one before she sat down. Then she held up her glass.

"La guerre est finie!"

"La guerre est finie," I responded and we touched the rims together and drank.

"The boche, they are bastards! Animals! You do not know what they do, but they have been in France for four years. They do terrible things and the French people know how bad they are; but maybe it will soon be over." Her eyes flashed as she spoke.

"I hope so."

She lowered her head, staring into her glass. For the first time in the half-hour or so since I arrived at her house, she seemed less aggressive, more pensive as she began talking again, in a soft, soothing voice which made the change just that much more noticeable.

"I had a daughter, you see, and before that a son. But I have not seen him since 1942 and nobody knows where he is. He went away to fight with the Resistance. He is nineteen now." She paused a minute. "My daughter joined the Resistance, too, and she worked for a year and a half, until she was picked up by the SS. They did terrible things to her and now I still have a daughter but she is like a little girl."

She took another sip of wine, then tossed off what was left quickly and stood up, running her hands nervously along her hips and down her thighs before she spoke again. This time her voice was more assertive.

"I will show you what they did to her. I'll be right back." She walked down the hall and into another room. I heard her speaking, softly, because her mood changed again. In a few moments she reappeared in the hall, walking slowly, and leading someone by the left hand, walking side by side, with her right arm around the person's waist. As they walked slowly toward me, she murmured a word or two, encouraging the other person. I saw that it was a young girl. Realizing this must be the daughter she mentioned, I stood as they entered the room while the woman led the girl to a chair, urging her to sit.

The girl's face had a vacant look. She took no notice of me and kept staring at the floor, sitting motionless on the very edge of the chair with her hands resting in her lap. Though her eyes were open, she seemed comatose, unaware of my presence.

"This is my daughter. She is seventeen and I will show you what they did to her to make her this way."

The woman kneeled and began to unbutton the girl's dress. As she parted the front of the dress, I saw hideous scars on her throat and upper chest and as the woman slipped the loosened dress over the girl's shoulders, I saw that her entire upper body as a mass of scars, circular reddish-blue blotches as big as a fifty-cent piece. Her breasts were flattened and thin, hanging like empty sacs. They too, bore the same horrible scars.

"Look at her back," the woman said, still speaking softly.

The girl whimpered.

The woman spoke quickly and very softly in French, trying to calm the girl. I understood enough to know she was saying that it was all right, that I was a friend and would not hurt her.

As the girl quieted, I moved close enough to see that her back was scared as badly as her chest but some of the scars were longer, three to four inches in length. It looked as if she had been lashed with a quirt.

"When she wouldn't inform, they whipped her first," the woman said, "then burned her with cigarettes in her flesh; and she was raped many times." She paused, "She was so beautiful" she said, "but it has been four months now." For the first time her voice choked on the words and she was silent for a long time before she slipped the dress over the thin shoulders and buttoned it again.

The girl sat there, not moving as her mother arranged the dress, alone in the terrible isolation to which she had withdrawn. The woman handed me a photograph wordlessly. I knew it was of the same girl but now there was a terrible difference and I wondered if she would ever recover.

Soon after the woman took the girl back to her room, the Resistance vehicle stopped in the street outside and it was time for me to leave. I started to shake hands with the woman but she gave me a big hug and the three kisses and told me, "Bonne voyage."

"Merci, et bonne chance, madame."

As I left the house in that little town, I thought about the young girl and her mother and I wondered how many other households in France had been torn apart as badly during the German occupation, and only vaguely wondered where the Underground would take me next, unable to dispel the memory of the forlorn young girl and her mother because for them the war might never end.

As we neared the center of the city, I spotted German troops on the sidewalks, their vehicles lining the streets. It was a bustling little place with French people mixing with the Germans. Most of the shops were open and enjoying a brisk trade.

We rode down a busy commercial street, slowing as we approached a building with German guards posted on either side of the entrance. I didn't worry about being seen; by now it seemed natural to be handcuffed between two cops.

A few French civilians glanced at us curiously, but none of the Germans paid any attention. Our truck slowed, almost coming to a stop as we turned into a courtyard across the street from where the German guards were posted. As we stopped, someone behind us raised a sagging gate just off the ground so he could walk without dragging it on the ground as he closed it.

The Gendarmes stepped out of the cab and ushered me into a downstairs room. I waited alone for ten minutes before a man entered and seated himself at a table near the center of the room. He motioned for me to sit opposite him.

When a second man entered, the first fellow began questioning me in English. The other man said nothing, just sat back and smoked, ignoring the lengthening ash on his cigarette while he listened intently. The ash was longer than the remaining tobacco before he finally flicked it away.

The guy interrogating me was young, smooth-faced, and casual. He knew what he was doing. He wanted to know when I last saw Metcalf. I suspected they hadn't heard from him and really wanted an answer from me. I told him all I knew, managing not to refer to Metcalf's chief as the "Belgian."

When the questioning ended, the young guy left, and I took a closer look at the smoker. He was older, perhaps in his forty's. He was about five feet eight inches tall and portly. His face was rectangular with piercing, black eyes, and angular nose, and very rosy cheeks with a big cleft in his chin and thin, red lips.

As I was observing him, a woman entered the room through a side door. He glanced at her, and introduced us in English.

"Lieutenant Woodrum, this is my wife, Sylvie."

"Hallo," said the woman, giving a quick little nod, smiling.

I returned the greeting, then looked at the man. "Why didn't you ask the questions?"

"We wanted the other man to get a good look at you first."

"I guess everything is all right then?"

"Yes, everything is all right. I am the chief of police here. One of the men who drove you from Versailles and again today, is my man. The other is not a gendarme." He paused. "They tell me you went through two roadblocks. Everything went well I understand, but my man wants to know why you smiled at the German corporal."

I laughed. "That was my first look at an individual German soldier up close. We hear all the propaganda put out about the mighty German Supermen. Aryans! Well, this little guy looked so much the opposite that when he leaned in and opened his toothless mouth, I couldn't help myself."

The chief laughed, too. "That explains it, then. We couldn't figure out why you grinned at him. My man tells me it was a pretty tense moment until then."

Sylvie brought a bottle of wine and three glasses. We followed her onto a bright, cheery patio with twelve-foot-high whitewashed walls on three sides, the other side open. Heavy timbers jutted from the inside wall, running horizontally overhead to pillars on the open side, beyond which I saw a field of gnarled apple trees and a chicken yard. Grape vines grew from patches of bare earth to form an arbor overhead.

Huge flagstones made up the floor of the entire patio, and large blue and yellow mosaic titles decorated two of the walls. We took seats at a massive harvest table, its top worn almost half round at the edges, which I assumed were square when it was new. The benches were as monstrous as the table.

Sylvie poured the wine, and I sipped it, with my arms resting on that big, old table. It's worn top bore testimony to the countless plates, pots, bottles of wine, and ashtrays which had rested there through the years as meals were served to hungry guests.

Wine spilled long ago left its stain, darkening the wood, and accenting the many gouges and dents on the table. The benches had worn smooth, but were comfortable and solid. Daydreaming, I decided that someday I should have a grape arbor with just such a table and benches if I ever managed to leave France alive.

Then the chief spoke:

"You were brought here from Versailles by a roundabout path so that we may put you on an aircraft back to England. We think the plane will come soon, but nothing is certain since the invasion."

I listened, hanging on his every word.

"They bring in many things now - explosives, guns, radios - and there are some things that must be taken out. We have priorities. Some individuals have so much information to deliver it is better if they are taken back first. Some of these same men will be trained in new skills and returned, by parachute, at night."

"They want to get you out, too, but with not so high a priority - and then, too, there is a danger in this." He paused, sipped more wine and I waited, glad to get the word.

"We will take you to a camp in the woods and I will tell you more about the individuals there tomorrow. For now, it's just a small camp, with less than ten men. It's easier to hide you. We've found that the German's easily discover camps with too many men. There is one American pilot in this camp already - a Mustang pilot."

He handed me a cigarette waiting to see if there were any questions before he continued. "Tonight we will eat right here, but later you will go to a room upstairs in the third floor of the gendarmerie. You will see that it is across the street from the Hotel de Ville, the City Hall, which is now occupied by the Gestapo and the military Chief of this district. You will see plenty of Germans, but don't worry. Do nothing to arouse suspicion and everything will be all right."

"Don't worry, I won't," I assured him.

Then he asked about my adventure before arriving in Versailles.

I told him in detail. When I mentioned Carlos and Maria by name, he suddenly raised a hand, palm out, in protest. "No names. I must not know. It is better." I told him about the bombing raid against the bridge when we went down, about my crew being captured, my first night, about the family at the garage and the wait in Carrieres-sur-Seine.

I told him briefly about the dogfight, the tanks, and the bombing raid by the RAF. I mentioned that after the tremendous concussions of the bombs, my hearing still wasn't back to normal.

"I knew about the raid," he said at last. "They told me about the agents who were captured, also."

"I didn't know for sure. Were they part of the transmitting team? How did the Germans find out about them?" I asked anxiously.

"Some Communists were picked up by the Germans and these people told them the names of others they thought might be involved," he answered.

I thought about it a moment. "Do you know if their leader in Versailles got out?" I was thinking about Metcalf.

"He is in a safe place, also waiting for a plane, just like you. His work in Versailles is finished."

"I hope his family is all right."

He didn't say anything for a moment, then, "Did you meet them?" I nodded.

"I hope they are too," he said quietly.

Then I thought of something else that bothered me.

"Chief, do you think I'll have to go through any more roadblocks?"

"Almost no chance when you leave here. I'm almost positive of it. It is not far and a car will precede you to make sure."

I felt relieved. I'd hate to get caught now, but I was also concerned about the two guys who'd helped me escape.

Then the chief asked another question.

"By the way, do you know of General Bradley?"

"Sure, he's leading one of our armies in Normandy right now."

"Yes, the radio says he is about to take Cherbourg which is well defended and a bottleneck for a port facility."

"I heard yesterday there was a force heading up the peninsula to take the city," I said.

"Where you are going, there is no radio. We will bring you news as often as we can." He thought a moment. "Another thing. The food will be not so good as here or in Versailles. You will have to steal some of it yourself."

There was a pause in the conversation which gave me the chance to ask a few questions.

"Chief, most of the gendarmes I've seen seem to be active in the Underground. Is that generally true? Are they all active?"

"Many of us, yes. There are some who do not participate but even they are sympathizers. All of my men are active as are others in many of the smaller towns and cities. I don't know much about the bigger cities, but I think there are many there, too."

Daylight faded to dusk as we talked. The grape arbor and courtyard were in heavy shade now and the sky had darkened to a reddish-orange. Sylvie said dinner was ready, and showed me to a bathroom where I washed my face and hands. Then I followed her to a table in a small room off the kitchen. Sylvie served a salad of fresh peaches, apricots, and apples. It was all grown locally, she said. The main course was braised meat and potatoes served with one of those fantastic French sauces I learned to like so much in Versailles and Carrieres-sur-Seine. There were two long loaves of French bread - whole wheat since white flour had gone out with the German occupation. I commented on the delicious meat.

"Lapin," she said. "We eat much rabbit in France now, and chicken, too—at least in the country. In the city, people are less fortunate."

"Ahh, but eggs," she signed, "Eggs are tres cher! I may be able to find some tomorrow morning, though." She rolled her eyes, as if to say we'll have to wait and see.

I ate everything on the plate, then followed the Chief's example and sopped up the extra gravy with my last piece of bread. Sylvie laughed approvingly as she poured the coffee.

It was late by the time we finished talking and Sylvie escorted me across the courtyard and up two flights of stairs to a huge room with a folding cot in one corner, two chairs, and a marble-topped table that seemed dwarfed in the expansive room.

I glanced around. There were two large windows partially open, lace curtains rustling in the breeze. I could just make out the German Headquarters across the street. A big Nazi pennant fluttered quietly against the building; its gaudy colors less distinct in the darkness. Four German soldiers guarding the entrance stood listlessly. The streets were empty.

A single window on another wall overlooked the courtyard. I closed the windows, turning the crank until they shut tightly and then I flipped the blackout curtains into place. Before I closed the courtyard window, I lit the candle stuck into wax on a saucer. It flickered ghostly in the cavernous room until the wax around the wick warmed, then it burned evenly.

Just then, there was a light rap on the door. Opening it, I found a girl, perhaps fifteen years old, peering at me curiously. She smiled, showing me a pile of sheets and blankets.

We made the bed, then she left for a moment, returning with a bottle of wine, an old Life magazine, and another candle. She placed everything on the table.

"Merci," I said. "Et merci pour le magazine, aussi." She giggled, and said the French expression for "until later," then closed the door and left.

My thoughts drifted as I leafed through the magazine and sipped the wine while the candle burned slowly. I finally snuffed out the flame and closed my eyes. The city was quiet and I wasn't a bit worried about the Germans across the street as I drifted off to sleep.

## Chapter 13

# THE OTHER AMERICAN

I glanced nervously around the room, trying to remember where I was. Then I noticed the bottle on the table; relieved, I rubbed my eyes, stretched, shook my head, and stretched again, my feet extending far past the end of the too-short cot.

I reached for the bottle, tilting it for a couple of swallows of wine before I swung out my legs and sat with my bare feet on the cool marble floor. I leaned back, extending my arms over my head, trying to work out the kinks. Then I took another swig. It tasted better than the night before.

I lit a cigarette and sauntered to the open window. Wearing only my shorts, I leaned against the window frame and looked toward the intersection a block or so away.

Gnarled sycamores stood in the space between the sidewalk and the street, their roots pushing up sections of the sidewalk, leaving it lying unevenly like a string of teeter-totters. Potted shrubs placed at intervals along the sidewalk looked scraggly and withered, their tubs in dire need of fresh paint.

Debris filled the gutters, completing the picture of neglect. I knew the French would make no effort to restore the pre-war beauty of this place until the Germans left. I didn't blame them.

Across the street was the entrance to the German headquarters. Along its front, plaster had crumbled in places, exposing red bricks beneath. At the gate leading into the courtyard, and at the archway forming the main entrance, German guards leaned casually with their backs against the wall.

The huge crimson Nazi flag was still there. I'd like to have that damned thing for a souvenir, I thought. I'd drape it on a wall to remind me never to get chicken-hearted again. Until three weeks ago, I never really believed all of the things I'd heard about the Nazis, but now I did, and hated them because of it.

It was no longer the impersonal war I'd known as a bomber pilot. Now it was just me and the French Underground against the Nazis, and so far, the Underground was making all the right moves. I was glad to be on the move again for the days of inactivity at Versailles were beginning to get to me. But I enjoyed my stay there, especially my hosts, the Brenners. I'll never forget that dogfight, I thought, cursing my luck again at not having been assigned to fighters. And I knew I'd always remember that bombing raid, especially since I still found myself asking someone to repeat a word or two I hadn't heard. The concussion did something to me, I was sure of that. But now, I was finally on the move again. Today, I'd meet another American.

I stared across the street, watching the two guards. The fat one nearest me stood by the main entrance, staring up the street. I noticed instantly what had snared his attention- a pretty, young woman crossing the street nearby. A tall, slender brunette, she walked with an easy, swinging stride, the furl of her flared skirt billowing around her legs. Her full breasts jiggled beneath a soft white blouse.

She passed the staring guard, not looking at him, and ignoring his remarks as she strode by. The guard turned a little, watching as she continued on her way, her swinging stride flipping the skirt from side to side as she walked toward the main boulevard. She had great legs.

The German was still watching the girl as she turned the corner. Suddenly, he looked up and realized I'd been watching him. He looked away abruptly, moving back to parade rest, clutching his Mauser stiffly.

I laughed to myself. What's the matter? You getting hard up in La Belle France? But then I thought, he'll get off duty soon. I was stuck right here watching Germans, knowing I was safe in the protection of the Underground.

There was a knock on the door. As I turned, a gendarme poked his head inside.

"Bonjour, Monsieur."

I returned the greeting and nodded when he asked if I wanted coffee. He returned in a few minutes with a cloth-covered tray which he placed on the table. I lifted the napkin and saw that the thick coffee was almost black. I added some sugar, took a sip, and was surprised to taste real coffee, not the mealy substitute.

There were three fresh croissants on the tray. I offered one to the gendarme.

"No, for you, peelot," he said, pointing at me.

I insisted, and he shrugged, grinning as he reached for the pastry. We ate for a while before he began asking questions.

"Pilote?"

"Yes."

"Monsieur, ah - you have killed Germans, no?"

"Yes."

He smiled, pausing to ponder this information.

"How many?" he asked.

"I don't know. Beaucoup."

Then he launched into the usual string of questions: what kind of aircraft, where was I from, how was I shot down and how many missions did I have. I answered them and when I told him, he seemed to think 35 was a lot. Then he sat back considering the idea of 35 missions against the Germans. It really wasn't very many when you considered that many pilots on both sides had been flying since 1939. I had been told there were several with 300 missions. But I could see the gendarme wanted to talk about it and I was sure he was waiting for a chance to fight the Germans himself. I grabbed the last croissant and gulped a final swallow of coffee.

From the street an automobile horn sounded as a German voice shouted, "Achtung!"

We stepped to the window as three German officers clambered out of the back seat of a bulky touring car. I could hear their boots clatter on the cobblestones as they crossed the courtyard to enter the Hotel de Ville.

"Gestapo commandant," the gendarme muttered. "Quelle bande de salauds ces boches."

As he cursed, he fanned his right cheek with the cupped fingers of his right hand, tilted his head contemptuously, making a "poof" sound with his lips. I smiled because it was a gesture I often saw in France, used seemingly by everyone when talking about the Germans. It was packed with defiance and I liked it. This guy did it as well as Henriette. In this simple motion, a national attitude was embodied. Once in a while, I used the gesture myself. I liked the French people's defiance.

There was another knock on the door, which surprised me since this time I hadn't heard footsteps. The chief, a rugged man in uniform, entered. He smiled and we shook hands.

"So, lieutenant, you look rested. You must have slept well."

"Yes, I did."

"That's good, because today, you travel again. But you do not have far to go this time and there will be no roadblocks. I can promise you that."

"I'm glad to hear that, but your people got me through those other two."

"Well," he said, "sometimes we are not so lucky. Today you will meet another American."

"You said he was a fighter pilot?"

"Yes. He was shot down north of Melun early in June. He had a badly sprained ankle from his fall, but he is all right now."

"He's at the camp now?"

"Yes. It is better if you don't know exactly where. You will wait there for the airplane."

"How soon do you think that might be? You mentioned some delay?"

"It is hard to say, but soon. Perhaps a week, maybe more."

I decided he really didn't know. But apparently he believed that sooner or later there would be a plane, and that's all I really wanted, or needed to know.

"When do I leave?"

"In a few minutes. A truck will come."

"Who's in charge at the camp?"

"A fine old man, you will meet him soon. He has done much for us. He has the Legion of Honor from Verdun."

Sylvie appeared in the doorway. She was staring at me and I suddenly realized I was still wearing only the floppy old shorts. She talked to her husband in rapid French as I turned to put on my trousers.

"My wife says that the truck is on the way here now. Perhaps a half-hour at the most," the chief said.

I put on my shirt and tucked it into my trousers, realizing as I tightened the belt that the seat of my pants was still too big despite Henriette's best effort at alterations. I tossed my gear into the musette bag, then stood in front of the mirror, arranging my beret the way Carlos had shown me. The gendarme watched, chuckling softly. I glanced curiously at the chief.

"What's the matter? Is it all right?"

"Yes, but you look like a fascist wearing it that way." He was grinning too.

"I've heard that before, but this is the way I was shown to wear it - by a Basque. He said to wear it the way he wore his."

"That explains it then."

"Shall I change it?"

"No, I don't think so. You see, however you wear it, you look more German than. French. It's all right."

I looked into the mirror. It didn't seem much different than the way most of the French wore theirs, but it was instantly obvious to the two gendarmes.

"If it doesn't look right, I'll change it."

"No, it's all right. You see, we know you are an American, but nobody else does."

He picked up my bag and headed downstairs, leading me to the grape arbor. Sylvie entered through the cellar door, pausing to shut it again. Then she handed a dusty bottle to her husband who wiped it clean with a cloth. He cut the foil off the neck and uncorked it. It was a thick, brown bottle shaped like Grand Marnier, and I wondered what it was, hoping it wasn't Calvados.

The chief held the bottle up and I was relieved to see an amber liquid. Definitely not Calvados.

"Rum," he announced. "A bottle I've been saving. It's from Martinique, 1935."

He handed it to me and I sniffed appreciatively. Back at McDill I'd drunk a lot of rum and cokes. It had a wonderful, rich aroma. He filled three glasses and we clinked them together. I took a sip and felt the warmth of the rum, then swallowed, feeling its heat creep through my body. I let it engulf me and tossed off the rest neat. I think it was the best rum I'd ever tasted.

The chief unbuttoned his tunic and offered me a cigarette. We sat there smoking while Sylvie went into the kitchen. The chief refilled our glasses.

He toasted, "To the United States." I nodded and we tossed them off.

This time, I felt the sensation in my toes. Sylvie came back and the chief filled three glasses again. I raised mine and said, "To the Underground, and especially to you two."

The liquid slid down easily and I thought: To hell with the Goddamned war.

"A little drink is good now and then, eh, Lieutenant."

"It sure is," I said without hesitation. "I've got a bottle of Armagnac in my bag but this rum is better than any I've ever tasted."

"Good." He held up the bottle. "Another?"

"No, thanks. If I'm going to ride with your people I don't think I'd better have any more." I reached into my musette bag and took out my pack of cigarettes, offering one to the chief. He took one and I told him they came from the Hotel Meurice via the black market.

"We must thank the Germans for all blessings, it seems."

"Yes, but not much longer."

"Je l'espere."

"I hope so, too." It was the first time the chief spoke French with me.

A vehicle rumbled in the street. I heard someone trot across the courtyard and caught a glimpse of a guard raising the gate. A truck nosed in at an angle, its engine rattling noisily.

An old man jumped down from the passenger's side of the cab and walked across the courtyard. His shoulders were rounded and he hunched forward slightly like someone who'd done heavy work all of his life and was forever marked with the burden. He reminded me in a way of my grandfather, only more sturdily built.

He removed a beat-up old Homberg from his head, banged it against his thigh a couple of times to shake off the dust, then fanned himself with it as he walked. The chief walked out to embrace him. As they talked, the old man's eyes scanned the courtyard until they reached me. The chief led him over, his arm around the man's shoulders.

I stood and shook his hand. It was rough, and surprisingly strong.

"Marcel, voila le Lieutenant Woodrum. Lieutenant, this is Marcel, the chief of your camp."

"Bonjour, American. Good day." He laughed, his eyes sparkling. "Je ne sais dire que Good day, c'est tout." He waved his hand excitedly as if he had forgotten something.

"Et, thank you, aussi." He laughed again, uproariously, and patted me on the back. The chief poured three glasses of rum. We clicked the rims of our glasses together and drank. Marcel's eyes widened as he swallowed his, savoring the taste. In the courtyard, the driver raced the engine, its rattling sound echoing off the courtyard walls.

Marcel motioned with his right hand to his ear and grinned. The chief turned and said, "Goodbye, lieutenant. Good luck. Do whatever Marcel says. He is the chief and I'm sure you will be safe with him. You will ride in the back of the truck under the canopy, and remember - say nothing."

I thanked him and followed them into the courtyard.

The truck was pointing straight out the gate. Marcel pulled himself into the cab as I hopped into the bed. The engine rumbled loudly as the vehicle rolled into the street.

The driver honked the horn frequently, even though there was little traffic. At the boulevard, he turned left into the main business district. We stopped at a traffic light where a cluster of German soldiers stood talking. Most of them were in their late teens, but there were a few older men in the group. The driver turned again, and two or three blocks later we reached the Seine.

Several barges were headed upstream, one after another, their wake sloshing against the stone walls of the riverbank. Further upstream were a few buildings and beyond them was open countryside. Across the river we turned abruptly to climb a long steep grade from the river to the top of a bluff. There were green fields east of the river, lined with poplars. It was a pretty view.

As we neared the crest of the hill, the truck's engine began to lug until we were barely moving. Unable to coax enough power to reach the top, the driver hit the brakes. He got out of the cab cursing, throwing his leather cap against the side of the cab in exasperation, and kicking the metal firebox mounted at the rear of the left front fender. He and Marcel began scrounging for wood along the roadside. While they shoved the wood into the box, I studied them.

Marcel seemed angry with the driver who should have stoked the engine at the gendarmerie. He began chewing the guy out in a loud voice and as he did, the man quit grumbling and began working harder.

The old guy was at least sixty, with a thick mustache that drooped at the ends. His bushy gray hair still had a touch of black in it, but looked mottled, as if lightly dusted with soot.

The soiled black Homburg perched precariously on his head seemed too small, obviously a matter of no consequence to him.

His face was seamed, wrinkled in tight time-etched lines. On either side of the upper flare of his nostrils, two very deep creases curved away and down past the corners of his mouth to his chin, deeply clefted in the center. His lower lip curled outward so that his mustache seemed to rest upon it even when his mouth was closed. Beneath his bushy brows, his eyes, which twinkled incongruously blue and bright, were startlingly alert.

Except for a white shirt, his clothes were entirely black. One bright spot of color stood out on his lapel where I could make out the rosette of the Legion of Honor, hard won at the Battle of Verdun as the chief had said.

I shifted to the back of the truck again and peeked through the flap. There was no one else around, so I opened it for a better view.

The town lay behind and below us, the roofs of the larger buildings visible some two miles away. It was peaceful and sunny on the hill, and I ached to get out and walk.

Suddenly I heard a whistling sound and poked my head out as far as I could to look. Four Typhoons with Canadian marking swooshed over the treetops at the edge of the woods. They came slanting down in a half-V formation, stacked upwards from the leader, only a few feet apart. They were so close to the truck and so low, I saw the head of the pilot in the lead ship.

From where we were parked, the broad, flat surface of the Seine ran parallel with the highway for almost a half-mile before the river turned eastward. Three barges were in the middle of the river, just starting their turn, their crews unaware of the imminent assault.

A red streak suddenly laced away from the nose of the leading Typhoon and I watched its lengthening plume glow for a moment before realizing it was a rocket. Its nose wavering ever so slightly, the rocket embedded itself furiously in the deck of the first barge, just ahead of the pilothouse.

Debris flew skyward as the rocket wormed its way into the hull and exploded with a searing orange-hot blast. The scene was instantly shrouded in a huge mushrooming black eddy of smoke. All I could see was a Nazi pennant on the stubby mast at the fantail.

Even before I heard the explosion, more rockets were speeding from the other planes and into the second barge, which exploded more terribly than the first. The third took only one hit, near the bow, but not within the hull. The Typhoons swooped upward gracefully, turning in unison away from town to avoid the German anti-aircraft guns.

But they came again. On the second pass, all four aircraft released rockets into the third barge. Its crew reversed engines frantically to avoid a collision with the two burning hulks ahead, but in an instant, the planes were back, this time with the whole length of the barge before their guns and rocket launchers. Then it disappeared, leaving only bulging pockets of greasy black smoke floating over the river to show where it had been.

The planes overhead roared away, and suddenly it was again quiet and lonely there on the slope of the hillside. I heard the faint crackling of flames from the burning barges and turned to watch them drift slowly with the current through the smoky debris of the one obliterated.

From the town came the sound of a belated air raid alarm, and I heard our driver curse again, more afraid than ever that we would be caught stranded here. He was poking furiously in the firebox, imploring the wood to burn.

As I watched the wreckage on the river, I thought of the dead men so suddenly dead, probably French bargemen carrying Nazi cargo. None of it made sense anymore.

In the past, whenever I thought about men dying, I seldom wondered when my turn would come. Before the suddenness of the sneak attack on Hawaii by the Japanese, the unseen, psychic scars, which mark all men exposed to combat, hadn't yet been etched upon my conscience. At the time, I'd viewed the attack with compassion for the dead and horror at the thought of how they died.

Now, all of the horror remained, and most of the compassion, but there was also a strange sense of detachment, and insulation to the day-to-day reality of death.

I wasn't one of the Typhoon pilots flying back to England. Now, I was a chance observer, staying behind in France, trying to get back home another way. Glimpses of all the airplanes I had ever seen blow up flashed through my mind, one after another, along with exploding bombs. I felt nothing but a burning desire to get out of France - to evade.

It made me feel impatient, nervously anxious for this truck to get moving. I turned to see Marcel dump another load of branches alongside the firebox. He was clearly eager to leave, but when the old man climbed into the truck, he calmly puffed his curve-stemmed pipe.

Then the driver climbed into the cab and started the engine. Soon we were moving again, leaving the river and its wrecked barges behind.

The road was a two-lane macadam highway running through patches of forest interspersed with unfenced, plowed fields. The trunks of even the largest trees were much smaller than in Northern California, none of them more than eighteen inches in diameter. Most resembled pines, others were hardwoods, shaped like oaks.

We soon reached a small village, passing several old stone houses before stopping in front of one of them. Marcel climbed out of the truck and motioned for me to follow.

Inside the house, he introduced me to his wife and two daughters. Marcel's wife poured us all a glass of wine. Speaking slowly in French, Marcel told me we would only stay five minutes.

A young man came into the house. Marcel introduced him as his son, also named Marcel. The kid grinned as we shook hands. Perhaps twenty, he was as tall as his father with the same swarthy complexion and long, coal black hair. I helped him carry boxes of canned food and fresh vegetables to the truck. Marcel followed us outside, joined by a second young fellow. As the three of us climbed into the truck, the kid introduced himself as Raoul, another of Marcel's sons.

We drove down the lane to the highway and turned south again. There were fewer than fifteen houses in the entire village. The fields beyond it were tilled on both sides of the road. There were no ditches or wells, but the soil was moist and I wondered where they got their water.

A few miles from town, the truck stopped.

Raoul handed the sack of canned food to me. He and his brother each grabbed a box and I followed them into the woods as the truck moved away. Their father had already crested a knoll and beckoned for us to hurry. We moved into the brush and crouched out of sight. An instant later, a German staff car sped past.

We followed Marcel along a beaten trail into the woods. Every quarter-mile or so we reached a firebreak, each centered with a well-worn trail. I realized they were all the same—a maze of well-used paths that wouldn't betray the camp's location. The old man paused at each intersection to check his direction.

After walking a mile and a half, Marcel motioned for me to follow him closely. Concealed by vegetation, we kneeled a few feet from the edge of the forest, a spot affording a good view. Beyond a plowed field, were a large barn and some smaller outbuildings. There was a tractor between the back door of the house and the barns. Neat rows of green beans and potatoes were growing in the field.

Marcel pointed. "No good," he said emphatically. "Milice!"

He spit the last word in contempt.

As I looked toward the big rambling house, a man came from the back door and got into a sedan parked near the tractor. Wearing a business suit, tie, and a hat, he was better dressed than most of the people I'd seen. Both Metcalf and Carlos had told me that Milice were traitorous French, collaborating with the Germans.

Marcel growled a curse I couldn't understand as he watched the man. Then we turned back to join the others, heading along a trail which paralleled the edge of the field. A quarter-mile later he turned abruptly from the trail to enter the forest.

A voice called out from the tree, startling me.

"Bonjour, Marcel, c'est bon, Passez!"

I was glad to know they posted guards. Tall, leafy trees and slender saplings formed a dense area of the forest leaving the entire trail in shade as we passed another clearing at the edge of a small pond covered with thick green scum. A hundred yards further down the trail, we came to the camp.

Set in a shady thicket, I could see a hut, a table, and several chairs. The hut was covered with brush, mud, old cardboard boxes, and a couple of pieces of corrugated metal.

The hard-packed earth, swept smooth and clean, covered a large area around a fire pit which had been built twenty feet from the hut and was close to the big table. Its sides were fashioned from stone and mud, sheet metal forming the grill.

Just beyond the table, between the hut and the fire pit, were five men. As we approached, their faces remained expressionless.

Raoul and Marcel set their food boxes down and I put the sack on top of one of them. The old man held up his hand, pointing to the group, then looked at me.

"Which man is the American? "he asked mischievously.

I was already wondering the same thing, but knew I was licked. What does an American look like, especially one disguised as a Frenchman?

I looked them over carefully. One was bare-chested and muscular. He seemed European to me somehow, and I thought he was probably in his thirties, too old to be an active pilot. Next to him was a young freckle-faced guy, with wavy red hair. The third was a husky, blue-eyed blonde, who looked away from me grinning, not returning my gaze.

Next was a dark-haired fellow wearing a beret. He looked straight at me, his face blank. The last man was slender and swarthy, with a square face and flat features. Too European, I thought, and too young. But I knew any one of them could be the guy.

I tried to think of them as aviation cadets, picturing overseas caps on their heads. I looked for class rings, unsuccessfully.

"This is going to be difficult, Marcel." I said, watching them as I spoke. Then I tried again.

"Well, I know one of you guys got your ass shot down flying a P-51. Which one of you is it?"

The blond man grinned slightly so I pointed to him. "That one."

There was a burst of laughter. The guy in the beret smacked a fist into the palm of his hand. "Karl, by God!" he exclaimed.

"Anybody but him and I wouldn't feel insulted." Grinning, the other American came over and stuck out his hand.

His name was Walter Kozicci, from Chester, Pennsylvania. He was flying top cover for a group bombing an airdrome near Melun when an ME-109 shot up his engine, which lost all its coolant, forcing him to bail out. What really made him mad was that he never even saw the guy who hit him!

Landing in an open field, he sprained an ankle badly, which forced him to crawl along a muddy ditch for a half mile before he found cover. Farmers hid him in a barn overnight but the next day they turned him over to Andre, the same Chief I'd met a few days earlier. Walt was moved directly to the camp and had heard absolutely no news since the day he arrived in the woods on D-Day! Now he was suffering from an acute lack of awareness. He understood Polish pretty well and talked with Joseph, the camp leader, who was Polish, but he didn't have any more access to news than Walt did. Joseph did translate the news passed on by Marcel when he visited the camp but that was very skimpy. Like me, he was trying to learn French.

We sat down and I began bringing him up to date. Our discussion continued through the evening meal, a thick potato and green bean soup. We talked far into the night, long after the others had gone to bed, a small fire glowing as we got acquainted. The usual stratus clouds drifted overhead and the night was cool.

I brought Walt up to date on the invasion, using his escape map to indicate the position of the advance into Normandy. I told him about the war in Italy and the Pacific—everything I could remember. Finally, we went into the makeshift hut and I crawled into a bunk made of saplings with rope slings and a straw tick, covered with a World War One GI blanket, a faded US stenciled on it.

During the night I found that other living things occupied the blanket beside me and I woke up covered with fleabites and probably lice. Walt was just leaving the hut. A moment later, I joined him at the table and poured myself a cup of coffee, neither of us saying much, all talked out.

We drank ersatz coffee and made toast over the coals. Raoul gave me some cheese, which I spread on the toast. I offered some to Walt.

"It's goat cheese," he said. "I don't like it."

"Tastes pretty good to me," I said.

The first camp member I came to know that day was Andre. He was almost twenty. His father was a Russian Jew who had come to France from Georgia in the twenties. When he disappeared just after the Nazi occupation in 1940, Andre's mother had shipped her son to the woods for his safety.

Andre had a pudgy nose, and a triangular face topped with a crown of curly orange-red hair. He had a pleasant grin and an open, friendly manner and he was a hell of a smart kid.

He said he wanted to speak English to learn the language but we had to switch to a mixture of French and English for better comprehension.

When I told him that lumbering, cattle raising and gold mining were the primary industries where I lived, he became very interested.

"Mining," he said, "you still have gold mining?"

"Yes, a lot."

"Have you ever found gold?"

"Yes, many times. In the fall and winter, when the creeks were full, we used to pan for gold or use a sluice box … sometimes nuggets but usually smaller flakes."

"How do you know where to look?"

"Most creeks have gold, and I know the location of the old gold-mining areas."

The business about the gold had Andre flabbergasted. He thought the gold had all been removed by the early miners. He couldn't understand why everybody in Shasta County wasn't out mining.

Walt sat listening, not entirely convinced that I wasn't giving Andre a big snow job. He listened dubiously, then asked a few questions but after I told him about having worked on a doodle-bug dredger, he became interested himself. We talked about gold mining a while before Andre changed the subject.

"Albert, you have car -- auto?"

"Yes."

"Ah -- you have house also?"

"Yes."

"And…travail…work, you have job?"

"I've had several jobs. But I have also worked for myself."

"You mean your own store?" He was really excited now.

"No. A small business - selling things - but not from a store. It was a truck route."

He leaned back, contemplating this bit of information seriously. Then he went through the whole thing, step by step, counting them off on his fingers as he went along.

"You have house. You have car. You have business?"

I nodded.

"Bon, I understand. Albert, you are a capitalist!" He made it a very positive statement.

Walter and I laughed. Andre grinned, glancing from one to the other as he waited for an explanation.

"I guess you're right, Andre. You could say that I'm a capitalist. But you don't have to have a car and a house to be a capitalist, just a lot of money."

"No house, no car?"

"Not necessary."

"But if you have money, you must have a car."

"With money you can buy a car. But you don't have to be a capitalist to have a car."

"If I had money, I would buy a car before anything else."

Walt and I shared another big roar of laughter. This was getting to be fun.

"A lot of people in the United States feel the same way," I said finally. "The first thing they do when they save enough money is to buy a car."

Walter spoke up. "Andre, if you were in the United States, you could buy a car."

"Me? No, I am not a capitalist."

"Maybe not now. But in America, you could get a job and buy your own car. Many, many people have cars."

"Workers own cars?"

"Sure," Walt said.

"Workers are capitalists?

We laughed again. I got a charge out of that one.

"Capitalist enough to buy cars, yes."

"I do not understand this," Andre said. "How can a worker be a capitalist?" He couldn't believe common workers could own cars. As far as he was concerned, they were never able to save money. Finally, he stood up and shook our hands resignedly.

"We talk again later, OK?"

"Sure, Andre, anytime," I said. "Anytime."

As we chatted, a tall, dark-haired man walked out of the woods and walked towards the hut.

"Who's that," I asked Walt.

Walt turned just as the man entered the hut, then looked back at me and laughed. "That's Francois. He'll come out in a minute and I'll introduce you. He's a riot. Marcel let him go back to the village with him last night. He's probably been shacked up somewhere. Says he's a real ladies man."

When we met, Francois asked me all the usual questions and then gave us the latest news he had picked up. A major battle was apparently shaping up and Francois thought he and his camp mates should be out making life tough for the Germans. It was a good thought but even though I'd only been there a few hours, I knew these guys weren't ready for any kind of combat. The Germans would eat them up. They had a few weapons but no training; however, Francois was adamant. I liked Joseph, too. He was a good camp chief, and was only waiting for the promised arrival of weapons to begin training. A member of the Free Polish forces, Joseph landed in the Dieppe raid and became stranded when he went inland too far and was unable to get back in time to disembark. He headed east and joined the Underground.

I asked about setting snares for birds but was told the water was so bad there were few birds in this particular forest. When I learned the only water available to us came from a green, scum covered, stagnate pool, I drank wine with every meal like everybody else. Our coffee water was filtered through sand and charcoal before boiling.

Life in the camp became a dull routine the next few days. Karl sulked, apparently homesick. François grumbled about not fighting and I could understand his reluctance to just sit around when I learned that before the war, he was a professional thief. I decided he would be a tough foe at night, especially after I saw how good he was with a knife. But he continued to argue for some kind of attack on the Germans.

The following Sunday, Walt told me the people from the village gathered at an open area of the forest to mingle with the men from the Maquis camp. There was a big blackberry patch there and everybody made a picnic of it. Walt and I went with them, staying close to Joseph. When we arrived, most of the villagers were already there. We were introduced to certain ones by Marcel who was waiting for us.

After Andre handed a wine skin to us, he sauntered away with Francois to join an attractive woman sitting with her two young daughters. Soon they were all sipping wine together. Even Joseph joined another group. Walt and I sat there alone, drinking the wine and talking until we got bored. We walked away and then took a short cut back to camp. Everyone returned by nine o'clock that evening except Andre and Francois. Joseph was furious because he was sure they had gone into the village with the women. Marcel Jr. was going into the village. Joseph asked him to tell Marcel about Francois and Andre.

Andre came back about midnight and said not to expect Francois until morning. Joseph was furious. He and Andre shouted at each other before the camp finally quieted down. Walt and I thought that this kind of disorder could screw everything up and worried about what might happen. Francois finally returned the next morning and Joseph jumped him immediately. For a minute, I thought they might try to kill each other. Karl had already indicated he thought they should get rid of Francois. But Joseph said to wait for Marcel.

When the old man arrived, he talked with everybody but Francois and then called him out of the hut. Walt and I sat by ourselves. Surrounded by the others, the two sat at the table as the old man laid down the law in no uncertain terms. He had a big revolver in his waistband when he arrived and sat with it on the table under his hand as he told Francois that from now on, he wanted no more grumbling. I think Francois was sure that Marcel would kill him if he gave him any lip. I thought he would, too.

Francois looked up from the blue steel of the pistol into the cold gaze of the old man. They stared at each other for a moment until Francois looked away, subdued.

As Marcel leaned forward slightly his voice softened just a bit. "We do not wish to lose you, Francois. Will you accept my orders from now on without question?"

"Oui, Monsieur, I always have . . ."

"No, Francois, you have not. You have gone to town without permission, not just to the village, but to Montereau. There will be no more of that, and if I send you somewhere with a message you will not stay out all night. I cannot trust you that way."

Francois may have been thinking of how he'd jeopardized the safety of the others, but I think he was reacting to the icy authority of the old man filling the roles of judge and executioner. The set, defiant look on the younger man's face melted into submission.

"Bien, Marcel. I will do as you say."

The old man reached for his pipe, fumbled with a match, and lit the tobacco. He sat leaning over, watching Francois, his right hand still hovering over the pistol. Then, as he called for Raoul to bring wine, Marcel leaned over to Francois. "This is finished," he said, almost cordially. "There is nothing more to say."

# Chapter 14

# THE TERRORISTS

Marcel raised his glass. "To the victory," he said.

We drank the toast, as we relaxed from the tension developed by the showdown. Marcel stood and raised his hand for attention.

"This afternoon we'll receive the weapons, and soon we'll also have more men. Then we'll begin to do the things you've all waited for so long. But first, you must learn to use firearms.

"Perhaps Walter and Albert will help?" He turned to us, already knowing our answer.

"Oui, Monsieur Taboulet. We'll help," we nodded.

He took several men with him to the woods. They returned an hour later pulling a heavy two-wheeled cart laden with heavy wooden cases, balanced carefully to trundle the cart through the woods easier.

Lying across the top of the uppermost box was an American-made Thompson submachine gun with two full pans of ammo. One of my favorite weapons, I'd always scored well when firing it in training.

Marcel directed the unloading. When the cart was empty, Joseph began prying the lids off each box. The men, standing nearby, were unable to conceal their excitement.

There was another Tommy gun, twelve Lee-Enfield rifles, six British-made pistols, and four American grease guns, each with plenty of ammunition. There was also a box of hand grenades.

The weapons were wrapped in heavy brown paper and covered with cosmoline, which came away on the paper as Walter and I unwrapped them. We spread the large papers on the table and placed the guns on top.

While busy at our task, we didn't notice Raoul grab a gun. The loud sound we heard as he pulled open the bolt was our first inkling that he had even picked it up. We quickly took it away, then we stopped working to give a quick lesson on gun safety. None of them knew the first thing about firearms except Joseph, and Francois, who knew about pistols - from his professional experience, I guessed.

We placed several heavy pans of water to warm on the fire, then fieldstripped each piece, starting with the rifles. We flushed the barrels with hot, soapy water, oiled the mechanisms, and checked the actions on each to make sure they worked smoothly.

We cleaned the barrels with oiled cloth patches until the metal gleamed when we peered through the barrels. We spent most of the day at the chore, showing the men what they needed to know to assist us. It was almost dark when we finished. Marcel seemed pleased with the instruction we provided.

While Raoul and young Marcel cooked supper, Walter and I began making training aids for use in teaching the triangulation method of aiming. For the bull's eye, we cut circles from tin and blackened them in the fire, then used one of the crates as a makeshift cabinet and stowed everything in the hut.

While putting the stuff away, I noticed with alarm that some of the grenades were missing. Marcel was about to leave, but I asked him to talk to the men before he went.

To our relief, he returned with the recovered grenades. Everyone wanted to keep one in each pocket, even though they didn't know how to use them. I was nervous enough each time they laid their hands on the guns, but their carelessness with the grenades was worse.

The guys were just too darn eager. They'd never worked with any kind of machinery and weren't mechanically minded. They had no experience with guns, but now they all wanted to be armed. I suppose they really thought that after waiting so long, they needed to carry a full arsenal to think of themselves as "real" soldiers.

For the next few days, we worked hard to teach that bunch how to use automatic weapons, bolt-action rifles, and pistols. It was a rough go all the way. They continued to disregard the safety mechanism. It was there, they knew what it was for, and we had demonstrated its use. They thought it was a nice addition, but refused to use it, insisting on waving the weapons about with a clip in the rifles and a round in the chamber - ready to go.

"Albert, we must be ready for the Germans," Raoul told me earnestly.

Fearing an accident, we called them together for a talk. Joseph ordered them to turn in all the ammunition. They were crestfallen, but we were mad as hell about their carelessness and they knew it. We were sure that once they understood that safety precautions were necessary, they'd do alright. The language barrier was a real obstacle although when I really chewed one of them out in English, he got the idea.

We taught triangulation in teams, the rifle in a fixed position and the bull's eye moved until sighted in and marked with a dot in the center of the bull. We kept them busy as they made smaller triangles with the dots until all knew how to sight their rifles properly. After some practice, they got pretty good and began enjoying their training. We kept them at it all day, every day. Finally, we issued each man five rounds, just in case, but with the understanding that none could be kept in the chamber!

When we began teaching the use of grenades, Karl boasted he could hurl one the farthest. He was a young, husky kid, always eager to show off his physical powers. But the first time he tried to hurl the weighted dummy grenade we used for training, he ignored our instruction and did it his way. The thing waggled through the air for about half the expected distance; and he threw out his shoulder to boot.

"Quel gamin," murmured Francois, shaking his head.

"What did you say, François?" I asked.

"I said "little boy," Albert. Karl is a little boy who can do nothing right."

"Maybe he'll learn," I said without much optimism.

"No, he'll never learn. Karl is stupid. Better to castrate him now." Francois made a little circle in the air with the tip of his pocketknife for emphasis.

I made no comment, but silently agreed.

Karl had finally approached me, about two days after my arrival at the camp, and began asking questions. One of the many things that bothered him was the height of the Empire State Building. He'd seen pictures of it, but didn't believe it was as tall as people said.

"It's 1,250 feet tall," I said when he asked. "That would be about one-third of a kilometer."

"One-third kilometer?" Karl asked in disbelief.

I nodded.

"Kilometers?"

I nodded again.

Karl looked around searching for something to judge the height. I pointed to a tall tree.

"That's about forty feet high, Karl. Put thirty trees, one atop the other. The Empire State Building is about that tall."

He started nodding his head up and down as he counted, one nod for each tree. He was looking almost straight up by the fourth or fifth nod. He paused; his face flushed. He stood there for another moment, and then walked away. A half-hour later, he was back.

"Thirty, Albert?"

"Yes, Thirty." Karl never trusted me after that.

Now, he stood there rubbing his elbow, flustered and mad. Francois spat angrily into the dust. I liked Francois. There was something intriguing about him. Since the showdown with Marcel, he was allowed visits to the village and always returned promptly, usually before midnight. He always came in half-loaded, but never drunk. He was content now; no longer at constant odds with Marcel.

I enjoyed many long conversations with Francois. He was undoubtedly, the biggest character I've ever met. It wasn't just his words, but his appearance as well that set him apart from the crowd.

To put it bluntly, he looked like a cadaver. The first time I saw him I was impressed with the abruptness with which his whole face narrowed just below the cheekbones, as if that part had been compressed in the jaws of a vice. The space between his temples was normal, but when looking at him head-on, his jaw seemed indented at least an inch on each side, giving a downward thrust to his thin, pointed nose and slit-lipped mouth which rested atop a narrow clefted chin.

His close-set black eyes flicked back and forth nervously, like a reptile's. The skin stretched tautly over his face and small, but conspicuous reddish-blue veins criss-crossed the bridge of his nose and the area under his eyes. Just under his temples, faint capillaries fanned out to paper thin, bright-red ears. His face was a monument to his debauchery.

And could he talk! Orating magnificently on almost any subject, his favorite pastime was to sit on one of the benches in the dappled shade and tell long, glorious lies to anyone who would listen. His favorite subject was women, and he was a regular Romeo.

Regardless of what I thought of Francois' appearance, he was, for lack of better description, a sex magnet. This was verified by others, especially Andre, whose one escapade with Francois had gotten him into trouble.

It seems that many of Francois' interludes weren't all his doing. When he went into the village bar for a quiet class, the women wouldn't leave him alone. He was a marked man.

He attributed all of his success in life, so he told Walter and me, to this power to attract women. He said that before the war, he combined this natural attraction with the pickpocket skills he'd picked up as a Marseilles street urchin, and parlayed the two into eminence as the top thief in his native city. He was a cat burglar, a second story man. He fondly relived his memories for us.

Once, he said, a certain European government hired him to remove the passports of wealthy Italian businessmen visiting the Riviera. Apparently, there was an urgent need for stolen Italian passports before the war.

When the women, usually other than the businessmen's wives, accompanied the businessmen on their holiday, Francois profited doubly, for he was not above a little blackmail. Depending upon the morals of the lovely lady involved, he hinted that he occasionally profited in yet a third way.

He vividly described his most unforgettable passport theft. He learned where one particular Italian businessman was staying and used his legendary skill to gain entry to his hotel suite, only to find the man in bed with his girlfriend. At gunpoint, Francois gagged the man and lashed him to the bed. Then, in full view of the helpless fellow, he dragged the woman into the next room, leaving his captive desperately tugging at his bonds.

Francois promptly forgot about the man tied to the bed and turned his charm on the woman who succumbed readily, apparently quite willing to switch from the fat businessman to a skinny thief. Her only concern was that they be quiet enough so the businessman wouldn't get too suspicious.

Francois told us it was the quietest seduction he'd ever enjoyed. He laughed at the memory and said he often wondered what tale she later concocted for her companion.

Still laughing, he elbowed me in the rib. "Ah, Albert, these Italian women, eh?" I had to like the guy.

Since our dictionary didn't contain many of the French words that comprised Francois' colorful vocabulary, he carefully pantomimed his stories, pausing frequently to utter a key word, sometimes in French, sometimes English, to illustrate his tale.

Every action was deliberate. His hands, eyebrows and even his shoulders were so expressive that words were unnecessary. He'd set the scene describing the woman, using his hands as easily as an artist wields a brush. Then he'd assume a pose and we envisioned the entwined figures, something like Rodin's Eternal Spring. Then he would graciously toast his love with champagne, stroke her hair, brush her cheek and breasts with his lips or plant a kiss upon whatever part of her anatomy was most convenient. He made each scene so vivid that we were on the edge of our seats exclaiming breathlessly, "Oui, oui, Francois, we understand, go on, go on!" Francois would smile, pleased to acknowledge the special bond of understanding.

No doubt this womanizer missed his rich life of abundant and rewarding crime living in the forest with us; but he didn't neglect his more lusty pleasures.

His unique background made him especially suitable as a courier with the organization in town. He looked forward eagerly to his visits there, but Walter and I anticipated them just as much. Watching Francois prepare for a sortie was true entertainment.

Our pool of still water at the camp was greener on the surface than the surrounding forest, but Francois would boldly disrobe, skim some of the growth off the top, and jump right in, hopping around as he scrubbed.

One or two of us would use sticks to keep the scum out of his way until he was finished. When he climbed out again, someone else would douse him with a bucket of clear water. Sputtering and hopping like a skinny jaybird, he'd scurry to the hut, toweling off as he ran. By then, water he placed on the fire earlier was hot, and he could shave.

It made me nervous just to watch. He lathered so thickly that every time he leaned toward his mirror, I winced as the old-fashioned straight razor disappeared into the sudsy cream. Considering his unusual profile, I always expected he would cut himself seriously, but all he ever came up with were a few minor nicks. Then he doused himself liberally with cologne.

Dressing for the trip to town was the highlight of the entire production. He was so obviously happy that his anticipation affected all of us. We gladly accepted the role of valets. From under his straw pallet, we pulled a pair of pin-stripe trousers already attached to a heavy pair of canvas suspenders - the kind American loggers wear. With the trousers on and the suspenders dangling down his skinny flanks, he slipped into a white shirt and stuffed in the tails before flipping the galluses into place.

Then he struggled with a celluloid collar too small even for his scrawny neck, and fastened the stud. He meticulously arranged a long black string tie, knotting it with wide bows to cover the stud.

A black coat emerged from the battered suitcase. Holding it at arm's length, he inspected it carefully, shaking off the dust and brushing daintily at the lapels. By now, he was humming a happy tune. Sometimes he'd disguise a moth hole with black ink. We held the coat for him as he shrugged into it so the padded shoulders rode evenly; then he wriggled again, smoothing the wrinkles around the collar.

His appearance was ludicrous before, but now it was real Charlie Chaplin comedy as he stood there in the antiquated coat with long tails. He looked more like a scarecrow than ever. But he walked proudly, preening before the cracked mirror hanging on a tree branch.

He paused to inspect his reflection. Satisfied, he placed an old black Homburg on his head, cocked it to one side with the jauntiness of a boulevardier, and flicked his fingers against the brim.

The center of attention by then, he'd strut around the table, confident of his magnificence, then bow with a flourish, flip us a cocky little salute and amble down the trail, disappearing in to the woods.

The Don Juan of the Forest of Valence was on his way to town.

After his first night out following his run-in with Marcel, Walter and I waited up for the details when he returned. First, he filled us in on the war news.

"L'Americain, le General Patton, c'est un bon combatant, n'est-ce pas?"

"Oui, bon General," we agreed, waiting for him to continue.

"Two, maybe three months, la guerre sera finie et il n'y aura plus de boches en France." He hunched over, silent. Suddenly his face brightened.

He grinned and pulled a bottle of red wine from his coat. We sat there sharing it with him as he relived his trip to town. He provided ample details with his mixture of French, English and gestures. When we finally went to bed, the only thing we didn't know was her name.

The next few days passed quickly with everyone working hard to learn all we could teach them about weapons. I could sense they were anxious for action.

Late one afternoon, Joseph sat in the sun wondering how he could raise the men's spirits and came up with a plan. There were only two non-smokers in camp, Karl and Raoul. The rest of us were beginning to miss our smokes. We made a habit of fieldstripping our cigarette butts and saving the shreds of tobacco to roll our own later. When we found a couple of two-inch squares of pipe tobacco, we doled them out bit by bit. But it barely satisfied our craving.

Joseph worked out a plan, but when he mentioned it to Francois, who was now his closest confidant, flaws were revealed. Together, they devised a secret scheme for a raid.

Joseph and Francois believed the French storekeepers who sold tobacco were just as unhappy with the German-imposed ration as anyone. So, they reasoned, all they had to do was convince the shopkeeper that if his stock was stolen, through no fault of his, it would be replaced. Thus, he would be out nothing and we'd have our smokes. The shopkeeper would be allowed to keep half the tobacco himself as reimbursement. Francois smooth-talked the guy into going along with the plan and they scheduled the burglary.

Walt and I asked why they were so sure the stock would be replaced.

The Germans, they said, would blame it on terrorists and replace it to improve their image with the town folk. Joseph said it would also give the group a good reconnaissance since the store they planned to rob was in another village, several miles away. When Joseph and Francois laid out their plan that night, the others were excited as children.

Time passed slowly for them the next day as they waited for nightfall. At dusk they gathered round the table and blackened their faces with charcoal. They all wanted to take their rifles with them but Joseph said no.

"Someone must carry the things we steal. You want to carry guns, too?"

"Yes!" they answered in unison, resentment evident in their voices. Joseph refused to give in.

They trooped into the forest single file. Francois brought up the rear and flipped Walter and I a farewell salute before disappearing into the thicket. We laughed thinking of the suave Marseilles thief stealing tobacco from a provincial shop - his only profit a few cigarettes. Walt and I sat around playing hearts with a well-worn, almost unusable deck. We walked to the edge of the field, waited awhile, and then strolled back to camp.

Darkness settled over the forest, and the silence I could never understand came with it. Moonlight glinted through occasional breaks in the overcast that lingered over the camp that summer, but otherwise, it was pitch black. We built a small fire in the pit and made a pot of coffee that left a grainy sediment in the bottom of my cup. It was thick and black because we had used too much of the erzats, but it tasted good anyway.

Finally, we went to bed. I was just leaning over to douse the lamp when we heard a strange noise. Suddenly the sound of laughter echoed through the forest, and I rose up on my elbow to listen.

We were always concerned about the camp's general lack of security. They'd stopped posting guards, and no one ever bothered to brush away their clearly visible tracks as they neared camp. They all said, "No risk. Don't worry."

"Woody, does that sound to you like it sounds to me?" Walt asked grinning.

"Those silly bastards are drunk - sure as hell!" I answered.

The men began to sing as they neared camp. They piled into the hut laughing and talking excitedly, all trying to tell us at once of their success and excitedly rattling off plans for other raids. Even Joseph lost some of his reserve. He slapped Walter on the back, shouted for someone to bring cups, and poured brandy freely.

Raoul and Andre dumped two big sacks of loot onto the dirt floor, handing us cartoons of tailor-mades, cigarette and pipe tobacco, shoes, cheese, wine, brandy and some clothing. They said a sack of meat and vegetables was still outside.

Francois, not to be outdone, made a production of opening a bottle of champagne which spurted wildly. He poured what was left into our brandy cups. The almost French-75 tasted pretty good.

"Where'd you get all this stuff?" I asked.

"They said it would not look good for just the tobacco store to be robbed so the store owners arranged to let us into two other places also." Francois beamed, happy to provide the information.

"They pointed out what we should take and what we should leave," added Raoul.

"Sort of robbery by appointment," Walt suggested as everyone laughed.

They were happier than I'd ever seen them. Even Karl was smiling. They'd made the same deal with the other shopkeepers, leaving half the "loot" with them and toasting their good fortune before leaving the village. They took their time coming back, but swore they didn't start singing until they neared the hut.

Walt and I hoped for all our sakes they were telling the truth.

A troubled Marcel arrived shortly before noon the next day. I knew something worried him but he said nothing until Joseph, Francois, Walter, and I joined him in the hut. Then he told us that a serious incident the night before might cause trouble. He said that a small village about seven miles from his village had been raided. Many supplies were stolen, but the worst part was, he didn't know who did it and was afraid that another group of Resistors might attract the Germans.

Walter and I remained silent, but we noticed the other two nod to each other casually during Marcel's announcement. Marcel fumbled with his pipe, tamping a small amount of tobacco into the bowl. Straight-faced, Joseph handed him a tightly packed pouch of pipe tobacco.

"Here, Marcel, have some of mine."

Marcel looked at the small square of fresh tobacco, a frown working into deepening wrinkles on his face. Francois handed him another package.

"Take this one, too" he dead-panned.

Marcel stared, then jumped to his feet.

"You!" he shouted. "It was you who robbed the store. And I didn't know!"

"Yes, Marcel. It was us," Francois said. "But don't worry. Nothing is going to happen."

Joseph began reciting the story as the old man drew on his pipe allowing the taste of real tobacco to soothe his anger. When the story ended, he thought for a moment.

"How much did you get?"

"Half the stock," Joseph answered quickly.

"Enough to last how long?"

"Oh, several weeks."

The old man grinned, then broke into a smile followed by a hearty Santa Claus laugh. Raoul, who'd been listening outside the hut, came in smiling, glad that Papa was happy. Marcel considered everything and decided there would be no serious repercussions from the Germans. As he prepared to leave camp that day, the men presented him with ten of the tobacco squares. He protested that it was far too much but they told him, after all, he was the chief. They added several bottles of wine to his load.

As it turned out, the raid was bad for everybody. The Germans investigated the theft and posted bulletins proclaiming that terrorists were plundering villages and instructing people to report any information. They warned that such terrorist groups would be hunted down like dogs. A couple of days later, the shopkeepers asked for replacement of their lost rations.

"You have used your ration," they were told.

"Yes, but they were stolen."

"That's too bad," came the final answer.

And that was that. No more open-door robberies. The "terrorists" were through.

Another day, while Walter and I sat whittling to pass the time, Marcel came to us for advice. He wanted to know the quickest way to stop and seize a motorcycle courier at night, leaving no trace of violence.

The Resistance wanted to waylay the courier near our camp, and confiscate his papers. They didn't care what happened to the rider, and were leaving that part to Marcel. He said we would be given a few hours notice before the courier was expected to reach a specific point on the highway.

While we whittled, Walter and I brainstormed possible ways of stopping the motorcycle. We discarded the noisy plans; and then threw out those requiring too much preparation. Finally, we settled on a cable stretched across the road. If it was pulled taut a moment before the courier passed, a stand-by crew could remove the rider and his machine within seconds of the accident.

We figured two men could drag the rider away, while two others moved the motorcycle - if it wasn't too banged up. Another couple of guys could clean up any remaining debris and haul in the cable.

Joseph quickly grasped our plan when we explained it to him later. He remained silent until we finished outlining the details, after which he turned to us, grinning. He called Francois to join us and repeated the details in French. Francois knew where to find a cable. He agreed it was the quickest way to capture the pouch.

Marcel approved the plan. He then told Joseph to assign men to each task.

Marcel came back a day later, and said the courier was expected either that night or the next. It turned out to be the following night. Marcel knew the courier's planned time of arrival, give or take 15 minutes, and his boss, after hearing the plan, picked the exact spot for us to stretch the cable. There were trees on both sides of the road where the cable could be anchored with loops that would be quickly tightened once the cable was stretched. Surrounding underbrush would provide good coverage on both sides of the road.

Calling the men together, Marcel warned them that they must obey all orders without question. They quelled their excitement and listened intently.

"For some it will be a real mission. For others a sortie with training you need, but you will all have a part to do," Marcel pausing to scan the faces before. "Tonight, we are going to waylay a Boche!"

Their enthusiasm kindled, the men began shouting out questions with machine gun rapidity. It was Andre who finally asked, "Why do we do this, Marcel?"

"There is information about occurrences to the south that someone wants. They must know if Germans expect something or have knowledge of it. There are other details we need to know. Those documents are being transported by the courier tonight."

"What occurrences?" Andre persisted.

"I do not know. Perhaps a battle."

Walter and I looked at each other. We were pretty sure that was it. The invasion of Southern France had been openly discussed for months now and everyone knew Churchill liked the "soft underbelly" approach.

Marcel said he would watch the proceedings from the edge of the woods. Joseph would lead the crew, giving the sign to pull the cable.

After the man was dragged from the motorcycle, he would signal each group to go about their tasks. Francois and Joseph would take care of the German; young Marcel, who knew a little about gasoline motors, and Karl who was husky, would get rid of the motorcycle.

"But we will not leave the bike in the woods. A truck will come by, heading south, to pick it up. It will be hidden somewhere else," Marcel added.

"The body will be buried in the woods, but on the other side of the highway. When the job is done, you will all come back here, and I will go back to the village."

"Are you sure you can get away with hauling the bike off like that, Marcel" I asked, after he finished with the others. He looked at me and grinned. "Things may change, Albert."

I shrugged back at him. He was way ahead of everybody.

When we rejoined the others, Walt and Joseph were going over last-minute details. Andre, who could read German, would read the documents.

"Do Walter and I go with you?" I asked.

"No. You must remain here." Marcel said. "You are the responsibility of the Resistance. If you are caught with us tonight in civilian clothes, you will be tortured. Otherwise, you will be treated as prisoners of war and that is how our Chief and the other bosses want it."

I thought it over, and it was OK with me. If they could get us out of France, we could fly again.

Marcel gave the men a pep talk before they hustled off into the woods. Walt and I tried playing gin rummy but quickly tired of that. Both of us knew many of the cards the others held because they were badly torn and stained.

For a while we just sat there, not saying anything. Our thoughts were with the others. I added wood to the fire and began thinking about the night's foray. Suppose the Allies were planning for the invasion of Southern France and the courier actually was carrying documents of value. Certainly the Germans would have out-riders. Or they might even use an automobile instead of the usual motorbike, or perhaps send a well-guarded staff officer.

Even if it was the usual courier, suppose just one guy in town talked at the wrong place? Not Francois, not Joseph and not Raoul, but maybe someone else.

If there were patrol vehicles of any kind, they might catch one of our guys and everyone's cover would be shot. What were our chances of getting out then? I wondered if Walt was thinking the same thing.

By eleven, I was dog-tired and decided to catch a few winks. Walt said he'd stay awake to keep the fire going and promised to rouse me if anything happened. The next thing I knew, Walt was standing over me saying, "Woody, they're coming back."

Still wearing my trousers and shirt, I got up and slipped on my shoes. Walt had the fire going and was boiling water for coffee. We could hear the sounds of the men as they approached camp, quietly this time.

Karl was the first to enter the clearing. He was grinning excitedly. "Bon," he said. "Tres bon."

Francois and Raoul came next, followed closely by Joseph, and the others. Except for Karl, they didn't seem as excited as I'd expected. Francois poured a cup of coffee.

"It went well," he said. "We have much success. Never have I seen anyone come to such a quick stop." He laughed and began savoring his coffee. The others continued their silence. At last, Joseph began telling us what happened, speaking very slowly in French so we could understand. When there was something he couldn't make us understand in French, he switched to Polish and told Walt who repeated it to me.

"When we reached the highway, it was a good place to hide, out of sight," Joseph began. "Some kept watch while Raoul and Pierre crossed the road to fasten one end of the cable around the tree. They dragged the free end of the cable across the road until it was lying on the pavement free of kinks. The loose end was positioned so that we could stretch it tight and hook the cable in place very quickly."

Joseph leaned forward, elbows balanced on knees, and continued. "We began to worry after a few minutes that another vehicle might come along before the bike and discover the cable - but none did."

"It was quiet there by the road and as we waited in the dark, we hoped the rider would be on time. He was. First, we saw the blue headlight, and then heard the engine puttering. When he was twenty meters away, Raoul flipped the cable to the correct height and hooked it into place. I was worried that I had signaled him too soon, he did it so fast, but the German kept coming. I don't think he ever saw the cable."

Joseph took a sip of coffee, pausing to look at each of us before continuing the account.

"He must have been traveling at least 50 to 60 kilometers per hour and I noticed that he was a tall man, sitting upright on the seat. But the cable easily cleared the handlebars of the bike, hit his arms just below the shoulders and slid up toward his neck. It all happened so quickly I could hardly think. It seemed that he continued forward a little before the cable tightened and hurled his body upward and back onto the road while the motorbike kept moving forward. The engine slowed to idling speed since his hand was off the throttle, but the bike stayed on the road for a short distance more before rolling off into the brush.

"Marcel and Karl were waiting nearby and caught up with it, shutting off the engine. Raoul dragged the cable back to the other side of the road while Francois, Andre, and I dragged the body into the brush out of sight. There was only a small bloody spot in the middle of the road to indicate any accident.

"The man's neck was broken and his throat was mangled where the cable hit. He was dead before we ever got to him. The dispatch case was still over his shoulder, and another bag with papers was in a basket on the rear wheel. Karl brought it back for Andre to read and then returned to help Marcel. We took the man's bayonet, his rifle, and his identity card while Andre scanned the papers.

"Then, just as Marcel said it would, a truck came along and stopped where Marcel was waiting on the slope, then moved slowly forward to where we were waiting. Two men told us to throw the body in back. Then the truck roared away quickly - without the motorbike. They weren't there two minutes."

"What about the motorbike, Joseph, what happened to that?" I asked, concerned.

Joseph looked puzzled and paused for a moment before he answered.

"That's what was so strange," he said. "When the truck stopped where Marcel was waiting, somebody got out of the truck. Young Marcel switched off the ignition. His father came across the road and asked if the bike would start.

They said "Yes, it had only a few scratches." The old man told his son to start it and stay there. Then old Marcel turned and called to a man hiding in the brush where the truck had stopped. He ran across the road to where they were standing by the motorbike. The newcomer was wearing a German uniform, a corporal, the same rank as the driver we had stopped. We stood there wondering what the hell was happening, but not worried since Marcel was talking easily in French to the guy while he checked the bike. Then the uniformed fellow climbed on, gave it the gas a couple of times and drove down the road and out of sight."

Joseph looked perplexed. "It was very strange. Why do you suppose the plans were changed at the last minute?"

"Did Andre say what he found in the papers?" I asked.

"No, just that it was interesting."

"Anything about the invasion?"

"No, but he was excited about the names of some informers."

Joseph looked at me seriously. "I wonder where they took the bike and the dispatch case?"

"Maybe they will make photos somewhere," I guessed.

"Maybe they have somebody inside the next German Headquarters."

"Well, it all worked out. You apparently got what the underground wanted and nobody got caught," I said.

The group had successfully completed their first act of aggression. They had another rifle and a bayonet to show for their efforts, as well as the papers that were apparently the reason for the whole escapade. We never learned what happened to the substitute courier, but there were no repercussions from the Germans as far as we knew, so there must have been more to the plan than we heard.

Andre later told us the papers had information of great significance to the Underground and refused further comment.

In early July, Marcel brought his Resistance boss, also named Andre, to our camp. Walt had met him earlier. Accompanying him was a woman he said was a countess, and a dentist.

I'd been suffering with an aching tooth caused by a lost filling. The dentist gave me a bottle of something containing oil of cloves that eased the pain. He said he was more worried about the wound on my left arm that refused to heal properly and was becoming infected. He promised to send some salve, the kind used for flash burns by the French Navy.

The countess, for her part, took one look at Walter and me and arranged to return with a barber. For a while, I wondered if that was the real reason, or if she really just wanted to see Francois again. I had a chance to see that lady-killer in action for the first time, and he played it to the hilt.

The moment the countess appeared, he automatically fell into his gallant gentleman routine. He simply couldn't do enough for her. I'm sure she had his number, but she didn't discourage him in the least. He played the role to perfection. I've seen a lot of wolves, but Francois was the king - even in his tired clothes.

Before leaving, the boss, Andre, told us he was sorry, but we'd have to wait at least a few more days for the aircraft. When they were gone, Francois started chattering about the countess right away.

"Oooh-la-la! Did you see those legs, Albert? Formidable!"

"The rest wasn't bad either, Francois," I added.

"Yes, but those legs…"

"You better go to the village tonight, Francois."

He did just that.

Two days later, the area boss came back. He brought some gummy stuff the dentist gave him for my tooth. After I filled the cavity with it, the stuff hardened and the pain disappeared. The countess was with him again.

But his real reason for returning was to direct Marcel to begin surveillance on the home of a known collaborator in a nearby city. The man was preparing to flee the country with his family, taking along his wartime loot and his pre-war riches. It was rumored that the guy owned half the town including a very solid bank.

He was in cahoots with the Germans, having done their bidding since 1940, and no one could touch him. Being a collaborator for so many years, he knew his life would be in danger if he remained in France after the war. He knew it was just about over for him, and apparently bribed the Germans to escort him safely to Spain. "The days of Fortress Europa are ending, and the rats are fleeing the sinking ship," I thought.

The Germans didn't much care what happened to the old guy, but since he'd paid their way, they continued to take care of him. As long as he was in France, he was still useful to them.

Marcel gathered all the information the Resistance had on the man, as well as his home. He was directed to study the residence carefully, then raid it, and confiscate everything of value.

Marcel enlisted the help of Francois, our professional thief, assisted by Andre and Joseph. For Francois, this was duck soup, especially since he was well aware that the collaborator, a man in his late 50s or early 60s, lived with a beautiful, young, redheaded mistress in a palatial red brick chateau. The whole place was surrounded by acres of tree-studded lawns and protected by a high stone wall with metal grills along the top.

Joseph and Francois took turns casing the place. Francois learned, through his village drinking buddies, details that would have been impossible to come by any other way. They staked out the place for a week and learned everything they needed.

Once Marcel knew all the details, he organized everyone and worked out the overall plan. He said he would stay home this time. He explained that the stunt would require quick action and tremendous physical exertion and that he was just too old to attempt such things any more. He put Joseph in charge again.

By this time, four more newcomers were in the camp. The original group plus two of the new men would go on the raid. The team left at dusk a few nights later. Walt and I again remained behind as the forest stillness settled in. But there was one difference this time, ever since the sortie with the courier, we now posted night guards as a matter of routine.

Walt and I both stayed awake that night, keeping the fire burning low and sipping coffee laced with brandy. We felt we were living in the lap of luxury ever since the "terrorists" made their supply raid. We even fixed a midnight snack.

On this rare night, the moon shone brightly and we could hear an occasional flutter of night birds in the forest. The group returned around three in the morning, lugging a load of men's and women's clothing, shoes, canned goods, tobacco and wine, brandy, champagne, some automobile tires, books, German marks and French francs. They also said two cars and a truck were turned over to another Resistance unit, along with the hoard of gold. They seemed more exhilarated than ever.

They said the house was huge, its high fence protecting the entire set-up. But they managed to gain access by waiting in shrubs near the front gate, until the collaborator returned home, just before midnight. He arrived in a car along with his two sons from a former marriage, and the young mistress. A hired man rode behind them in a truck. When the guard opened the gate for the car to pass through, Joseph and Pierre jumped into the truck's cab with the driver. Francois silenced the guard and then locked the gate himself from the inside.

When the happy family entered their home, they were suddenly confronted by our six grim-looking, trigger-happy, and heavily armed "terrorists." The men were quickly bound and gagged as Joseph, Pierre, Raoul, and Andre searched the house for gold and money. They found it in a chest hidden in the man's office.

They also found a wall safe which they opened after much pleading by the old collaborator whose gag was loosened as Joseph pressed his blade against the man's neck, ordering him to talk. The safe contained a generous amount of francs, marks, heirloom jewelry - and something else I didn't learn of until later.

The mistress was as beautiful as our reports had indicated, and under Francois' close supervision, she prepared a meal for the raiders, who leisurely carried out their mission. They worked silently, motioning instead of speaking, and never calling each other by name when the family was within earshot.

They loaded a trunk, cramming it to capacity. The old man screamed pitifully when he realized they were taking his gold, and Joseph quickly stuck the gag back into place. The collaborator gurgled and moaned when they finally managed to open the safe, but they couldn't understand why, since it appeared to contain only worthless paper, documents, and letters, along with a few pieces of jewelry.

The man ignored the plight of his sons, but feared the raiders would rape or kidnap his lovely mistress. Francois later described her as "formidable," with green eyes and a luscious body.

"You wouldn't believe it, Albert, never have I seen such a beautiful body." This coming from François, I was impressed.

The next day, everyone in camp was reliving the adventure and inspecting the loot. Francois was almost lyrical as he spoke of the titan-haired mistress. Even Karl was chatty. It was the first time he had ever seen such opulence, and was flabbergasted. Andre, though, was silent and preoccupied. After lunch that day, which was very fancy for our maquis camp, Andre disappeared for a while, but later returned and spoke quietly with Walter before they both came over to me.

"Woody, do you know anything about bonds?" Walter asked quietly.

"A little, why?"

"Andre may have stumbled onto something last night. He says he's got a whole sack full of bonds from the safe. Joseph saw them first but tossed them aside. Andre picked them up and asked if he could have them. Joseph said sure, if he was crazy enough to lug them around. Then Andre found a lot more in the safe," Walter explained.

"Holy smokes! Where are they?" I gasped.

Andre left, walking away from the camp; after a moment, we followed. Crossing the camp toward the spring, we saw Andre near a heavy thicket that afforded some privacy. He was carrying a large, bulging sack shaped like an overstuffed pillowcase.

Inside were bundles of certificates, some individually folded others secured with rubber bands holding a half dozen or so per packet. Walter and I scanned several of the packets. The first one I opened was in French and English. It was stock in the Bathurst-Gambia Railroad, redeemable in Paris or London. The coupons were still attached.

Walter handed me another certificate, this one a pre-World War I issue of czarist oil stock with a fancy embossed emblem of the Imperial eagle on it. I figured it was probably worthless now that the government there had been overthrown.

"I think we can chalk this one up to Ivan," I said, handing it back to Walt.

"Yeah, that's what I thought." He kept it anyway, stuffing it into his pocket.

Everything I picked up looked interesting. There was real estate stock in Paris, hotel stock from all over, oil company stock in the Philippines, Indonesia, and Venezuela, gold and silver mining stock in Canada, and stock in a company in South Africa whose product I didn't know. I wondered if it was diamonds.

It was overwhelming. I paused to look at Walt and let out a long, soft whistle.

"Congratulations," I said, turning to Andre. "You did all right. You've achieved your goal - you are now a capitalist. A gross capitalist, in fact." Walt laughed and Andre looked at us excitedly.

"So? Is that right? It is good?" he asked, unable to conceal his glee.

"C'est bien, tres bien, old buddy. Woody's right. You are a big capitalist," Walt told him thumping him hard on the back.

"You're rich. You have a fortune here. You don't even have to dig," I added.

"For-mi-da-ble," Andre said, drawing the word out phonetically.

We quickly figured the total value from the first bunch at more than $75,000! The rest, which we were less sure about, totaled about $400,000.

It took some arithmetic, but we tried to determine how much the franc might be worth after the war. We guessed it would be pretty low. We then translated the dollar and pound values on the coupons into francs. The result averaged at least $2,000 from all the certificates we weren't certain about.

The three of us sat thinking about how long it had taken the old man to accumulate such wealth. Since many of the certificates dated back to World War I, we guessed he'd been at it for 20 or 30 years. We didn't understand why Joseph had tossed them aside without a glance - but they were all Andre's now.

"What are you going to do with that money, Andre?" I asked.

"I will go to the university after the war with my share."

"With your share - what do you mean?"

"We go together – equal - us three."

"Andre, are you sure?" I looked at him closely and he nodded.

"You're a real capitalist now, Andre," I reminded him. "But if that's the way you want it, it's fine with me."

"Yeah, it's OK with me, too," said Walt, laughing. "Let's put this stuff away and hide it somewhere."

Andre handed us a piece of oilcloth taken from the collaborator's garage and we stacked the bonds on it until it was about two feet square. Then we folded the oilcloth over the edges and tied it tightly closed with string. Andre pulled a roll of adhesive tape from his pocket and we sealed the corners to protect the papers from moisture and insects.

Reflecting on this good fortune, I figured about $25,000 each could be had immediately by cashing the coupons. We'd have the remainder over a period of time at a hefty monthly income. My salary as a first lieutenant at that time was less than $400 per month and I really couldn't visualize what I'd do with that much money. I was stunned. I hadn't done a thing to earn it except meet a Resistance kid while hiding from the Germans.

Andre took the package and said he'd bury it nearby. Walt and I offered to help but he refused. I was as excited as the terrorists were earlier, but my exhilaration didn't wear off.

I knew the stocks and bonds were of no value to the Underground as long as the war was on. They could only be reclaimed after the Germans had departed France. But I didn't want to do anything that might cause trouble, even though Joseph had given the stocks to Andre.

My exhilaration stemmed primarily from knowing that some cut-throat collaborator, who certainly hadn't taken any risks while selling out his friends and his country, would have to stay and face the music since the Resistance now held all his gold, as well as his francs and marks. Without his wealth, he was just another guy to the Germans and would likely never escape France alive.

Walter and I agreed to meet Andre in London after the war at one of the banks listed on the certificates. We decided to stay at the Dorchester Hotel. Walter and I would take the stocks back to England with us when we left and put them in a safe deposit vault there. The three of us would meet at 11AM six months after the war's end. I don't know why we picked that time; it might have been because of the World War I armistice. We asked about leaving the stocks in the village somewhere, but Andre nixed that idea. He trusted us and wanted us to take them back to England. It was hard to get back into the routine of the camp that day, knowing that package was out there waiting for us.

When Marcel came to the camp that afternoon, Walt and I asked him if we could hike around a little, just to get away from the camp where we were beginning to go stir crazy. He told us that it would be all right and suggested we go down near the highway where we could check the vegetables in the fields since the camp supply of green beans, stolen from the field earlier, was running low.

It was a sunny day and Marcel walked to the road with us. Not long after we reached the edge of the woods near the highway, the same old truck which brought me here nearly three weeks earlier came down the road and picked up Marcel. Walt and I lounged around for a while, seeing only a few German staff cars and trucks. The warm sun felt good. Going back to camp, we walked through the first little clump of forest and turned down the path toward the vegetable field.

Suddenly, a man stepped from a trail about two hundred yards ahead, then turned toward us.

"Damn it, Walt. Look up ahead!" I hissed, then added quietly, not looking at Walt, "Just keep walking, there's not much we can do."

As the man came closer, I had an idea.

"You pass him on one side of the road; I'll go on the other. Make him walk between us," I whispered. "If he says anything, just nod."

In my pocket, I switched open my knife. As we neared the stranger, I was apprehensive. Drawing closer, I saw he was wearing a sport jacket, a snap-brim hat, with something under his right arm. His hands were in his pockets too.

He was medium height, stockily built with a thick neck, his light blonde hair thinning and his face was round and pudgy, with rosy cheeks. He strongly resembled a man I knew at home who came to California from somewhere near Heidelberg; enough like him to be a brother.

A few more steps and I saw the object under his arm was a double-barreled shotgun. He grinned as he approached us, saying nothing until we were only a few feet apart, then smiled as he said, "Bonjour."

We smiled and nodded, parting so that he walked between us, which didn't seem to bother him. As soon as we passed him, I turned to watch. The man never turned or wavered from the path, just kept straight on. But I was plenty worried now. From the next corner we took a different route back to camp from the one we had planned to use.

Upon our return, we immediately told Joseph who sent Raoul to the village to get Marcel. When they returned, we described the man for Marcel.

He said he didn't recognize anybody like that from the "La milice" house, but would check further. He looked worried when he left.

Jittery and apprehensive after seeing such a well-dressed man on the trail, especially with a shotgun, I had to have something to do. When Raoul started supper, I helped, cooking fried potatoes with bacon pieces and some greens. They tasted pretty good and everybody kidded me about my future as a chef. But that night, I had a hell of a time getting to sleep.

# Chapter 15

# ON THE LAM

Walt and I were training the new men when Marcel arrived with six more men, all young fellows dodging labor press gangs. No one in camp knew them, but Marcel said the Resistance took them in from small towns around the area, after they had been checked out.

One was a slim, young black kid about 19 years old and when he learned I was an American, he walked over and said, "Hey, man, Louis Armstrong. Jazz, hot jazz."

His English seemed flawless and I began chatting, but his face took on a blank look. It was the only English he knew.

None of the recruits knew anything about firearms so Walt, Joseph, and I began from scratch - again. The veterans in the camp became big shots, the new guys envious. By now, our first students were doing well at what we could teach them, which, of course, did not include actually firing a weapon. They even sounded off when the new guys ignored the safety, as they had.

With the new men came a second delivery of weapons, enough to provide an automatic weapon for everyone. We kept the guns ready.

Marcel indicated four more men, the last for our camp, would arrive soon. After training all morning and most of the afternoon, Walt and I sat at the table in the shade. Walt whittled on a pair of Dutch wooden shoes, a remarkably good copy, and I was talking with Andre. Suddenly, two ME-109s flew right overhead. They hurtled by so fast there was no time for anything more than a quick glance.

Since they flew perfectly level, Walt and I guessed they didn't see the camp, it was probably just a chance flyover, nothing to worry about. Our fire was out so there was no smoke to catch their attention, and trees screened most everything else. If they were searching for a camp, the Germans would probably use smaller, slower planes. These two were going flat out.

But we still wondered. First, the well-dressed stranger strolled the path with a shotgun under his arm, then two Messerschmidts flew overhead. It did nothing to ease my apprehension.

Marcel came that evening and said there was a break near Caen with a heavy attack by British forces. We thought some sort of breakthrough would occur soon and still figured the best line of advance would be south of Paris. That would put us right in the middle. I asked Marcel the date and he said July 5. I'd already been down for over a month!

The next morning, at about 10:00, two men came into camp without escort. They were Americans, one a staff sergeant from Cleveland, and the other a B-24 co-pilot, who was a second lieutenant from St. Louis, named Robert Brown.

They were directed to the camp by people from another resistance group who dropped them off on the road with a crudely drawn map. Our guards brought them in and they immediately asked for Marcel. Joseph sent someone to get him while Walt and I talked to the Americans.

They asked us when and where we were shot down. I told them when, but not where. When Walt didn't respond in detail either, I realized he also was doubtful about the pair. The sergeant said little, leaving the talking to his buddy. He seemed much quieter than most Americans would be under the circumstances.

They asked why we stayed at the camp instead of trying to walk out through Spain. We said we were following orders and didn't want anyone from the Resistance caught by blundering around and being captured.

The lieutenant wanted to leave immediately, with or without the Underground. They used escape maps to show where their B-24 was shot down, asking us to indicate where we went down. We put them off. They said they went down two weeks before near Le Mans.

The lieutenant said if we stayed with the Underground and were caught, we'd be shot as spies. He told us a story about 11 evadees who were caught with the Underground near Valenciennes in northern France near the Belgian border. A bunch were caught in an armed Maquis camp, wearing civilian clothing. Even though dogtags were around their necks, the Germans lined them up and shot them as terrorists.

"You guys don't want to stay here. If you get caught, they'll kill you," the lieutenant said.

"How did you learn this story, Brown?" I asked.

"At a place we were two days ago. The guy in charge told us and said it was confirmed."

Walt and I didn't know whether to believe him or not, but I didn't think the Underground would have told them even if it was true. I didn't trust these guys. As if to clinch our trust in them, Brown suddenly switched the conversation to baseball.

"Did you guys know the Browns were leading the league?"

He gave us their batting averages, leading hitters, everything. I didn't trust him at all after that. It was too pat. But Marcel later verified that he'd expected them. None of it made sense, especially the map. The Underground never used maps.

We ate lunch and as Marcel prepared to leave, Brown said they'd leave with him and work their way out, on their own. I didn't say much, just stuck out my hand, and said goodbye, relieved to see them go. Brown talked too much and hadn't figured things out yet. I just didn't think they were authentic. I thought they just as easily could be English-speaking Germans wearing dogtags from some shot-down crew - guys already captured and in a German prison camp - or dead!

When they left, Walt and I discussed their visit in detail and concluded they were imposters, despite what Marcel was told. Why else would they try to learn so much about us, where we were shot down and all about our group? Before he left, he gave Karl permission to go home for a few days, if he promised to stay low and stay out of sight. I thought Karl was homesick and tired of the camp. And maybe a little nervous around the new guys.

The next day dragged. I'd been here almost three weeks, but it seemed like months. I went potato digging with Marcel and Pierre. When we were sure it was clear, we crawled into the field, filled a sack full of spuds, went to another field for the beans, then scurried back to camp.

Andre went to the village with young Marcel. He wanted more packing materials and paper for writing instructions about the bank.

Late in the afternoon, Walt and I were talking about the chances of the other two Americans walking out on their own, if they weren't phony as we thought, when Marcel dashed into camp, almost out of breath. He placed a hand on Walt's shoulder.

"Come. Get your things. You go now," he wheezed.

We raced to the hut and grabbed our packs. I slung mine over my shoulder. Outside, Walt was already telling Joseph goodbye.

"Something wrong, Marcel?" I asked.

"No. No. The airplane comes tonight but it cannot land here now, so you go to another place."

I looked at Walt and cursed.

"What's the matter, Woody?"

"Andre is in town—we don't have the package!"

"Son of a bitch!" he groaned.

We made sure we took everything else, including extra tobacco. We said quick goodbyes. Francois ran up and gave us each a hug and three kisses. I was going to miss that ugly lover.

Raoul went with us when we left.

This time I kept up with the old man easily. I was back in shape. We hurried on at a fast pace, silent until we reached the woods near the highway and started across the field. We'd just sat down in the roadside brush when I looked up and saw Andre emerge from a small thicket on his way back to camp. I called to him and he stopped short, motionless until he recognized us. He trotted over, wondering what was happening.

"You go?" he asked.

"Yes Andre, we're leaving. Tonight the airplane will take us back."

We shook hands. He watched me, wanting to say something but didn't have the words, so I spoke, "Andre, not London. Under the Arch of triumph instead. Same time. OK?"

"OK," he said grinning. "Arch of Triumph."

Marcel pulled a bottle of wine out of his bag. We passed it around.

"Marcel, thanks for everything. You are a real friend."

"De rien, Albert."

Andre held out his fountain pen, his most prized possession. I didn't want to take it, but finally put it in my shirt pocket.

"Merci, Andre."

I tried to think of something I could give him but had very little. I slipped off my watch and handed it to him. He was flabbergasted but I knew he felt as I did when he handed me the pen.

Andre looked at Walt and me. "No worry about the package. I'll meet you Arch of triumph, same date."

"Apres la guerre, eh?"

"Oui. Après la guerre!"

The old truck rattled around the curve. Andre sat next to the driver and motioned us into the back. We tossed in our packs, then climbed aboard, pulling the flap aside to wave farewell.

Marcel climbed in beside the chief and the truck rolled away. At the next village, Marcel got out and walked away without a backward glance. When we were out of the village, the driver accelerated. Within minutes, we reached a small town and the truck stopped along the main street. The chief motioned for us to get into a car parked in front of the truck.

The car started immediately and we rode through several towns for what must have been almost an hour when we entered a larger town with a road sign proclaiming it "PROVINS".

We were led to a building where a man in a brown leather coat instructed us to follow. We walked several blocks to the kitchen of an antique shop where we sipped coffee from dainty china cups, so white they glistened. The frilly window curtains seemed to be from another world. I felt strange, uprooted. I peered at Walt.

"Walt, you look like hell, you know that?"

"You don't look very damned good either."

"I didn't realize how dirty we really were."

"No, it just catches up after a few days in camp."

We sat there, saying little, both of us apprehensive. After an hour, Andre came into the kitchen. He wore the same beige jacket with leather patches he had the first day. His sandy, faintly red hair was short, almost in a crew cut, and he'd started a beard. He sat down.

"There won't be any airplane," he began. "My whole organization is crumbling. Someone talked, but we don't yet know who. The Gestapo has picked up a lot of our people - using SS troops. There's no telling what will happen next. I had to get you out immediately. I told Marcel, and he is going back with the others. They have already been warned."

"Did Marcel mention the man we saw on the trail?" I asked.

"Yes, he did. I didn't think it was anything, now I'm not so sure. You still have your papers?"

"Yes, everything is either in my pocket or my bag," I said.

"I will take you to a house. It is safe. I will take you there but will not enter. They are expecting you. Just open the door and go into the house."

We were even more apprehensive now, knowing we could be picked up at any minute. Ten minutes later, we left the shop and drove a short distance to the house. We got out of the car and climbed a flight of steps, entering the house through a massive wooden door. As I pulled off my beret, I noticed a woman standing there.

"Bonjour," she said. "Vous parlez français?"

"Un peu." I said. "Albert."

Walt gave her his forged ID name, "Andre."

"Tres bien." She led us into a parlor where a man and a girl about 15 years old waited. The woman made introductions, using only first names and asked us to sit. They were big, soft, upholstered chairs.

After trying French, the mother and daughter switched to English. Then we tried a mixture of both languages. Again, we waited but this time we had a chance to wash our face and hands. I really scrubbed.

We stayed until dinner, which was the best I'd eaten since Versailles, and the best ever for Walt. The highlight of the meal was a melt-in-your-mouth artichoke.

Andre returned later and told us things were getting worse in his area. He was worried - some of his men had already been executed. He thought our camp was still all right though.

We were shown to a bedroom, where we found a radio. We fidgeted as we listened to the news. We'd won a battle near Caen and things were shaping up. We still thought our guess about the advance heading our way was correct. We worried about the guys in our camp. We hoped Andre could return soon with some news.

If things were going as badly as Andre thought, they'd get hit, too. We didn't want that to happen, but I couldn't forget the guy with the shotgun, the two supposed-Americans, and the planes.

At midnight, the chief returned. He talked with the family downstairs first, then with us. He was tense and worried sick. He'd just been warned to leave his own house, because the Germans had learned he was a Resistance chief. He fled his apartment just in time by scurrying over rooftops. He made a few checks but was unable to get in touch with his key people. Fearing someone might have informed on them, he came here to brief the family on what to say if the Germans came, and instruct Walt and me. He said the Germans might discover this house, too.

He showed us two rear exits and told us to run through the garage into the alley if anything happened. He would try to have a car parked around the corner and one of his people would drive us to a safe place. He'd spend the night trying to learn what was left of his group, and return the next morning.

Walter and I took off our shoes and slept in our clothes with our bags ready. But we'd forgotten how soft a real bed was and slept soundly until the owner of the house shook us awake.

"Descendez," he said, and I could tell he meant in a hurry. We jumped up, put on our shoes, grabbed our canvas bags and went quickly downstairs. Andre was at the back door.

"Hurry," he said.

As we crossed the backyard, I wondered how close the Germans were. We walked through a garage, then quickly down the alley as we heard cars screech to a stop in front of the house. Someone shouted orders in German and I thought this was too damned close for comfort. We piled into the waiting car, its engine idling quietly. The driver sped away, turned a corner, and took several more turns only a block or two on each street. Andre told us he thought the Gestapo came to the house on a hunch and said he didn't really believe they'd learn anything about us there. I didn't believe him.

We got out of the car and climbed into a truck which drove on for another half-mile to an open area on the Seine, before following a poplar-lined driveway to a gravel parking lot by a large building. Andre entered with us and led us to a basement. The top portion of its windows were above ground with a view of the courtyard.

He gave us a few instructions, then told us the Germans were raising hell all over the area. He said a lot of people were rounded up; some stood against a wall and shot. He was leaving to get the two other Americans, then return. He told us to wait.

It was getting light as he drove away. We went upstairs and checked the rest of the building. It was vacant except for a few pieces of furniture here and there. On the ground floor, glass doors led onto a patio overlooking the remnants of a beautiful lawn, which curved to the edge of a river. On one of the walls, we spotted a framed certificate indicating the place was a gun club.

We sat around talking about the close call with the Gestapo, but mostly we were silent, thinking about the guys back in camp and wondering if they were safe.

Daylight soon flooded the basement making it hot and stuffy, so we went upstairs and sat in old chairs watching the road leading to this place. I browsed around the second floor and found a nice bar and lounge, covered with thick dust. It must have been great before the occupation. I saw a skeet house out back with shooting positions arranged in a semi-circle. Posted prominently were pre-war notices in French, English, and German about gun registration. The Krauts knew exactly where to go to collect every gun in the country when they took over.

By 10:00, we were jumpy as hell, starting to worry that the truck might not return. We snapped at each other a couple of times, realizing the tension was getting to us, but within the hour, the truck nosed into the lane and parked in front of the building.

The chief got out, followed by two men who came inside as the truck drove away. They were the other two Americans we'd heard about for so long. Bill was a tall blonde from Wichita, Kansas, a B-17 pilot. The other was a B-24 co-pilot from Chicago named Martin.

The chief said the family we'd stayed with was released after a night of questioning. In the meantime, he'd dyed his hair dark brown. His clothes were older, and rumpled, and he seemed a different man. He knew that more of his people were captives and feared they would be killed. Old Marcel had been picked up, but Andre hadn't heard anything from the camp as yet.

The driver would return in 30 minutes to drive us to a place nearer Paris. Orders had been issued for us to hole up and wait for the Allied advance in the city. He left, walking back to the road. We looked at each other speculatively. It was a whole new ball game.

While we waited again for the truck, we talked to the two other Americans. Martin said he'd bailed out of his B-24 and was captured near Dusseldorf. He was thrown into an old warehouse used as a temporary prison.

The RAF came over the first night he was there and blew up part of the building. Martin and about 20 others escaped through holes punched in the walls and fence. He walked to Holland. People there helped, and eventually he rode south on a stolen bike and contacted the Underground near the Belgian border. He lived in a barn part of the time and in the woods, alone, for a while. He said he hadn't eaten a decent meal since he left England. I think he may have been dirtier that even Walt or I were. Bill was neat and clean.

His story was a lulu. He was leading a B-17 flight against an airdrome south of Paris when his plane was hit by flak. He turned the controls over to his deputy group commander, flying as co-pilot, while he went to help a gunner put out what he thought was a minor fire in the bomb bay. The bays were open. About that time, the trapped bomb exploded, and that was all Bill knew for a while.

They were above 20,000 feet when he was blown out. By the time he awoke and popped the chute, the chute oscillated only a couple of times before he hit the ground - hard. He was semi-conscious when someone propped him up and gave him a drink. He took a couple of hard swallows before his mouth started burning like fire and he gasped for breath. His first drink of Calvados brought him around fast.

Other men ran to help. They hid him for a day before Andre came and took him to the chateau Marcel had told us about, the one owned by the countess. There, he lived the good life! He'd just left there this morning. He thought that his plane returned without him, and he might be accused of bailing out on his crew.

"If we get back," he said, "I have to volunteer to finish my tour."

"You think that co-pilot got her back, huh?" we asked.

"Andre said there were no other chutes and no B-17s crashed around there that day."

"I see what you mean. That's quite a predicament," we agreed.

We swapped stories and discussed our chances. But we all agreed the best thing to do was stay with the Underground and do what they told us.

The truck returned just before noon. The chief came inside and gave us instructions. "Things look better now," he said. "You will be taken in the truck and when you get there tell the man you meet I will contact him as soon as possible. Your ride will last about an hour. Now go."

I rode in the cab with the driver, the other three in the back. The driver smoked madly, a cigarette perpetually dangling from the right corner of his mouth. He was silent at first; then started a discussion using short, two-or-three-word phrases, spoken slowly enough for me to understand. He'd obviously been around shot-down Americans before. Every time we passed a German soldier, he muttered, "Salaud de boche."

At the edge of the city, he turned onto a country lane but within 10 minutes, we were back on the main route rolling smoothly past cultivated fields and gentle hillsides. The driver was a stocky guy, with a big black mustache, a leather cap and heavily muscled arms. He tooled that beat up old truck along expertly. I tried to keep the conversation going, but he was too tense, apparently thinking about some of his friends who, at that moment, were in the hands of the Gestapo.

I was wondering where the hell we were going when I noticed the snouts of several 88-millimeter guns in a field, to the right off the road. We passed another emplacement, then another. I took a closer look. The crew was sitting in position, ready to fire. As we passed the second emplacement, our right front tire blew. It made a hell of a noise and the truck bumped unevenly down the road, the driver fighting the wheel.

I realized that we were going to come to a stop almost opposite the third battery, manned just as the others. As the truck came to a stop, the gun nearest the road was 20 feet to my right sitting on ground a few feet higher than the level of the road. A young blond soldier in a black uniform lounged in the steel seat at the breech of the gun grinning at the unexpected entertainment. Other Germans were also watching us.

I slipped out of the door as we slowed, ran around to the back, pulled the curtain aside, stuck my head in, and held a finger to my lips for silence. Then I whispered.

"Don't say a damned thing. We're only 20 feet from an 88-millimeter gun and a whole SS crew is watching."

They slid out of the truck and followed me around to the front wheel, ignoring the gun crew. The driver was obviously scared to death we would say something in English. I motioned to him for the jack. He dashed around and got the tools we needed. I jacked up the wheel and it was no sooner above ground when Bill went to work with the lug wrench, twisting those damned nuts off so fast I knew he'd logged service station time back home as I had. The driver and Martin already had the spare waiting and when Bill got the last nut off, he rolled it toward the other two without looking and placed the spare on the lugs, tightening the nuts again.

I lowered the wheel to the ground, Walt took the jack to the back of the truck and climbed in. As I got into the cab, the tall, young German grinned at me, his long blond hair streaming in the breeze.

"Rapide" he said.

I shrugged and kept quiet. Then he spoke again, too fast for me to understand. The driver, standing on his running board, answered quickly for me.

The German laughed and pushed the air with his hands as if to say, "Get the hell out of here." Our driver got that old bucket going immediately. As we drove away, he turned to me and smiled, then broke into a big belly laugh. I know it was the fastest tire change I ever saw, and I think he thought so, too.

He turned to me, wiped his brow with an exaggerated motion, and smiled, his leathery face aglow. He pointed out a few areas to me along the way, noting we were on the edge of the best champagne country in France. The vineyards were clean and cared for, the furrowed soil rich red.

At last, we came to the outskirts of a small city. The driver knew exactly where to go, deftly navigating through the streets until we reached a narrow lane where he pulled up to a garage and honked his horn. The doors opened immediately and closed behind us as we entered a courtyard.

A man came out of the house, motioning for us to go inside. A woman there indicated where we should sit. She picked up a telephone, talked for a moment, and told us "Monsieur" would join us in five minutes.

I hate just sitting around when I don't know where I am or what's going to happen - but I waited, fidgety as hell. For all we knew, the Gestapo might be minutes behind us.

## LAGNY

When the man arrived, he greeted us in English and introduced himself as Paul. Young and jaunty, he talked with the driver, and laughed when he heard about the tire change. I asked him to translate what the young German said when we drove away.

"He says the German asked him how long he thought the tire you put on the truck was going to last. He told him it didn't make any difference because he has four more old tires in the back. He does, too. It's the only way we ever finish a trip.

"Have you heard anything from Provins?" I asked.

"No. Did Andre give you a message for me?"

"Yes, he said he would get in touch with you as soon as possible but didn't know when that would be. He told us they picked up a lot of his people."

Paul said we were just west of Paris, in Lagny and that we'd spend the night here. He was a British agent on his fifth undercover mission in France. This one was already in its fifth month and going smoothly. He said he needed to interrogate us. Bill and Martin were taken to another room.

First, he told us we were safe here - to quit worrying. He asked how long we were at the camp, then asked us to recall everything we could think of that might indicate the Germans were on to the camp's existence. We described everything in detail. I told him I didn't think we posted guards early enough, and when I mentioned brushing away tracks, he was surprised they hadn't been doing that prior to our arrival.

We told him about the "Don't worry, no risk" attitude, but he didn't seem surprised. We gave him a list of weapons that had been received before we left. Paul indicated there was one man in the camp who worried him, but he didn't hint at who that person was.

He said he was aware of the two Americans who walked in alone. He was confident at the time that they were genuine but thought they may have been picked up and could have still had the map on them. I told him they said they would get rid of it on their way out of the woods with Marcel.

Paul wasn't concerned about the Messerschmidts either. He said the Germans generally used Fisler-Storchess to search wooded areas for Maquis camps. He said that a lot of new changes were going to be made to improve camp security in his area. He told us we would remain in Lagny for another day or two, then continue on to Paris.

"As a matter of fact, I could use your help right now," he said. "We must take a cart of weapons all the way through town to another house."

We went into the courtyard with him to a garage where two young French couples waited. The men were in their early 20s and the women seemed younger. They were loading weapons into an old two-wheeled, rubber-tired cart. There were several cases of rifles, some grenades, four grease guns, and a Tommy. After loading the weapons, we placed short lengths of wood tied into bundles on the cart for cover. I made sure the Tommy was within easy reach.

We pulled the old cart from the garage, easily at first, until we reached the cobblestone street where pushing became hard work. It was easier again when we reached an asphalt street through the town square. A big crowd was gathered there, with many German soldiers mingling with French civilians. Some kind of celebration was underway. Nobody paid any attention to us as the French kids talked and we Americans kept silent. We struggled to push the cart up a hill, and I took off my coat, sweating in the warmth of the afternoon sun.

When at last we arrived at our destination, we shoved the cart into a shed, latched the door and went into the house.

We flopped down at a kitchen table about 12 feet long with benches on both sides. The woman of the house, aided by two girls, served us huge bowls of vegetable soup, sandwiches, and jugs of hearty red wine.

"What do you think of this soup, Walt?" I asked.

"Damn it's good. After all those beans and cabbage at camp, this is strictly gourmet," he answered, not breaking his spoon-to-mouth shoveling.

It made me curious about Martin. His life in the Underground had been rough until now and I noticed he never said much unless spoken to directly.

"What have your meals been like with the Underground, Martin? I asked.

"Never much at one time," Martin answered. "Mostly vegetables, never any meat, and no coffee."

Finished with our meal, we thanked the women and smoked a cigarette. By this time, the older woman had taken a good look at us and determined beyond a shadow of doubt that a bath was definitely in order. Three of us were filthy.

She instructed the girls to help her set up tin bath tubs in the kitchen and heat water. While that was being done, we were taken to upstairs rooms to undress and given old robes to wear. We drew straws to see which two of us would bathe first. Bill and Martin won.

While they were downstairs, I opened the Armagnac bottle and Walt and I sat on the balcony in our robes watching the crowd still gathered in the square below, two blocks away. We tried to relax after the last two hectic days watching German soldiers wander through the sidewalk stalls, buying trinkets and enjoying themselves.

As we stood there rubber-necking, an air raid alarm sounded. In a few minutes we heard the belch of anti-aircraft guns to the south before the batteries near Lagny opened. As the barrage continued, we saw the first of many aircraft heading almost due east, a mile or two south of us. Big four-engined RAF Lancasters. They were flying at about five thousand feet, very low for them, and in formation. I was surprised to see them in broad daylight, in France, and flying so low.

Flak was bursting all around them. Just east of town, one of them was hit. Black smoke gushed from an engine as the pilot nosed down away from the flight for 2,000 feet or so, and finally straightened out. As the smoke dissipated, the bomber continued on course. Minutes later, we heard the unmistakable rumbling as their bombs detonated only a few miles east of Lagny.

Just then, Bill and Martin came upstairs and Walt and I trotted eagerly downstairs to soak.

The woman and two girls were refilling two big, metal tubs standing in the middle of the kitchen. Each tub was long enough so even I could stretch out. Already the steam was rising invitingly.

We helped them bring more big pans of water from the hand-operated pump on the back porch, and placed them on the stove, confident that the first tubs of water would turn black the instant we stepped in.

That proved true. We scrubbed a bit then emptied the murky baths, poured in more water, and climbed in again. Naturally, we invited the two girls to join us but they declined, giggling. This time I washed my hair first, and really scrubbed. The woman of the house came in with a bottle of brandy and a bottle of liniment for our chiggers or lice or whatever kind of vermin were nibbling on us.

As we soaked in the hot water, we sipped the brandy, which felt as good inside as the bath did outside. When we got out, we rubbed liniment on our legs and bellies. It stung like hell but it got rid of the bugs.

That night, Paul ate dinner with us and reported that Marcel had been captured by the SS but he didn't know what happened at the camp. He said he'd tell us as soon as he heard. Walt and I listened to the radio in our room after dinner, down in the dumps about that fine old man in the hands of the SS or Gestapo.

When he returned the following morning, Paul briefed us about a train ride we'd take to Paris the next day. Again, silence was the key, but the biggest risk would be in Paris when we took the "Metro." The Germans periodically rounded up men in the subway stations.

Paul was businesslike and full of confidence. I liked his attitude as an agent, and marveled at how assured he was, operating behind the lines as he did, always in a new area each time he returned, and knowing that the Gestapo would love to get their hands on him. He always answered our questions fully.

After the briefing, Paul talked to Walt and me alone. Marcel was dead, he said, killed by the Germans. It happened when the Gestapo made a sweep with SS troops. They picked up a lot of people, most of them suspected of Underground activities. One of them revealed that he thought Marcel was a leader so they picked up the old man in the village. The guy who squealed was shot as soon as he told them, and his wife and daughter raped.

Paul said his informant told him that some of our camp mates were also captured. That was all of the information he could get that day. The SS picked up Marcel while we were still in the gun club, even before we left Provins for Lagny.

They apparently tortured Marcel all day long, launching their attack against the camp just last night. Paul said the strangest thing was that after the German attack, they found the body of a blond French kid about 18, dangling from a rope noose. Apparently, he was hanged by the French before the Germans arrived. Walt and I looked at each other.

"Karl" I gasped.

"Yeah. He must have talked somewhere."

"He was away from camp when we left."

We told Paul about Karl and of his envy of Francois. He said he'd check out that angle. Walt and I thought Karl might have gone into a bar looking for some of Francois' girlfriends and talked too much in the wrong place. A couple of drinks would be enough. Whatever happened, the guys in camp must have held a necktie party. But why were they still there when the SS attacked? We thought they'd flee if they suspected trouble.

It was a sad time for us. I hated to think about Marcel being killed and we didn't know anything about the others. Some of them could have gotten away. Paul said he would try to let us know. Also, he gave us a telephone number to call in London when we got back.

"Call this number, either my mother or sister will answer," he said.

Walt scribbled it on a scrap of paper and stuffed it into the lining of his coat through a small hole in his jacket pocket.

## ARRIVAL IN PARIS

The next morning, we got up early, gulped a quick cup of coffee with the family and after saying good-bye, walked down the hill with our guide to the train station. It was crowded, but there were only two German soldiers in the tiny depot.

Bill and Martin sat four rows ahead of us on the same side of the aisle while the guide sat across the aisle with his back to the window, able to observe all of us at a glance. As the passengers streamed onto the train, the seats quickly filled.

Minutes later, I broke the cardinal rule. A well-dressed man holding onto a strap began speaking to me. I understood, but only nodded when he said the train was crowded.

When he started another conversation, I gave him a blank look and said, "Ja." A startled look came over his face, which began to redden. He turned away, rigidly grasping the strap as he stared down the aisle, not giving me another glance. The eyes of other passengers flicked toward me, then away. No one said anything.

In the Paris station, we followed our guide through the crowd to the sidewalk where he turned us over to another man with a nod of his head before quickly walking away. The new guide folded his paper, gave us a little nod, and walked ahead.

As we neared the curb, I glanced back to make sure Bill and Martin were behind us, when suddenly I bumped into someone. I saw a black uniform, Gestapo or SS. I moved back a step, focusing on the silver flashes on the collar, taking in the polished boots, the swastika armband, and the peaked cap. The man was at least four inches taller than I, peering down at me. A smile formed on his lips as he watched me. I scowled at him, but his smile broadened as he moved into an exaggerated little bow, his boots clicking together. He made a flourishing motion with his right arm for me to go on.

"Pardonnez moi," he said.

I stepped past to walk on, still scowling, but I got such a good look at the guy I knew I'd never forget him." (Three and a half years later, while stationed in Germany, I ran into this guy again. Having been cleared, he was holding down a good job working in a plant which manufactured products used by the U.S. Army. I reported him to the CID who picked him up. He was returned to France where he was tried as a war criminal.)

By this time, Walt was 15 feet ahead of me. I slouched along to catch up but for a moment, I'd thought my evasion had come to an end.

Further down the street, the guide stopped, asked us if we spoke French and when we gave him the standard, "A little," he realized we didn't and motioned us on. The Kraut officer had acted so damned superior I was mad as the devil, but cooled off as I began thinking that I was lucky to still be walking at all.

When the guide stopped again, he gave us each a ticket. "For the Metro," he said. We walked downstairs and followed a long corridor to a ticket stall with a metal fence that funneled passengers through the gate.

A train nosed into the boarding area within five minutes. We followed our guide into an almost empty coach and rode for almost 15 minutes. The coach was dingy and the graffiti on the walls looked like it does all over the world. We went through several stations before our guide stood up and walked toward the door. We followed him outside, through another long corridor, then upstairs to the street.

He stopped, pointing to two men. One was on a bicycle and the guide said to follow him. The man nodded to us and we could see the other begin walking down the street with Bill and Martin.

We tagged behind the bicyclist along a wide boulevard with multi-story buildings edging the sidewalk for several blocks. Between the sidewalk and the street, stubby sycamores grew. Every tree was severely pruned. I never saw such a stark, forlorn looking row of trees in my life and wondered why they were in that condition. I also wondered what street I was on. I turned around and looked down the street. Not far away, I spotted the Arch of Triumph, probably the most recognizable landmark in Paris with the exception of the Eiffel Tower. It looked magnificent, and I felt a quick surge of emotion.

"Walt, look behind us."

"What's the matter?" he asked, suddenly nervous.

"Nothing. You'll see."

He looked back for a moment, then flashed a mischievous grin. "At least we know for certain now that we're really in Paris."

"That's for sure. I wonder where he's taking us."

"Beats me. Just have to follow to find out."

The street ahead led to a wide bridge and continued into another broad expanse of pavement. At the next corner was the street sign "Avenue de la Grande Armee."

The guide peddled ahead slowly, letting us keep pace. Before we reached the bridge, the street name changed to "Avenue de Neuilly." At the bridge, the guide told us to cross and said he would meet us on the other side. Then he sped off. We strolled along, taking in the scenery. When we reached the other bank, we found the waiting guide.

This was a street, not a boulevard, and the buildings weren't as ornate as across the river. Some of the side streets were cobblestone.

German vehicles passed headed out of Paris, and I saw another one of those small square-looking vehicles with a hood that sloped to the

front bumper. Along the way we passed kiosks with posters in French
and German. Some of them had red swastikas at the top and bottom.
I assumed they were official notices.

After a while, we reached a spot where the street narrowed and a
side street branched off at an angle leaving a triangle of ground between
them. Near the point of the triangle was one of those "pissoirs" I'd
heard about.

Just before we started to cross over, a group of Panzer tanks lumbered
up behind us. We stopped at the curb waiting for them to rumble on
when suddenly, one of them stopped right in front of us. The hatch
popped open and a young soldier climbed out.

His blond hair was so long whisps of it fluttered along the sides
of his forage cap. His black uniform and armband indicated he was
SS. As he jumped down from the tank, we moved across the street. By
now the cocky young German was on the ground alongside the tank.
He watched us closely as we crossed the diagonal, edging quickly away
from the tank. Starting toward the "pissoir" he stopped, then spoke to
us in French.

Walter kept right on going and I took a couple of steps, but then
slowed as he growled something. I just stared, and he spoke again,
shouting this time. I kept staring, not comprehending. Then he yelled
"Ou passé?"

I knew I had to do something since he was concentrating on me. I
looked at him as impassively as I could and offered that well-rehearsed
shrug.

I looked at that SS'er thinking, "Get back in your God-damned
tank, you son-of-a-bitch, and leave me alone." For some reason I wasn't
a damned bit scared. As I held the shrug, he stood there. "Go on into
the crapper and let this poor little old Frenchman go," I begged silently.

He glowered at me for a hell of a long time before he growled "Ah,
passes," motioning to me as if saying, "Get the hell out of here."

I moved away as he unzipped his fly, and took out his penis, holding
it between his fingers while walking toward the "pissoir" still 20 feet
away.

If he wasn't about to wet his pants, I'd probably be in a prison camp before nightfall. I caught up with Walt, still following the guide who was pedaling harder now. Walt didn't speak at first, then he asked "How in hell did you get out of that one?"

"I gave him the old shrug."

"They told us not to say anything."

"I didn't say anything, but that character wanted some kind of response."

"Well, it worked."

When we reached our destination, he led us into a house and downstairs to the basement. He shut the door and then spoke softly.

"I am Monsieur Paris," he said.

We told him our names. Then he asked me what the German said before waving me on.

"He growled and said "passez," I told him.

The man grinned and said, "You are very lucky."

We'd have to wait in the basement for several hours, maybe all night. Our new hosts were out of town for the day.

He left us there and we just sat. There was nothing else to do; nothing to read and we couldn't even whittle. I tried to nap but couldn't. About 2 in the afternoon, Mr. Paris returned with a woman who brought us a bowl of soup. When they left, we just sat some more.

I tried watching passers-by outside. German officers were going in and out of the house next door. It took us awhile to figure out it was a German brothel. Also, we noticed a few French people wearing tri-colors on their lapels. When Mr. Paris returned that evening, I asked him about it.

"Today is Bastille Day in France, a national holiday. We couldn't show the tri-color because of German orders but today, many people do this anyway."

He returned an hour later to say the other people were not yet home from their trip. He said he'd try one more time.

It grew dark outside and darker in the basement. I was getting antsy, just sitting around. At last, Mr. Paris returned and said we could go. The curfew had been extended, and we just had time to reach our final destination.

We followed him upstairs and to the street. He wheeled his bike along as we walked up the hill. Finally, we turned onto "Rue de Dunkerque." Mr. Paris said we were now in Nanterre. We entered a yard through an iron gate surrounding a tan stucco house: #6, Rue de Dunkerque. We followed him into the courtyard and waited as he knocked on the door. A man opened it. They talked for a moment before Mr. Paris motioned for us to follow.

The owner of the home turned to greet us. Facing me, he took my hand, looking me squarely in the eye. He was about 5'-8", with a round face and thinning brown hair. He wore wire-rimmed glasses, and his eyes were taking me in fully. He had a warm smile when at last he said "Bonjour."

He ushered us into their living room. His name was Louis Berty. A woman entered, carrying a tray with a bottle and some glasses. She placed them on the table along with some lighted candles. The city had already turned the electricity off for the night.

The woman was Mr. Berty's wife, Marcelle. A moment later, a small boy bounded into the room and was introduced as their son, Pierre. Walt and I were introduced by our evasion names, Andre and Albert.

Louis poured a glass of wine for everyone and we sipped, making small talk until Mr. Paris said he had to leave if he was to reach his own home before curfew.

After he left, Marcelle took Pierre to bed. When she returned, she asked us to join them in a light meal.

In the kitchen, we met another young fellow, Charles, Louis' half-brother. We drank a cup of tea while the Bertys explained that it was the first time any of them had worn the tri-color since 1940.

As we continued talking, it became obvious that Louis had a dry sense of humor. I liked him immediately.

Charles asked a lot of questions, and we answered a few that night, telling him we would answer the rest in the morning. Marcelle was a gracious hostess, and amazingly adept at deciphering our peculiar

French. After the meal, Marcelle led us to our bedroom. Its window overlooked a courtyard and the double bed looked welcoming.

Thankfully, the bathroom was nearby. We wouldn't have to worry about the chiggers, or lice or whatever we had accumulated along with layers of dirt during our stay in the woods. Now, we could enjoy the luxury of a bath every day.

# Chapter 16

# NANTERRE

When I opened my eyes the next morning, sunlight streamed through the window and I heard the muffled street noises of civilization. I took my kit into the bathroom, determined to shave every day now that I was no longer roughing it. Walt was still asleep so I dressed and went into the kitchen where Marcelle was bustling about with another woman, making breakfast. Marcelle glanced up and smiled at me.

"Bonjour," she said. The other woman looked at me, but turned back to her work, saying nothing as I replied.

Marcelle was pouring me a cup of coffee when Walt came in and sat down. She offered him some coffee; she then spoke quickly in French to her helper. The other woman's eyes widened and flicked toward Walt and me, eyeing us closely as she listened. Marcelle led her over to the table and introduced her as Suzanne. Until that moment, she hadn't known that Louis and Marcelle intended to hide shot-down American pilots in their home.

Suzanne worked there three or four days a week. She smiled as we shook hands, and gave a little nod. Her look told us she took the responsibility of this secret very seriously. Marcelle and Louis told us they'd talked it over and were confident Suzanne would not betray our hideout. She was another willing conspirator against the Germans.

From that first morning, Marcelle somehow managed to understand our garbled French, often interpreting for others who'd never heard their mother tongue fractured so badly.

Marcelle was a thoroughly practical and serious woman. Louis had a practical side as well, but kept it concealed under a coat of humor. He was always cracking jokes. Even as new visitors in the home, we instantly realized that Marcelle adored her husband and child. Her kitchen was always neat and clean with sparkling white floor tiles. Even while we talked, Marcelle was constantly busy.

After finishing our coffee and toast, I stood up and looked outside to check the view. The entrance from the courtyard was covered with a glass-paneled roof with side panels screening an entry porch. The front gate was wide enough to admit a large vehicle. On the opposite side of the courtyard was a building with several rooms, and across from it was a second building with big windows through which I watched Louis and Charles work. Louis was a "charcutier," a pork butcher; Charles was his apprentice.

They were closed because of the war and thus Charles was stymied. A few days each month, Louis made sausage, pate' and salami. Watching them at work, I wondered how young people like Charles viewed the German occupation. He was about 19 and had already spent a most important four years of his life under severe restrictions. I imagined that trying to grow up under such conditions must be hard on French teen-agers.

The rest of the morning Walt and I investigated everything, finding English books, drawing pads and charcoal pencils. I discovered that Walt was a damned good artist. He picked up a pad and finished an excellent sketch of Marcelle in five minutes flat. We also found a radio and a much-needed French-English dictionary with a map of Europe, which we started using to pinpoint German targets we heard on the radio.

At lunchtime, we discovered why Louis' products were so much in demand before the war. Marcelle served his pate'. I really didn't know how good a meat spread could be until I tasted his, then I couldn't get enough of it. He made damned good salami, too.

I didn't realize it at the time, but they were still checking me out, wondering if I was authentic. I was tall, with straw-colored hair and a square jaw like most of the Germans in the city. And I had a habit that was dangerous for Americans in France just then. I'd frequently drawl "yeah" instead of "yes," sounding too much like a German saying "Ja." And I still wore my beret in the Fascist style.

They thought maybe I was slipping and said "Ja" without thinking. They questioned Mr. Paris, who double-checked with his people and verified that I was indeed Lt. Henry C. Woodrum.

Late that afternoon we had visitors: a man Louis' age and a young blonde girl, about 16, with a bubbly personality. They arrived on bicycles, entered the courtyard, and were brought into the house by Charles. The man was Raymond Besse, his daughter was Jacqueline.

Louis said they were also hiding two Americans. I thought of Bill and Martin, but they said no, these guys were 8th Air Force gunners. Jacqueline was going to the dairy, so Marcelle went with her while Mr. Besse stayed with us. He had a great sense of humor, like Louis. They were a couple of characters, laughing, joking, leading each other into all sorts of schemes, and then laughing about it.

In the early days of the war, M. Besse was on a French naval vessel. At Dunkerque, he got away from the beach after his ship sank and came home to his family. When his daughter returned with Marcelle, they prepared to leave, saying, "We will see you tomorrow." I didn't know what they meant.

After dinner, we listened to the radio, trying to learn something about the raid we saw at Lagny. If it was covered at all, we never heard it. The front at Normandy was already consolidated; the entire peninsula was in Allied hands since Bradley took Cherbourg. Buzz bombs were still falling on London and both the 8th and the RAF were hitting Berlin and other major targets. I guessed the 9th (my Air Force) was hitting targets nearer the front.

The next morning, Walt and I strolled around the back of the courtyard. There was a high fence around the yard and we could walk unobserved.

At noon, Marcelle gave us some coffee and said, "We will not eat now. Later."

Two borrowed bicycles were waiting outside for us and we were going to ride to the Besse home for Sunday dinner. They instructed us to smile, nod and keep riding if anybody said hello. "Don't speak!"

We peddled out of the courtyard around 2:00, the first time I'd ridden a bike in years. The Besses' house was only about four blocks away. At the first corner, the Bertys met some friends who called and waved. Walt and I smiled and nodded while Marcelle and Louis stopped to talk for a moment as we kept going. The Bertys caught up with us at the corner where we waited, turning in circles because we didn't know which way to go. Pierre was on a little bike of his own. He could have led us to the Besses if necessary. He was really sharp for a 7-year-old.

The Besse home boasted a large front yard with flowers in full bloom. We went inside and were introduced to the gunners. The first was a fairly tall young blonde kid from Baltimore named Jack and the other was an engineer-gunner named Stone from some place in the mid-west. They'd been down about a month, and had spent almost a week with the Besses - holed up just like us.

Madame Besse wore an apron around her waist, and was wiping her hands on a towel. She smiled when we entered, but as we shook hands, her smile grew even warmer. She was an extremely pretty and jovial woman who had as much fun joking as her husband. They made us feel right at home. Mr. Besse was also a butcher - poultry and rabbits. The meal they served was a feast, far beyond the usual wartime fare.

Marcelle helped them set a big table since there were 11 of us. They began serving the meal prepared by Madame Besse and Jacqueline. First, vegetable soup with bread and red wine, followed by a plate of sliced tomatoes and cucumbers, then a big platter of braised rabbit with a delicious herb sauce, potatoes, vegetables, and a lot more wine.

M. Besse offered the toast, holding aloft his glass: "A la fin de la guerre!" As we drank, a female voice added: "Les boches sont des salauds!" and as everybody laughed, Madame Besse grinned.

Dinner was a noisy affair, with constant chatter and laughter, reminding me of the holiday meals back home. Walt couldn't get over the delicious meal, and kept repeating, "Damn, Woody, that was really good!" I had to agree.

In late afternoon Louis arose and clapped his hands "Allons faire une promenade!" he said, motioning for everybody to get up. With much groaning and laughing, we put on our jackets and berets and made it to the courtyard. They said we were going to see the view from the old fort.

Putting several wine bottles and some glasses in a basket on one of the bikes, we pedaled down the main street.

We reached a well-kept lawn covering the entire hillside sprouting white crosses near the crest. At the crest of the hill, a massive stone wall guarded the fortress. German soldiers guarded the huge gate. Near the entry, there was a large expense of lawn without crosses where other families were already gathered. When we found a place apart from the others, Charles unfurled a couple of blankets and we all sat down on the lawn.

Through clusters of trees studding the lawn, we could see the rooftops of Paris. Louis said the town directly below was Puteaux. Suresnes was just to the right, and the Seine River separated both from the Bois de Boulogne, beyond which was Paris. I could see both the Eiffel Tower and the Arch of Triumph.

The crosses indicated this was an American and Canadian cemetery from World War I. The American caretaker had been placed in custody December 7, 1941, when the war between the US and the Germans began so the place was now cared for by French civilians. It was immaculate, the lawn well-trimmed and lush. German troops strolled up the walkway to the main entrance. I watched a couple of officers saunter to the gate, giving casual military salutes to the guards as they entered. I asked Louis the name of the fort.

"Fortress of Mount Valerian," he replied. Later, I came to know it as one of the most dreaded places in France, where the SS and Gestapo tortured and executed over 4,500 people during the war, using firing stakes in the basement. (Now, a colorful memorial signifies what the place means to the French.) Relaxing on the green lawns that day, Walt and I knew nothing of the murders.

At dusk, we went again to the dairy and while Marcelle and Madame Besse bought milk, the rest of us watched the Parisian skyline as the sun set.

By the next morning, Walt and I had already established a routine, as we had at camp. We rose at 8, had coffee with Marcelle and sometimes Louis and Charles.

I enjoyed talking with Pierre, nicknamed Coco. He was a smart little boy. One day he told me about the serious talk his father and mother had with him before we arrived. They'd told him that we were allies, fighting the Germans. He was very impressed with the admonishment from his father that he should never say anything to reveal the presence of American flyers being hidden in his house. Louis told him that he was old enough to act like a man- and he did - always. An amazing little guy.

One day, Walt and I asked Marcelle if we could join Louis and Charles working in the shop across the courtyard. She checked the gate, and then gave us the go-ahead.

Louis and Charles were washing tables, some wooden, others steel, all with raised edges to keep water off the floor. There were a couple of big cooking vats and a large gas range in the first room with the tables, and beyond that another room with meat hooks dangling from a rail along which pork carcasses could be hung and moved. The last room led to a cold storage area.

We asked Louis if we could help and he said no, because we would get dirty. We looked at each other, rolled up our sleeves and began to help anyway. He laughed and when we were finished, Louis pointed to a showerhead in a semi-enclosed area of the porch and motioned for us to take a shower if we wanted. We were hopping around like jaybirds as the cold water splashed against our naked bodies.

I looked up just in time to see a woman open the gate and enter the yard. She glanced at us as we ducked inside; then she hastily turned away while calling out in a high, sing-song voice "Bonjour."

Louis poked his head out the door and answered, "Bonjour, Madame," without cracking a smile. He indicated with a wave of his hand that she should see Marcelle in the kitchen. Louis tossed us towels and we scurried to the back room, out of sight.

When she was gone, Charles went out to bolt the gate so anyone else would have to ring the bell. Once we were back in the house, Louis decided that we should not go to the shop until afternoon when they were closed.

It was a good thing we established that rule for the following Saturday morning a German truck rolled to a stop at the gate and several soldiers climbed down. One of them rang the bell. Their Saturday morning visit had been a regular routine since 1940. They were from Fortress Valerian and came to borrow Louis's sausage machine, a request he could not refuse.

Marcelle saw the Germans as they entered the yard and told Coco to alert us. We were asleep, so Coco bent over me, shaking me awake, a finger to his lips, demanding silence.

I got up and slipped on some clothes, not saying a word. Pierre and I quietly walked into the front room to watch as the Germans lugged the machine out to their truck and drove away. They looked just like draftees anywhere. They came back a time or two after that, but we were always well out of sight. Later events proved that Louis had established some sort of friendship with the French-speaking German who always headed the group. It would save his life, and maybe all the rest of us, too.

Later that afternoon, Mr. Paris came over with his wife and little boy on a very fancy pair of matched bicycles. He came to make sure everything was all right but he got all shook up when he learned the Bertys had taken us to the Besses and to Fort Valerian. He apparently felt that such sorties would jeopardize the Underground. He told Louis not to do it again and they had a long discussion. Louis didn't want us to go stir crazy. He could see no harm in a bicycle ride. Besides, he figured he could always outwit the Krauts.

That day, Louis contacted the head of his FFI (French Forces of the Interior) group, a man named Andre Caillette. Louis introduced us when he came to the house. Andre spoke no English so our discussion progressed slowly. Afterward, he said he saw no reason we couldn't take short trips as long as we were careful. I was glad because I enjoyed getting out. Andre himself even took us on a memorable trip later.

The following Friday, Andre returned with his niece, Denise. She was a willowy blonde in her early twenties. She'd studied English in a university before the war and she spoke it quite well considering her short time of study. We spent the afternoon talking and she told us a lot about life in Paris. Things were rougher in the city than we thought. Also, she said she would obtain some materials and begin teaching us French, surprised at the vocabulary we had acquired along the way during the last month and a half, but she laughed uncontrollably when we tried to pronounce many words. She said she'd teach us some grammar so we could do more than just string a few words together.

Marcelle was a good teacher, too. She taught us new words daily, correcting our fractured pronunciations. At almost every meal we'd have a lesson. Someone would hold up a knife and we'd say "couteau" and then go on to other words. Butter, water, cup, saucer, fork, spoon, and anything else at hand. I memorized the word, but my pronunciation was bad. Walt's was better.

Like the Brenners, the Bertys kept a garden plot a mile or so from the house, and we had plenty of fresh vegetables. All cooking was done by gas—electricity was too unreliable and before the war, too expensive. When there were long periods without power, Marcelle used the refrigerator as an icebox.

I began to feel right at home with them and understood enough to know what was happening. They were very hospitable. I thought of them as my second family. We had long discussions, covering a variety of topics. Whenever we hit a barrier, it was usually Marcelle who made the breakthrough.

One Sunday we had an early lunch, took the bicycles and started off for a park they told us about. We rode past Fort Valerian, down through Puteaux to an apartment where Marcelle's cousin lived. We stopped for a short chat and then continued along the bank of the Seine and into a residential area.

I got tired as the devil pumping that old bike, so Walt and I changed off from time to time. We reached a crowded park, where there were thousands of bicyclists riding any imaginable kind of bike. A few German soldiers strolled the sidewalks and along the river.

Finally, we came to a beautiful, tree-studded area and turned into the woods. We rode slower, for there were many pedestrians. There were more German soldiers, too, some with French women. As we moved along slowly, following each other in a line, I saw a group of about seven or eight German soldiers in grubby uniforms walking toward us. As we neared, they popped to a stiff attention in motion legs rigid as they marched. Suddenly their right arms shot out in the political salute of the Nazi party, shouting, "Heil Hitler," in unison. Just in front of us, two young officers in spic-and-span uniforms with gleaming boots and high, peaked caps responded with a casual semblance of the Nazi salute, obviously more interested in the stunning brunette who walked between them.

I was surprised because it was the first time I'd seen the political salute used since Versailles. But those two Krauts had good taste in women.

We followed Louis down a wide path that curved through neat lawns to a cul de sac in front of a huge monument with two tall towers on either side and a sort of arch between them. Steps led from the drive up to a wide, sweeping expanse of concrete around the base. As we neared, I saw chiseled into the arch overhead, "ESCADRILLE LA FAYETTE."

We parked and chained our bikes, then walked along the huge concrete base, and I paused to look up at the words on top of the arch. "A LA MEMOIRE." Below that was a pair of pilot's wings etched in the stone. Sure! This was the memorial to the Lafayette escadrille from World War I, the bunch of American pilots who came over early and flew for the French. I felt a surge of emotion.

Aviation was always my big interest. I'd read stacks of World War I flying stories and knew a lot about the squadron. Now, as we entered their shrine, I recalled many of their aerial feats. The names of each battle were carved in one prominent pillar and the name of every member was carved in another, followed by the decorations awarded to each marked after his name. Louis beckoned and we followed him down a stairway. Lining the walls were photos of flyers, aircraft, and aerodromes, along with props and wing insignias. There were group photos of American aviators standing alongside Neiuports and Spads, a jaunty bunch.

At the lower level were caskets containing bodies of many of the volunteers, and bronze plates identifying the pilot inside. Slowly, I toured the perimeter of the dimly lit tomb, noting the names of people I'd read about as a kid growing up with aviation.

At the last niche I saw a simple bronze plate upon which the name "Raoul Lufberry" appeared. I was reminded of a time when war in the air was new, and pilots wore no parachutes. Lufberry had been killed when thrown out of his aircraft at low altitude because he wasn't wearing a parachute! I realized again how lucky I was to get out alive when we were shot down. Now pilots used the "Lufberry Circle" often, and one P-51 jockey had told me not long ago that he owed his life to it. Lufberry had been one hell of a pilot! Standing in the tomb of these heroic pilots produced an intensely emotional feeling. I'd forgotten this place existed, and was glad the Bertys had thought of it. We left the building and started home, finally arriving at the vista point near the dairy where we stopped to rest.

A German staff car pulled up to the curb. A portly field-grade officer and a female lieutenant stepped out. He took out a Leica, snapped a few pictures, then stood gazing out over the landscape as we were. Suddenly the man glanced at us, asking in French how to get back to Numero Trois. Louis waved a hand, indicating the proper direction as if the German was just another tourist.

The next day, Yankee Doodle reported that an attempt had been made on Hitler's life, and as a result, the Nazi salute was now the only one used in the German Forces. The old Army salute was now "verboten." It was good, knowing even some Germans wanted that maniac dead.

Denise began our French lessons that week. We thought we'd have plenty of time to learn since the military lines weren't advancing as quickly as we expected. We were sweating it out. We listened to the radio while there was still electricity, keeping abreast of what was going on. From the reports, we knew that air activity centered over Germany.

One day we visited Bill and Martin. Marcelle took us to their place and left us with them for the afternoon.

Their hosts were a man and wife with a little boy about four. They lived on a third-floor apartment two blocks away, but higher on the hill. Since their apartment was the only one on that floor, the roof of the second floor served as a kind of patio area. They could relax out there, listening to the radio, or playing ping-pong. A chaise lounge and a table with an umbrella hugged the outside apartment wall. They hadn't left the building since arriving here.

We told them about our trips and Bill said he was going to check with Mr. Paris to see if they couldn't get out, too. They were glad to see us. I understood why they were going ape; the place was bedlam most of the time.

The kid was into everything, crying like mad whenever he wasn't given exactly what he wanted. When his mother shrieked at him, which was often, he bawled and took revenge on the cat by kicking it and when that tomcat yowled, you could hear it for blocks. Only once while we were there was there any peace and quiet, and then only because the kid fell asleep out of sheer exhaustion.

When the old man came home, he was more volatile than his wife and tended to go into shouting sprees. It was quite a household, and I could see why the two pilots were beginning to go stir crazy, especially Martin.

We were wondering what would happen if Paris was laid to siege. We could only wonder. None of us thought Germany had enough air power left to undertake a lengthy defense against a siege. But if one came, famine would be generated in just a few days for there was already a great food shortage within the city. Many people spent their time on bicycles going to the country to obtain food.

In an aerial bombardment, the city would be left a shambles. If we were stranded, it would increase the chances of the people talking care of us getting caught. We talked to Andre about leaving on our own if something like that materialized.

That night, we discussed it with Louis and Marcelle. When we finished outlining our thoughts, Louis considered the problems and then told us that as a member of Andre's group, Zadig, he would take part in whatever organized uprisings were undertaken. We asked what activities they had in mind but he didn't know the specifics. We guessed they might seize key utilities, but knew if they faced Panzer tanks, their success was doomed. They had only pistols, rifles, grenades, a few grease guns, and Molotov cocktails. Louis showed us an old handgun, once carried by his grandfather in the Franco-Prussian war.

Marcelle listened attentively but didn't speak. She wore a determined look on her face, though, and nodded agreement that the Underground would be foolish to fight tanks given such limitations.

As the days passed, our ties with the Bertys strengthened, bringing us closer than I was to some of my own family. We kept track of the invasion by radio and posted the latest advances. The battle at St. Lo was a major breakthrough and indicated the Allied advance was moving in our direction.

But we had a lot of free time, and one of the things we did was design our post-war dream homes. We leafed through every magazine we could find and decided the ranch-style house was the one for us. I wanted a U-shaped place, wrapped around a patio, with an old-fashioned porch in front and around one side.

Once we started on floor plans, Walt began sketching exterior views as he visualized them. He was really good at it and came up with some drawings of professional quality. Mine were pretty mediocre. But we both kept going and eventually came up with some good designs. Marcelle joined us one day, studied our work critically, and selected one for herself.

Then Denise came up with an idea. She attended a cinema to see if there were any Germans around, and having checked several showings, decided it would be safe for us to go to a movie. Andre gave us the go-ahead, and the Bertys agreed.

Walt went first with Denise, Marcelle and Madame Besse. The showing was in the middle of the afternoon. They rode bicycles to the theater. There was a short line at the ticket office and plenty of seats once they were inside.

There were two German soldiers in the audience with their girl friends but they paid no attention to anybody else.

The first film was a German propaganda newsreel, showing destroyed American tanks in the hedgerows of Normandy and a few clips of their anti-aircraft gunners shooting down American planes. They said the invasion was a failure and that invading forces were doomed to miserable deaths. During the main feature, the power went off and the manager had to fire up an emergency generator. Walt said it didn't make much difference because it was a lousy movie anyway.

M. Paris was furious when he heard about this outing. Andre and Louis calmed him down, but he was convinced the entire organization was in jeopardy.

But it wasn't long before Marcelle and Louis proposed another sightseeing adventure. I'd go first this time. When the day arrived, Marcelle announced, "Albert, today we visit the Trocadero."

"What is the Trocadero?" I asked.

"A place near the Eiffel Tower. Many things to see. A museum." She turned to Walter. "You must stay home today. You will go tomorrow."

We left at 10 that morning, riding our bikes until we reached "Avenue Henri Martin" teeming with German officers and their families. It was a nice section with attractive apartment buildings confiscated in 1940 by the Germans. Soon we reached a large plaza with four or five streets emptying into it and what looked like a museum on the right, beyond it was the Eiffel Tower.

Sidewalk cafes were crammed with people. We locked our bikes in the racks and entered a crescent shaped building. Inside, huge pictures were on display, and I turned toward a cluster of seascapes, some depicting famous French naval battles. Before going further, I glanced at Louis and he nodded. I strolled toward a painting of a sailing vessel in a harbor. A lighthouse was visible on a spit of land in the background and men worked on boats in the foreground.

As I stepped back, admiring the work, someone came up and stood on my left. I paid no attention until I turned to walk to the next painting. I then realized it was a German soldier.

He was in his 30s and seemed a little raunchy, square-jawed, and tough. His helmet dangled from a hook on his belt, and he wore an overseas cap. A Mauser was slung over his shoulder, butt up. His uniform was disheveled, as if he just arrived from the front. Maybe he's on R&R, I thought. But he looked more like the kind who'd head for the nearest bar instead of a museum. Another soldier stood on his left, younger but dressed about the same. When they saw me turn and pause, they turned too. In unison, we moved a few feet, turning to inspect the next painting.

Just as they moved again, another German stepped over to stand on my right—an officer boasting a crisp uniform and a whole smear of decorations. He looked at the painting for a moment before turning to me as if to speak.

I quickly turned toward the soldiers and again we moved away, right in step! I was in another one of those sticky situations I couldn't seem to avoid. The two Krauts on my left apparently didn't give a damn about me, but the one on my right looked like he wanted to make small talk. Dammit, what can I do?

Again, we moved in unison. I wasn't even really seeing the artwork as I stared at it. I concentrated on the hot shot on my right who was nodding his appreciation and seemed ready to walk to another painting. I girded myself for the confrontation, when suddenly I felt a little tug on my right hand. I looked down and there was Coco.

I smiled, nodding. With all the seriousness the little tyke could muster, he peered up at the German earnestly and spoke a few soft words with great solemnity. The German nodded and Coco and I moved away, across the corridor and through the foyer to the huge plaza in front of the museum. We avoided Louis and Marcelle, until we were certain we hadn't aroused any suspicion.

We rejoined the group and continued our tour.

After a few minutes, Marcelle kneeled to speak with Coco. He had a smug little grin on his face, obviously pleased with her praise.

"What did he tell that German?" I asked.

Marcelle looked up at me, her eyes laughing. "He simply explained that his father is a deaf-mute," she said.

There were several hundred people strolling around the plaza and among the beautiful gardens below us. The Eiffel Tower loomed magnificently at one end of the plaza. Some of the tourists were German soldiers, and we paused to watch a group of officers, men and women, who stood near us admiring the view. The men were in their 40's and 50's, with a lot of gray hair. The women were all young and pretty.

One of the officers was a portly, white-haired fellow boasting a chest of decorations and trying his darndest to impress the ladies, who all seemed to be doing a good job of apple polishing themselves. Everyone was snapping pictures of everyone else, and finally they all clustered for a group shot.

I watched the old colonel pose by himself, the Eiffel Tower in the background. He took a deep breath and sucked in his gut as the shutter clicked. The women gathered around him like a gaggle of geese telling him how good he looked.

As he watched, Louis made little comments under his breath, only some of which I understood. They must have been good because Marcelle and Coco giggled until Marcelle finally tapped the little boy's arm, still smiling and warned him to be good.

I was privately thinking this guy with the bulging belly better get all the souvenir pictures he wanted, because Paris wasn't going to be the German treasure much longer.

Just as they strolled away, three ME-109s swooped in from the south to buzz the tower. I think the leader had planned to fly under the base of the grids, but at the last minute, he and one wingman veered to the right. Then all three pulled up and began a wide, upward turn while the German audience in the plaza "oohed" and "aahed" in appreciation.

We continued our tour of the garden and the aquarium where I saw some rainbow trout just about the size I used to catch on the McCloud River back home. We strolled to a sidewalk café where Louis checked the menu before deciding not to eat there. He said something to the waiter who said, "It's the war," shrugging his shoulders. Marcelle looked at the food being served to others and said it didn't look very good anyhow.

We returned to our bikes and started down the street. There were more cars on the "Rue De Henri Martin" then I'd seen in all of France. It seemed to be an affluent neighborhood. Louis said it had been one of the nicest areas of Paris, but the Germans took over many of the buildings when they arrived in 1940.

Waiting for traffic at an intersection, I noticed an unusually pretty woman strolling with a tall, young German officer. She clutched his left arm with both hands, and was gazing into his eyes, talking animatedly until they reached our corner. As they stopped, she looked straight at me.

She was brunette, with flashing eyes and satin-smooth skin. I did a double take. It was Maxine. I'm certain. I hadn't seen her in years, but there was a glimmer of recognition in her eyes as she looked at me. I gave a little nod, and thought I saw her smile a bit.

The traffic cleared and we rode through the intersection. I turned, and she was still watching me, looking perplexed. I'd bet all odds that it was the girl I knew years before in California.

The rest of our trip was uneventful, but I had a lot of fun telling Walt. He went a day or two later, accompanied by Denise and they stopped at Andre's apartment in Neuilly on the way home.

Walt and I were visited by a young RAF gunner shot down in a Lancaster. Mr. Paris brought him to stay at the house until he could find a permanent place. The gunner was a young guy who thought he should be well out of France by now, and was really glum. We explained the effect the invasion and the expected advance was having on evadees. He spent the day with us and we brought him up to date on recent war activities.

That evening, Mr. Paris picked him up. He would live with seven other people from the RAF at a big place just outside Paris.

Bill and Martin also came over and spent most of a day with us, enjoying not only Marcelle's good cooking, but the peace and quiet as well. They'd been allowed to leave their apartment only once before, to visit Mt. Valerian as we did.

Denise was teaching us the conjugation of verbs. Memorizing them was easy, but pronunciation was still a challenge.

All invasion news was good and seemed to get better every day. Seemingly, the hopes of the Parisians soared, too. Jacqueline came to the house daily and we noticed the change in her first, then in the others. Even Yvonne, from the apartment where Bill and Martin were staying, was noticeably enthused about the prospects of liberation. After more than four years of German occupation, it was hard to believe that freedom was so near - it took awhile for the feeling to build.

Once it started, it was contagious. For days, all Jacqueline talked about was what she would do. First, she wanted to hang big French, British, and American flags from the window. Then she decided to make a new dress, with flags of those nations as the motif. She was certain there would be a gathering at the Arch of Triumph, the Place de la Concorde and city hall.

The more we talked, the greater their realization that the day actually was near. Soon, each woman was designing a dress. We learned that Marcelle once worked for a fashion designer in Paris. Madame Besse and Jacqueline consulted with her on the dress for Jacqueline. They decided it would be white, with a full pleated skirt. The blouse would be decorated with flags of France, Britain, and the United States.

Louis and Charles would wear armbands with the words "Live Free or Die" and the tri-color. Somebody asked Walt what we'd wear; he said our regular clothes with a big American flag on our backs.

Louis had another idea. That night after supper, while we waited for the electricity to come on, he asked some questions.

"Albert, in Carrieres-sur-Seine, you know the name of the people?"

"Yes. Carlos and Maria Filipotto."

"They have a bar?"

"Yes, on the Rue du Moulin. I think they called it "The White Stallion.""

"That will be easy to find. Your uniform is there, no?"

"Yes, it is. You are going there?"

"Maybe," he said, noncommittally. "Also, Albert, your pistol. You hid it in some concrete blocks - but at another house near the bar, no?"

"Yes, that's right. About six blocks away."

"You can show me?"

"I think so, yes."

I drew a sketch of the streets, remembering that I doubled back from the garage before I started up the hill after meeting Jacques. I drew the rail station at the approximate direction from the house. Then I remembered Claude's words.

"Louis, here is a drawing of the area as I remember it. The Red Cross man who was my first Underground contact said they knew exactly which house it was. If you can talk with Carlos, he can find out, if you can't locate it from my sketch.

"Good," he said, looking it over, "Facile."

"How far is Carrieres-sue-Seine from here, Louis?"

"Bicycle, 30 minutes. Easy."

"It would be great to have my uniform and my pistol back. What a great souvenir that would be, that is, if we don't have to use it first."

"We will see. Tomorrow I go."

Walt didn't say anything, but I knew he wished there was some way to get his uniform. I asked him about it and he said he knew the place, but that it was too far away. Nobody in the room gave any indication that they understood what we were talking about, but I noticed Marcelle was casually taking everything in. She probably learned more English than I learned French while there.

Sometimes I'd get so mad at myself for not being able to communicate, I'd cuss myself out, and she'd laugh, then tell everybody what I wanted to say. She was usually right.

When the power came on that night, we learned that the Germans were starting a counter attack at Avranches. We heard that Brest had been captured. Avranches was the key now.

Louis left the next morning at 10. I hoped nothing would happen to my friend just because he was trying to get my uniform. At lunch, Marcelle kept up the conversation, telling us there was really nothing to worry about. I was most concerned that he would be successful, but then be stopped by the Germans on the way home and having to explain why he had the uniform and my pistol.

Louis was back by mid-afternoon with not only the uniform, but also the pistol and the extra clip of ammo still in the shoulder holster. "Facile" he said simply, grinning.

We sipped cognac while he told us about the trip in a mixture of slow French and English.

First, he went to the bar. It was just as I'd described. He made sure no one was around before speaking to Carlos. He told him I was at his house and described some of the events that had brought me back to Paris. Carlos was interested in the news and called Maria. All three sipped wine as Louis related his story.

They listened attentively, but Carlos refused to acknowledge that he had the uniform or ever heard of me.

They talked a long time before Louis convinced them he wasn't a German. The clincher was that Louis knew where the pistol was hidden. They realized I'd never give the Germans that information. Since they still weren't positive, Carlos said of course he knew where the American pilot landed just before D-Day, everyone in the town did. He directed Louis to the house.

"If you find the pistol, stop here on your way back," Carlos said.

Louis found the house immediately. He parked his bike, went through the gate, climbed the steps, and knocked on the door. A young woman answered and he told her he was an official of the Underground, now taking care of the American flyer who'd landed on their house just before D-Day. The woman's face tightened, guessing he might be a German. She invited him in, and introduced him to an older woman who said she was at home that day.

"I heard a noise and went to the back porch. I noticed this strange young man in the backyard. I shut the door and went back inside because he should not have been there. He was blonde and I thought perhaps he was a German. But a moment or two later, the Germans were pounding on my front door."

The Krauts questioned her all afternoon, she told him, and then took her to their headquarters. She said they slapped her face and poked her, pretending they didn't think she was telling the truth. Finally, they let her go the next day. But they made her describe me, which she did. Other people in the crowd gave descriptions of me too, and the Germans were able to sketch an excellent likeness that was posted all over the neighborhood for days.

The woman told Louis to look through the yard for the pistol, but they were sure it was useless because the Germans had conducted a thorough search. Louis said he thanked them and went outside, peeking into each stack of concrete blocks, finally discovering the pistol. He reached into the cavity, pulled it out, and slipped it under his coat, walking back to the gate.

The younger woman was standing on the porch and asked, "Did you find something?" Louis flipped his coat aside to give her a peek of the pistol. He hopped on his bike and pedaled straight to the bar.

Carlos let him in, locking the door immediately and escorting Louis to the bar where he poured more glasses of wine. He set a glass in front of Louis and asked carefully, "Well, what happened? Did you find the house?"

In reply, Louis pulled the .45 from his belt and placed it on the bar, still in its holster.

Carlos picked it up, studying my name on the leather holster. He looked long and hard at Louis, then reached behind the bar and pulled out a bottle of fine cognac. Convinced that Louis was authentic, Carlos gave into his curiosity, and asked a string of questions about my activities since leaving their bar.

Maria went upstairs, but returned quickly with my uniform, wrapped in a neat package. Louis placed it, and the .45, in his backpack for the return trip. He said he enjoyed the uneventful trip home.

Bolstered by the success of her husband's trip, Marcelle sprung her surprise; she and Jacqueline had decided to go to Melun to get Walt's uniform.

It just wouldn't do, they argued, for a shot down American to attend the liberation ceremony without a proper uniform. By this time, they were certain some kind of celebration would be staged.

Louis said he'd think it over before allowing them to travel the 70 miles to Melun. He finally agreed.

My uniform, bare of its insignia, wasn't too impressive, just green trousers, a shirt, and the Justin flight boots. I described the Lieutenant's bars, the prop and wings of the Army Air Forces and the pilot's wings for Marcelle. She said if Walt could make a sketch while she was gone, she'd sew it on to the uniform when she returned.

The women left early the next morning.

Walt kept his fingers crossed that their journey was safe; I was equally apprehensive. We knew their cover story was good since food in Paris was short and hundreds of people left the city daily to scrounge supplies. They wouldn't be alone, and two women traveling together would not arouse suspicion. Nevertheless, it was still a long trip. I still don't know how they managed it in one day. But they did.

They arrived home just after curfew. They'd found the place easily, following Walt's directions, and quickly convinced the people there that she was authentic. They gave her the uniform, as well as some food to insure her cover story. They also told her about Marcel and the trouble at the camp.

It was true, they told her, someone informed on Marcel. He was picked up in the village and tortured. The Germans learned from their collaborators that Marcel was the head of the camp, but they were unable to pinpoint its location, only the general area. Marcel agreed to lead them to the place. Shackled, they took him to the woods. As they neared the camp, Marcel shouted: "RUN BOYS, IT'S THE GESTAPO!"

An SS machine pistol ended Marcel's life in one chattering burst. The men in camp had heard his warning, the burst of gunfire, and immediately scattered into the forest. The Germans had fanned out in advance, however, and were able to round up most of the men from camp that night, and the rest the next morning.

The people who told Marcelle this, didn't mention the Germans finding the body of a young blonde man hanging from a tree limb. We knew only that Marcel was killed and the others captured or killed. Some of the loot from the collaborator's house was found, too, but Walt and I doubted that they located the square packet of certificates stashed by Andre. Only if he somehow survived whatever the Germans did to him, would anyone ever find it.

A day or so later, Andre came by and said he was going to take us on an outing. He belonged to a boat club allowed to operate on a restricted basis. He proposed rowing on the Seine. It sounded great. After lunch, we picked the best two bikes from the shed and rode to the river. The place was near Colombes.

When we reached a large building surrounded by a high security fence on the river edge, we parked our bikes and followed Andre to a locker room where we changed into swimming trunks and sweatshirts.

Upstairs was an elaborate bar and a spacious sun porch with tables. We took a seat outside and Andre ordered beers. While we were drinking, two young German officers sat at the bar at the far end of the room, otherwise deserted except for a lone bartender. We finished our beers and Andre told us to go down to the dock and wait until he rented a scull.

We wandered across the lawn to a long finger of floating docks tied between two posts protruding from the waters. A string of boats was moored on both sides. At one end of the dock, two benches flanked a ramp leading to the lawn. Walt and I sat down, lit a cigarette, and waited for Andre.

Something caught my eye near the end of the dock. I couldn't believe my eyes. I stared.

A woman emerged from the water, slithering onto the ramp. She rolled half over, resting on one elbow for a moment, before standing. She seemed quite naked.

I nudged Walt, "Get a load of that!"

Even at that distance, I saw she was tall and voluptuous. Slowly, she stretched, extending one arm, then the other, first to her side, then over her head, languorously, like a cat. The ballet ended with her standing on tiptoe, every muscle taut, and her silhouette distinct against the pale blue sky.

She lowered her arms and I heard Walt catch his breath before letting out a long, soft whistle of appreciation.

She turned, walking toward us along the 120-foot length of dock, each step purposeful, flowing on her long, long legs. Her hips curved deeply into a tiny waist. Her large breasts jiggled rhythmically with her stride.

As she neared, I noticed, covering just her nipples, a small patch of cloth connected to slender strings that tied behind her back. At her loins another little triangle of beige material was held up by nothing more than a string wrapped around her waist.

Her belly was flat and she walked with just the right amount of lateral hip movement for a woman confident in her sensuality. Her gorgeous body was tanned a light gold, and her glistening black hair hung far below her shoulders. Still 30 feet away, her eyes locked on ours and never left as she continued her feline stroll.

As she passed, she gave us the briefest of nods, and in a slightly husky whisper, added "bonjour."

Andre came up behind us and she said a few words to him in passing as he approached our bench. We were still watching the girl when Andre sat down, laughing.

"Formidable, eh?" he said.

"Oui, formidable, Andre," and because it was necessary, I asked "What kind of swimming suit is that?"

"Oh, it started here in Paris in 1940. They call it a bikini."

My first glimpse of a bikini was an unforgettable experience, and being as horny as a rocky mountain billy goat by then, only added to the impression it made on me.

Andre had obtained a four-man scull and after a little instruction, we were soon rowing competently down river.

We returned to the dock after an hour or so, showered, dressed, and returned to the lounge. We took a seat at our same table and admired the view.

The two Germans were still there, apparently engaged in some serious drinking. I wondered if they knew they would soon leave Paris and were drowning their sorrow. I could sympathize for a moment, relaxing here, enjoying the view.

I pondered this for a while, waiting for our beer, then looked at Walt.

"We'll have to figure out a way to stay here after the liberation," I said.

"That's a hell of an idea if we can manage it," he agreed.

"We'll have to figure out a way. Andre will line us up with some dolls just like that one." Andre grinned, understanding at least some of what we said.

"Introduce us to some girls in bikinis, Andre," I said in French.

He grinned. "Apres la guerre."

"Toujours, toujours," we kidded. "Its always after the war."

We finished the beer and wheeled our bikes outside, then started home. I didn't know it then, but I was about three miles or so from the Filipotto's bar in Carrieres-sur-Seine. We turned up Numero Trois towards Nanterre and everything was peaceful until about a half-mile up the road. Then came the rumbling of vehicles behind us and we turned to see a convoy of German Army trucks approaching. Andre immediately turned up the curb to a little bar with benches on each side of the entrance. We leaned our bikes against the wall and sat down while Andre went inside.

He came back out with three soft drinks. We sat sipping and smoking as the long line of vehicles rolled slowly by on their way into Paris.

As I watched the first few trucks pass, I realized for the first time how devastating the St. Lo bombing must have been and visualized the depth of the fighting, perhaps at Falaise, or the tank battle we'd heard about at Mortaine and its effect on German troops. The equipment rolling by was really beat up, patched hastily to keep moving, most of it ready for the scrap heap. Shrapnel holes left jagged, uneven edges, contrasting curiously with the round, smooth holes drilled by machine guns. Some trucks were charred from fires, and others were missing fenders and hoods.

Tree branches still protruded from some trucks, pitiful remains of earlier camouflage attempts. I knew that others, destroyed, had been left behind. Men clung to the sides of the metal hulks, or lay draped over hoods, and in the bed of each truck: twice as many men as it would normally handle.

I saw the look in their faces - defeat and despair. Their one hope: not to be bombed in Paris, now their refuge. But in some of the faces, I saw something else, too. Although they were crushed and beaten, they were even more ruthless. With a sudden, sickening feeling, I wanted to get the hell away from there. These guys would kill you if you even blinked.

To me, they represented Nazism and I was thinking of Marcel and the other guys in the camp as the last of the vehicles creaked past.

I caught sight of a German officer watching the convoy. He was standing in the entry of the courtyard across the street from our benches. He turned to go inside, then turned back, his jaw out-thrust, almost like Mussolini, and shouted at one of the guards who snapped to attention. The officer walked over to the man, leaning forward so that the brim of his cap was almost touching the soldier's helmet, shouting at the top of his lungs. He stepped back and brought his right hand up in a wide, swinging arc, striking the man a blow against the side of his jaw so hard, I heard a sharp crunching sound. The officer strode back inside, furious.

Oh, oh! I thought, the Krauts are coming apart at the seams. Let's get the hell out of here. Andre had the same idea.

"Allons-y partons!" he said

We rode quickly up the street into Nanterre, glad to get off the main drag and to the Berty's house. As we arrived, two neighbor ladies were talking to Louis at the gate. We walked our bikes through the gate, with Andre saying hello to the women.

Walt and I nodded, and ducked inside. Later, Louis told us that the ladies thought we were very impolite. He apologized for us, explaining we lived in Normandy and were temporarily deafened by the bombings.

We used that excuse another time too, when we went to the local tennis club where we sat among many of the Berty's friends to watch a tournament. After the game, Louis and Marcelle greeted some friends and a conversation started. They told the people we were deaf.

As we were sitting at the table, a guy came by, saw Walt's watch, and asked what time it was. We both understood, but when neither of us blinked, the guy asked again, this time a little louder. I decided to let Walt take care of this one all by himself. Finally, the guy leaned over and shouted the question again.

Walt couldn't take it anymore and turned to the guy, really pissed off, and held up his left wrist about 10 inches from the guy's face. The man glanced at the time, said thank you, and walked away quickly, looking perplexed.

I couldn't help laughing, especially when Walt leaned over to me and muttered, "That silly son of a bitch, doesn't he know I'm supposed to be deaf." A French couple sitting at the next table, watching all this, held their hands over their mouths, giggling. Hearing Walt speak English, they finally understood what was going on, and were in stitches too.

Now, settled down in the Berty's parlor, we discussed the condition of the German troops we'd just seen.

"They sure got the hell knocked out of them somewhere," said Walt.

"Maybe at St. Lo; they couldn't have come from Avranches already - that's 150 miles away," I agreed.

That night when the power came on, we learned a major battle was underway at Falaise. The line now stretched across the base of the Brittany peninsula as far east as Le Mans, then angled back to the vicinity of Falaise with a jog back to a point on the Seine. Le Mans was only 110 miles from Paris.

We talked about what it meant, and concluded one thing - the women had better hurry and finish their dresses if they wanted to wear them to the liberation.

We went to see Bill and Martin the next day. Their host told us rumors indicated German non-combatants and some troops were leaving Paris. We didn't know what the man did for a living; but we guessed he was a black marketer. Regardless, his information was usually good.

We hadn't been there long when Charles came to get us, saying Andre wanted to see us at home. Andre arrived soon after we did, accompanied by two other men. He introduced the first as a French air force general and the other, the general's aide, as a lieutenant colonel.

The general, charged by General Eisenhower's headquarters with setting up landing areas north of the Seine, 20 miles downstream from Paris, for paratroops, gliders and C-47s, needed our help. The force would be large enough to establish a bridgehead on that bank for use by our troops to avoid running out of reinforcement as the German troops were now experiencing.

The general needed authentic data on the shapes, size, and color of ground panel signals to be displayed for the glider and C-47 pilots.

We thought it over and gave them some basic information before making a few suggestions of our own and asking permission to work on the ground during the operation. He apparently liked our suggestions.

While the officers talked to Andre, Walt pulled me aside.

"Woody, that would be one dandy way to stay around Paris for a while after this is over."

"Yeah, Walt, it sure would." I turned to the aide.

"Would we be assigned to the General's staff?"

"Yes, I think so," he grinned, "it would be what you call detached service." He knew we wanted to stick around.

"That would be great. We have a lot of French friends we want to say goodbye to before we leave."

Thanking us, they left to see about acquiring some of the equipment we suggested, saying they would return in a day or two.

The gals worked on their dresses which were nearly finished. Marcelle stitched our insignia from Walt's sketches. When Marcelle finished the first set of pilot's wings, I was surprised at how good they were, she'd used only scrap materials since nothing new was available.

Liberation fever was rampant. Everyone realized the long-anticipated day was close at hand. The Germans, unable to stop the Allied invasion, were given no hope of stopping the liberation of the city. Already Walt and I were walking unescorted to visit Bill and Martin.

When the general returned, his aide said it was their understanding that the Allied invasion of Southern France began that morning and was proceeding well. They asked us to accompany them, and said they'd already received word that the airdrop of the portable radios we had recommended was in the works.

Late that night, the radio reported that, yes, the invasion news from the south was correct, and advances inland were quicker than expected.

Louis cheered and broke out a hoarded bottle of liquor, saved for a special event. We drank as we listened to Raymond and Louis cracking jokes. They even took time to explain some of them to us, grinning, and laughing.

The next morning, a man visiting us said he'd run into roving patrols of Germans on his way to Paris earlier. They were armed with machine guns and fired on any house displaying the French flag. They suppressed crowds gathering in the street with commands: "No crowds, or you will be shot!" He said an organized withdrawal of non-combatants was underway.

Truckloads of badly shot up German troops struggled up Numero Trois, a few at a time, in bad shape, barely able to move. In the city, German troops manned bunkers built during the last four years. It seemed there would indeed be a battle for the city. That night, Andre visited and spoke with Louis and Marcelle privately. Later, Louis removed a box from hiding and started oiling the old revolver he'd told us about.

He didn't like war. But worse, he hated the idea of his country being occupied by Germans. It was a matter of honor that he do something to help rid the land of Germans. While we were talking, a radio broadcast reported a Canadian victory at Falaise. We knew it was a big victory, but that night, we didn't realize how big it really was. Street fighting broke out in Paris. Germans fired machine guns into buildings, and Molotov cocktails were hurled back in retaliation.

Explosions surrounded us through the morning. Some sounded like cannon fire, others we thought were dynamite blasts. Here and there we saw thick black smoke boiling up, changing first to gray and finally to white. The Molotov's must be successful. Radio bulletins warned citizenry to stay off the street because reprisals would be swift against those bearing arms or involved in acts of terrorism. The electricity was on most of the day to make the radio bulletins available.

That afternoon, Louis took us to a house three blocks away and introduced us to an elderly couple. The man, he said, was a retired taxi driver who hauled civilians to the front in World War I when the Germans neared Paris. If anything happened within the next few days, he wanted us to move quickly to this house and stay out of sight. The couple would expect us and had already been given certain contacts.

While Louis made contingency plans, the women continued work on their dresses. Marcelle's was nearly finished. Jacqueline's was done except for sewing two flags in place. It was going to be a colorful celebration. The radio announced that the police were about to go on strike and I wondered what the result would be if that happened. The firemen would have a terrible time if there was a siege. Another rumor said the Americans were in Chartres, only an hour from Paris.

On August 18, the radio was on when we got up. Downtown hotels occupied by the Germans, were closing. That afternoon, we heard of a particularly sad event. German vehicles parked in the Bois du Boulogne where the troops were bivouacked, had been sabotaged, but not without consequences. Thirty-five teen-aged French boys passing the camp on their way to a nearby soccer field apparently made disparaging remarks and gestures that were seen by the fuming and hapless Germans. The Germans rounded them up, huddled together, in the soccer field, then lobbed hand grenades into their mist. Those still alive when the dust settled were shot.

We also heard the prefecture was occupied by police and learned that the French flag was flying over various public buildings. But obviously, it was still too early to move about the city freely. We saw German fighter planes for the first time in several days, then a flight of low-flying B-24s heading northeast just north of Nanterre.

The next day, Louis and Charles were working in the shop, when a man ducked inside and spoke briefly with Louis. Their unit was on alert and they had to leave. They said private goodbyes to the family, shook hands with us, and left.

Marcelle looked worried, dissatisfied with the orders. She wanted to be alone, so Walt and I went to Bill and Martin's place. We told them what had happened. Wherever Louis and Charles were going, they didn't have enough firepower, regardless of their mission.

The firing increased. It seemed to come from somewhere along the Avenue de la Grande Armee. The day dragged as I worried about Louis, Charles, and Mr. Besse. Just after noon, we caught glimpses of a half dozen or more trucks coming up the hill from Puteaux going to Fort Vallerian.

A man we'd never met interrupted our visit and said we were to return to the Berty's immediately. At the house, we found Marcelle in the parlor with Coco. She said Louis, Charles, and Mr. Besse, were German captives. She didn't know where they were now, but said to pack our things and to go to the taxi driver's house that evening.

We dashed around the house gathering everything that might reveal our presence, the drawings of houses and insignia, our packs of clothing, everything. While we packed, Marcelle told us that the men had occupied the Neuilly City Hall for a couple of hours before the Germans brought in tanks to blow off the doors. Our three guys stayed upstairs providing rifle cover while the others escaped through the sewers. Andre had escaped and rushed over to warn Marcelle. She didn't know if they were still alive.

We exchanged quick goodbyes, Marcelle fearing for everyone's safety. We stopped by to see Bill and Martin on the way. When we told them what had happened, Bill just shook his head.

"That's it. I'm afraid they've had it." Martin said he had to agree.

I was wearing my shoulder holster. I wasn't planning to jump any Panzer tanks, but I wanted to be prepared if anyone tried to give us any argument. I'd evaded too long to become a prisoner now.

Bill said they'd heard that our Underground force had killed about 20 Germans, and 30 French had escaped, but 20 more were captured.

# Chapter 17

# COUNTDOWN

**B**efore their capture, we'd counted the days until liberation, now we counted the hours until Louis and the others were free again.

It seems that the sewer plan had been the key to survival for those who escaped. The Germans did their utmost to locate the men, but to no avail. They twisted beneath the streets of Paris before exiting through an outlet on an island in the Seine near Andre's factory. The few women who waited for them there undoubtedly saved the lives of several men with the first aid they rendered.

At the taxi driver's house, he told us of his World War I experiences and how desperately he now wanted to see the Germans run out of Paris. His deep-rooted hatred of the miserable Boche crept into his every breath.

The next morning we went to see Bill and Martin. Marcelle had sent a food parcel for us there. It was a misty, dreary day, and I felt more despondent than at any time since I'd arrived in France. I kept thinking about the prisoners, feeling that they would be killed. Finally, I pulled Walt off to one side and told him about a plan I'd just come up with. He pondered for a moment, then agreed. When we told Bill and Martin, however, they advised against it. We said the hell with them and went to see Marcelle and Andre.

When we reached the house, Marcelle's eyes were red and swollen, but her face had that determined look, and I knew she would never stop trying. We stood in front of her, both of us taking hold on one of her hands. We told her our plan.

"Marcelle, tell the intermediary that the Underground will turn over two American pilots for Louis, Charles, and Mr. Besse," I said.

She started to cry, but then looked at me more defiantly than ever. "No, no. It is not good!" she said.

We told her we'd only be prisoners, that we'd be shipped to some camp in Germany and that would be that.

She wouldn't hear of it. She started gathering together the things she was going to take to help convince the Swedish Council that a cease-fire was in order.

She had been told that all the captured men were being held at Fort Valerian, inside the walls beneath which we had picnicked only a month before.

The next day, August 20, was bad, the truce was already broken, but the following day, August 21, was worse. German patrols were shooting everybody who moved, trying to suppress further uprising. I sat on the patio, engulfed in the somber mood of the world somehow reflected in that dull, gray sky.

Walt came out to join me.

"I don't think Louis will talk, do you, Walt? I asked. "He'll hold out a long time, but they can make anybody talk if they want.

"Yes, but those Germans in the fort are smart enough to know their days are numbered. They have to get out now or stand off the Resistance and hope they can last until the Americans and British forces get here. If the French get them, they'll probably be knocked off. I think the Germans would have already raided this house if they knew who Louis was, Woody.

"I'm sure they haven't identified him yet. Maybe he's still all right."

Andre told us in the morning that they were still alive, the German Commander was still honoring the truce, but we both thought all the random firing might change his mind at any moment. I wondered what I'd do in his place. I knew I'd hold out as long as possible, otherwise the men under my command would be prisoners of irregular troops, and they'd probably not live through the day, especially because of the war killings. I'd wait as long as I could to surrender to the Americans, hoping my men would be sent to prison camp, not shot.

Later that day, Marcelle said she had learned the captives were still alive because of the action taken by the Swedish council and General Von Choltitz. The exchange rate was still three to one. Marcelle was composed, tense, but determined, and now spent all her time contacting anyone who might help.

Mr. Paris came by and told us to stay put. He expected a battle for the city since the German defensive positions were manned. At that time, there were few street battles underway, and since Nanterre was clear we walked safely back to the old taxi driver's home, each evening.

Soon after we arrived there, Andre drove up in a big, black BMW sedan. It had two jump seats, and sliding glass panels between the front and back compartment. He asked us if we wanted to take a short ride to look around the area near the fort entrance.

"Sure. But where did you get the car?" I asked.

He grinned. "From the Germans. This one was Stulpnagel's." He was the commander before Von Cholitz.

"The general's car?" I asked incredulously.

He nodded. "Nothing but the best."

He was obviously pleased with his stolen vehicle, and we were delighted to take a tour; Walt and I had an idea, and wanted to see the fort. Neighbors craned their necks to see what was going on.

As we neared the fort, it seemed eerily quiet. No guards were posted. I stared at the place, knowing Louis and our friends were inside without any idea of what was happening anywhere else in the city. At the foot of the hill, the Resistance had erected a barricade out of a hodge-podge of materials including old furniture, heavy timbers, junk cars, and, right smack in the middle, a World War I 75 mm cannon. I decided it would last about as long as it took for the first Panzer to come along.

There were a lot of old guys hanging around, and Andre told them we were American pilots. They broke out bottles of cognac, patted us on the back, and we all drank. I looked up the hill at the main entrance to the fort. One lone soldier was standing atop the gate with a machine pistol cradled in his arm, just watching the people at the barricade.

When we returned to the Berty's that evening, Marcelle wasn't home yet so we poured ourselves another cognac and sat in the kitchen.

"Woody, are you thinking what I'm thinking?"

"Hell yes. It looks like it would be even easier than we thought."

"It would be a cinch," Walt agreed.

"All we'd have to do is get an American flag somewhere, put it on a pole, and set it up at the foot of the walkway leading up the hill. Then we go up the hill with a white truce flag and wave it like hell as we walk to the gate. We say we want to see the commander to deliver a note, calling upon his surrender. We wait out his decision. If he accepts, his aide can come part way down the walk with their own white flag."

"Then they escort us inside where we take over the fort. We'll meet there, take the surrender in the name of the United States Army, then we'll have one of their radio experts shift over to one of our frequencies. We'll broadcast in the blind. Every air base in the UK and Normandy will pick us up and we'll take over command, release the prisoners, and get some help from Andre and his guys to keep the place locked up until our troops get here," I looked at Walt.

"How will we keep the French civilians from killing them once we take them prisoners?" Walt wondered.

"We'll just keep the place locked and notify the Resistance through Andre that we have taken over the fortress and the German POWs are inside," I said. "Let's talk to Andre about it."

Marcelle and Andre arrived later. Marcelle immediately upon hearing our idea, told us to forget it, we'd never get up the walk. Andre thought it had potential. He left, but returned later to let us know the Resistance didn't think much of the idea either.

Marcelle said the very idea of two fellows she had gone through so much trouble to protect, just marching up a hill and expecting the German's to suddenly surrender, bordered on the ridiculous. Andre's people were sure it would work but Fort Valerian, of all places, had to be taken by the French.

Defeated, we returned to the taxi driver's house and hit the sack.

The next afternoon, someone delivered a message that we should return to the Berty's home. We weren't too surprised since we'd been told earlier that it was probably safe by now. When we reached the house, Marcelle seemed to be feeling a little better. The delegation of wives of captives had been able to talk to the Swedish council again and had been assured progress was being made.

A brief newscast that evening indicated that many more German soldiers were captured at Falaise than had been announced before. It was also reported that allied forces were only 60 miles from Paris.

Walt and I talked over a course of action if a battle should start in the city. We thought it best to take off on our own and relieve our French friends of the responsibility. We talked about flying, and I said I intended to keep flying as long as possible.

Walt said that's exactly what he had in mind as well.

I laughed. "You're just hungry Walt, you're still pissed that you never saw the guy who clobbered you. You want another shot, don't you?"

"Well, maybe," he conceded. "We'll see when we get back to London; it might not be much longer."

"I'm not going to stay in Europe, I know that," I said. "I'll go home and volunteer for fighters."

We shared our conversation later with the other two Americans, sitting on the patio outside their apartment, listening to Glenn Miller on the Yankee Doodle. Martin was adamant that he was never going to fly again.

"I've just seen too much damned death with airplanes, I've had it," he said.

The conversation was interrupted, however, by the clatter of small arms fire nearby. Several rapid bursts of cannon fire, followed immediately by the explosions of the shells, drowned out the initial shots. A black puff of smoke spewed skyward somewhere near the Arch of Triumph. We guessed a Molotov cocktail had found its mark on some unsuspecting vehicle.

More gunshots, cannons, and machine gun fire. Then more grayish black smoke from the downtown area.

"Sounds like an ammunition dump," Martin breathed.

"Hell, they wouldn't have one there, would they?" Walt asked, looking at me.

"Probably not. It might be something they didn't want the French to get."

All four of us were standing on the patio along the edge of the roof just outside their apartment, looking over the city, watching the heavy clouds of smoke roll furiously upward. We noticed other families standing on balconies, watching. The whole city was holding its breath, waiting for something to happen - - tense with anticipation.

The fire in the distance continued to burn, dominating the skyline as the smoke piled up and wafted over the city. Small arms fire continued it's even spat, punctuated by cannon fire.

The radio announcer interrupted the dance music with a bulletin.

"Ladies and gentlemen, we have an important announcement, Paris has been liberated, we repeat PARIS HAS BEEN LIBERATED!" The words, spoken by a professional news announcer in a deep voice choked with emotion stunned us.

Suddenly, we looked at each other incredulously and began laughing simultaneously, deep belly laughs. Obviously, the station had fouled-up somehow. How could they have gotten the news so wrong?

We calmed down a little, and another announcer came on the air describing the jubilation as Parisians danced in the streets after four long years of war. We listened silently now, wondering when they would correct the error.

Instead, it continued.

Lily Pons was singing "La Marseillaise" live from New York. We listened to her voice rise above the sound of firing in the city. As her rendition ended, cannon fire stuttered loudly from somewhere near the Seine, followed by the whirring, whooshing sound of flak flying across the corner of our patio, knocking a small chunk out of the stucco.

We switched to the BBC and heard the same liberation report.

"Maybe someone forgot to tell the Germans," Bill said sarcastically.

"They sure as hell didn't get the word." I agreed.

We switched back to the Yankee Doodle where the librarian of the House of Representatives was reading a poem he'd written especially for this occasion which would soon be entered into the Congressional Record.

"They must know something we don't," Martin observed.

We laughed for a while, then forgot about it. It wasn't true; obviously, someone jumped the gun. (Later, I learned that a pre-recorded tape by Charles Collingwood had been released inadvertently.)

Andre came by a little later and took us for a short drive. The streets were deserted. He said he thought Louis would be released from Fort Valerian within 48 hours. We drove by the barricade, the crowd manning it more boisterous than ever.

We stayed with Marcelle again that night and the news was good. Marseilles was occupied by the Americans, and the British had taken Deauville.

August 24 dawned just as the days before, with a dull, misty gray sky. We sipped coffee to pass the time, and then later strolled to the apartment to see Bill and Martin. We sat and waited, feeling a little more apprehensive than usual. There was less firing now.

The Yankee Doodle net had been correcting the report since the night before, and we wondered what could have happened to cause such a boondoggle.

After lunch, Walt and I were summoned back to the Berty's. When we arrived, there was a gathering of people in front of the house, and as we worked our way through, the first person we saw on the little side porch was Charles!

When he spotted us, he ran over, throwing his arms around us and shouting in French "Andre! Albert! I got three, maybe four.!!"

We hugged him back and patted him on the back as we walked quickly into the house. Louis was just going into the parlor, Marcelle hugging him like she'd never let go. We all traded bear hugs. I never saw anyone look as happy as Marcelle, she absolutely beamed.

They'd been released early, along with Mr. Besse. I'm sure the neighbors, swarming around the house noticed us and wondered, "Who are those two guys?" We continued with our deaf story until Louis finally introduced us to some of his closest neighbors. They were surprised that they'd really believed our line.

When things calmed down, Charles told the story of how they were kicked and beaten when they were captured. One young fellow who possessed a pistol when he was taken prisoner, was killed instantly by the Germans.

The rest were taken to the fort and thrown into dirty, stinking dungeons. They were questioned repeatedly, but never gave in. Since they carried no identification, the Germans were never able to find out who they were.

After one of the early interrogations, Louis was being dragged from his cell. As they yanked him down the hall, they passed a Wehrmacht soldier he recognized as the man who came to his house each Saturday to borrow the sausage machine.

The soldier recognized Louis too, and although he knew his name and address, he never said a word to his superiors. They took Louis to a yard, tied his hands behind his back, and made him kneel, facing a tripod-mounted machine gun set up only a few feet in front of him so he was staring right into the muzzle.

The gunner activated the charging handle, forcing live ammunition into the chamber. Louis watched as the gunner swung the barrel, aiming directly at his chest. They let Louis sweat for a moment, then demanded the name of the others in his group. Louis remained silent, saying his prayers. After what seemed like an eternity, he was led back to this cell. His captors told him he was lucky the officer decided to let him live another day.

This scene was re-enacted six more times. Once a blindfold was added. They clubbed him as well, apparently trying to determine Andre's identity more than anything else.

When they released him, Louis thought it was some kind of joke, that they would try following him to learn what they couldn't scare out of him. But when he saw the barricade down the hill, he realized that things had changed while he was a prisoner and hurried down to the waiting crowd.

Finally, that afternoon, Marcelle had to put an end to the well-wishers, telling them Louis was exhausted. Everyone was happy, but maybe even happier than Marcelle, was little Coco. He was ecstatic and trotted on his father's heels, never letting him out of his sight.

Andre came by later that afternoon with a friend from the Resistance who wanted to take us on a short ride to show Louis, Charles, and Mr. Besse what had changed while they were in prison. Marcelle was apprehensive, but Louis assured her they'd be all right. There were seven of us in the car when we drove up the hill and around to the barricade set up at the entrance. Things were much the same except there was more of a carnival atmosphere than ever. They knew the surrender was at hand, and celebrated each new bit of information.

This time, Andre drove down the hill into Puteaux, and over to Numero Trois where a few people were beginning to stir. We watched two ME-109's fly over very low, coming right up the main street from the Arch of Triumph.

When they reached the river, just a half mile from us, they veered away, headed northeast. Less than five minutes later, we saw another plane, smaller, and much slower, fly up the Champs Elysees, and down the Avenue de La Grande Armee, then turn back toward the Arch.

"Walt, that's an L-5," I said.

"It sure is, maybe we can go over there."

Andre tried driving in that direction, but we couldn't cross the bridge because of street fighting rampant on the other side, so we headed up Numero Trois instead. Gone were the struggling German convoys that had passed the bar there a few days before. Andre stopped to talk with several rifle-armed men. They said no German vehicles had passed that way since early morning. We returned to the Berty's house less than an hour after we left. After seeing the L-5, Walt and I were both confident that the Allied troops were in the city. We ate dinner, serenaded by the gunfire and occasional cannon fire outside. Then we heard something else.

It was very faint at first. The deep, resonant sound of a bell that could be heard for miles. Each time its reverberation reached us, we waited for the next. It came rhythmically. I wondered why it was ringing now, for the first time since we'd been in Nanterre. Louis said it was the bell at Notre Dame.

Then it was joined by another bell, a little higher pitched, with a shorter interval between each resonating beat. Within minutes, others joined, all ringing, clanging and booming in a steady, pulsing clangor. The chorus of bells continued until the air was filled with the song.

"What does it mean," I asked quietly.

"The liberation. It has to be. The Allies must be here now," Louis said.

Someone next door turned up the radio, and a neighbor called to us, "Turn on your radio, they are in the city!"

Charles dashed inside to turn on the French station, turning the volume up full. The ringing strains of "La Marseillaise" poured into the night, merging with the sounds of other radios all over the city.

The bells tolled on, immersing us in their sound for a long while. As the sound gradually faded, the frustrated firing of German troops trying to drown out the French triumph echoed over the streets.

We drifted slowly apart, not wanting to break the magic feeling, which began with the ringing of the bells, and the emotion generated with the sound of the "Marseilles" playing for the first time in four years.

Everyone was filled with hope for peace. For Walt and me it meant a trip back to the UK was forthcoming. For all of us, the countdown was almost over.

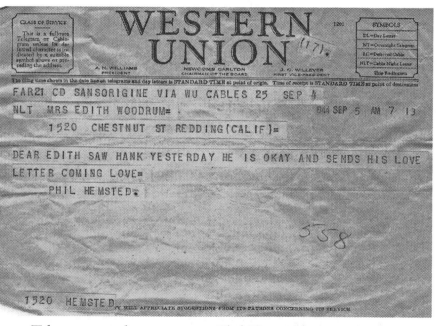

# WESTERN UNION (17)

1201

The filing time shown in the date line on telegrams and day letters is STANDARD TIME at point of origin. Time of receipt is STANDARD TIME at point of destination

FAR21 CD SANSORIGINE VIA WU CABLES 25 SEP 4

NLT MRS EDITH WOODRUM= 1944 SEP 5 AM 7 13

1520 CHESTNUT ST REDDING (CALIF)=

DEAR EDITH SAW HANK YESTERDAY HE IS OKAY AND SENDS HIS LOVE
LETTER COMING LOVE=

PHIL HEMSTED.

558

1520 HEMSTED

THE COMPANY WILL APPRECIATE SUGGESTIONS FROM ITS PATRONS CONCERNING ITS SERVICE

Telegram sent by my cousin, Phil Hemsted, to my mother
after he had seen me on my return to England.

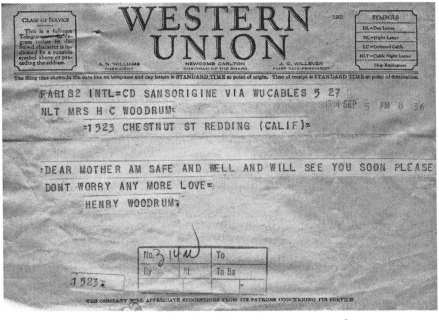

My cable to family telling them I was safe.
Sent after return from Paris.

# Chapter 18

# LIBERATION

Early the next morning, expecting to hear the intermittent cannon fire of the night before, I dressed and went to the kitchen where Louis was sipping coffee. He said last night's celebration was a little premature since only a few tanks had actually reached the city center, although French and American units were poised on the outskirts.

"They are fighting in the city," he said. "No Germans here, now. They left Nanterre, except those in Valerian."

The sky was bright and clear, a relief from the gray overcast and drizzles of the last few days. Marcelle bustled about the house until the Besses arrived.

The two men went somewhere by themselves with an admonishment from their wives. They laughed and said not to worry.

A half-hour or so later, Andre brought them back in the BMW open sedan. They told us Nanterre was in the clear, absolutely, no Germans anywhere. We listened to the radio as Marcelle put the finishing touches on our uniforms.

When they were done, Walt and I donned our outfits with the insignia and wings in place, and rode down to the Numero Trois Bridge with the other guys to see what was happening.

En route, Andre drove to the barricade at Fort Valerian where the perpetual celebration was in full swing. Cases of wine, and cognac were opened and bottles passed to us. The crowd was jovial, but sober; they wanted to be alert when the garrison at Valerian surrendered.

Andre drove us into Puteaux. He stopped opposite a square where he said a farmers' market was held every Saturday in good times, and we went into a bar. It seemed good to be there in uniform but better to see the men already there greeting our friends, laughing and clapping them on the shoulder. Everyone knew they'd been prisoners in Fort Valerian only a few days earlier.

We joined them in a toast they offered. Then Louis stepped between Walt and me, put his arms around our shoulders, and said, "These two are American pilots!" The bar erupted in cheers.

Americans were already fighting in Paris, but we were the first these people had seen. Everybody gathered around us, shaking hands, patting us on the back and shouting in French so fast I didn't understand a word. The proprietor dashed behind the bar to set up another round on the house. Everyone raised a glass while the proprietor gave the toast.

"Vive l'Amerique!"

When things settled down, our glasses were refilled and we raised them again, "Vive la France!"

We finally got out of there, still sober.

Andre drove through Puteaux to the bridge that Walt and I had walked across when we first came to Paris. We were told to turn back, however, because of fighting near the Arch of Triumph. We turned down Numero Trois instead. Andre found another bar filled with his Resistance friends, and again led us inside.

There were fewer people, but the greeting was just as enthusiastic. We stayed some 30 minutes, and then quickly returned to the bridge.

At a French checkpoint in Neuilly, we talked to the guards about the Germans holed up in an apartment building nearby. Within minutes, the Resistance team surrounded the place ready to accept a surrender or fight their way in. While they were waiting, the other Frenchmen were busy removing the champagne, brandy, cognac, Armagnac and wine from the basement.

We loaded our car with at least a dozen cases and took the liquor back to the house. We then picked up another load in Neuilly before we were finally able to drive all the way down the Avenue de la Grande Armee to the Etoile at the entrance to the Champs Elysees.

We parked our car just in front of an American jeep. A GI sat at the wheel, ready to move quickly if called, his carbine propped up against the wheel, ready for use. There were 10 other trucks from his unit parked 50 yards away, and another 4 or 5 jeeps and several Sherman tanks at other points of the Etoile, all facing down side streets coming into the circle.

The GI told us sniper firing had ended, but they didn't know if all opposition was silenced or not. He said more vehicles from his unit were enroute. Both American and French units were there, the 2nd Armored units on the other side.

Walt and I talked with a couple of GIs who wondered about our uniforms. They'd guessed we were shot-down pilots. One guy said we were the third pair who'd approached him, but in other cities, to identify themselves as shot-down Americans. We were the first he'd met in Paris.

The soldiers still weren't used to their new role as the liberators of Paris, and were still prepared to fight. They didn't want to take any chances by relaxing just yet. But they were all taking a look at their surroundings, getting ready to cut lose when the time came. They said they'd met a lot of German resistance on the way in.

There were very few civilians in the Etoile then and not many more on the Champs Elysees, so we walked around freely. Most of the soldiers were under cover, watchful of snipers. Their machine guns were set up, manned, and ready with tanks in strategic places. I saw three L-5s, one with American insignia, the other two with French marking. They used the Champs Elysees as a runway!

We talked a supply sergeant out of two packs of Luckies, asked how to send mail back to our folks, and were given a few V-mail envelopes. A captain told us to come back the next day as they were expecting more fighting any minute. We ducked back into our car and drove home to unload the booze into Louis' storehouse.

The making of a good Liberation party stood ready. Andre left the car parked in the driveway and left with Mr. Besse.

Later that evening, someone called to say the troops in Fort Valerian had surrendered to the Resistance who agreed to turn them over to the French 2nd Armored Division. Everybody gave a big cheer at the news.

Dinner was late that evening, and when we finished, Louis popped open a door I'd hardly noticed before, revealing steps leading into the basement. He came back with a large, brown bottle covered with a thick layer of dust. As he cleaned it, he told us he'd kept it since 1940 for the liberation. Now, after seeing the Allied troops around the Etoile, this was the time.

Marcelle set out tumblers while Louis removed the cork. Then he began pouring, almost filling each of the glasses, a smaller one for Coco, with a little soda. We held up our glasses.

"To the victory," said Louis.

"To the victory," we repeated.

We drank, and with the first sip, I knew it was the best rum I'd ever tasted, even better than that served by the Chief in Montereau. I knew why Louis saved this bottle.

Walt and I gave the next toast together, "Vive la France!" The others joined in, echoing our words.

Nobody said anything for a moment, as we each thought quietly about the meaning of this long-awaited day - it was finally here. Glancing from face to face, I saw only happiness.

Charles held up his glass, grinning mischievously, "Merde les Boche," he shouted.

We laughed, clinking our glasses yet another time before we sat down, helping ourselves when we wanted a refill. We listened to the BBC, then Yankee Doodle, then the French station, all now operating freely. They all carried the news that tanks of the French 2nd Armored and the American 4th Infantry Division were fighting in Paris and already occupied certain key points. Finally, they carried the news that Von Choltitz had surrendered and there remained only token resistance. The end of the German occupation was official.

Charles stepped outside, but dashed in a moment later calling excitedly. We went quickly into the backyard where he stood gesturing. The city was ablaze with light! It was the first time the lights had been turned on since the war started in 1939.

Louis shouted, and we all piled into the BMW and drove to an observation point up the street near the dairy. We got out, mingling with other families gathered there to see the city lights.

Charles had brought a bottle of cognac and we drank as we watched. As I stood there, it began to sink in that with the liberation of the wonderful city, my evasion was coming to an end. What started as an attempt to stay free for just one hour, then one night, then a full day and finally a week, had now grown into a three-month period. I'd made it! When the lights were doused a little later, we went home, but stayed up a long time talking.

Louis woke us early the next day, August 26. He told us French and American troops now occupied the Champs Elysees. He and Mr. Besse were on their way over there, and told us to hurry. Louis drove quickly, speeding along the magnificent avenue that was free of traffic. Along the way, Mr. Besse pointed to the remains of a burned building - all that was left of the Grande Palais.

We parked near the head of the Champs Elysees, and talked with American soldiers parked along the boulevard. Many more troops had arrived over night. Several hundred people were there with more arriving by the minute.

Sidewalk cafes opened as the street filled with people. Walt and I stopped to talk with a GI sitting on a tailgate. He looked us over and said, "Well, I think I recognize part of the uniform. What can I do for you, Lieutenant?"

"We'd like some American cigarettes. Where can we get some?"

He pointed down the row of trucks and told us to see the captain standing there talking to a noncom. He finished his conversation, then looked us over.

"You guys been shot down?"

"Yeah. That's right."

"What can I do for you?"

"We'd like to get some cigarettes and find out how we can get the word back to the States that we're OK."

"That's easy." He gave us both five packs each. Then he gave us some more V-mail blanks. "Fill these out and we'll have your names in London tonight. They'll send a TWX from there."

"Great. Thanks a lot, Captain."

"OK. How long have you been shot down?"

We told him and gave Louis and Raymond Besse each a pack of cigarettes. We borrowed a pencil from the clerk and wrote a V-mail note using the tailgate as a desk, and gave it to the clerk.

As I finished writing, a gorgeous brunette walked across the sidewalk with a young GI, peering into his face, smiling. She was dressed to the nines and giggling at something the GI said.

Suddenly, two burly women and a couple of men grabbed her and dragged her away, across the sidewalk. The GI stood gawking, unsure what was happening. The captain called out to the women in French, and after they answered, turned to the GI.

"Leave it alone, soldier. Let the French take care of it. They say she's a collaborator."

By now, the women were yanking at the girl's clothing, tearing off her dress, and ripping away part of her slip, then her brassiere. As her breasts swung free, they forced her down on a bench, face up. One of the beefy women used a pair of scissors to begin whacking off long handfuls of the glistening black hair, letting it fall to the sidewalk as the young woman screamed agonized obscenities, kicking and scratching until someone pinned down her arms.

When her hair was only an inch or so long, someone ran a pair of hand clippers expertly over her skull. In a very few minutes, she was practically bald.

Some of the crowd stopped to watch, but others glanced only casually before walking past. Someone explained that she'd been a collaborator and a whore of the Boche until just two days ago.

After the last bit of black stubble was clipped away, they let her stand. The bald scalp starkly white against her tan face and body. As she stood, she realized her breasts were exposed and clutched her arms to cover them as someone led her away, around the corner and out of sight.

The GI, apparently her last customer, disappeared around the line of trucks. I knew how the French felt about collaborators, but this was the first time I'd ever seen such a stunning woman reduced to such a pitiful sight so quickly and so publicly.

A burst of handclapping erupted as a French soldier climbed out of his tank, then reached to pull out a girl. The couple immediately went into a clinch, holding their kiss, oblivious to the crowd. A hand-printed sign on the tank said its crew was home for the first time in five years.

Little vignettes like that were being played out all around me as soldiers reunited with their families. We continued down the boulevard as we heard a ragged cheer grow into a roar, as a huge, French tri-color was unfurled from the top of the Arch.

People stopped us, and when Louis told them Walt and I were Americans, we began getting kisses from the crowd too. By now the streets were blanketed with joyous people covering the sidewalks and streets. American GIs struck up conversations with French people, all using their standard-equipment French phrase books.

Firing had ceased, and I couldn't help wondering where the Luftwaffe was - they were sure letting a good target go to waste.

The boulevard was already filling with jubilant Parisians. The women wore their special dresses, most featuring the flags of France, Great Britain, and the United States. Flags and banners were everywhere. We had been among the first to arrive, but now Louis wanted to rush home to get the others because General Charles De Gaulle was expected to march from the Arch of Triumph down the Champs Elysees that afternoon. He wanted them to see the march.

Returning to Nanterre took much longer than the drive in, because of the people streaming along the main avenues. It was still early so we stopped for a quick drink in Puteaux. A lot of people we'd met the day before were there again, and again we were treated to a couple of rounds and some hearty backslapping.

Our next stop was Fort Valerian. We drove into the courtyard and Louis explained to the guard that he had been a prisoner there just two days before. They escorted us downstairs to see the cells. Louis had described the place correctly. It was filthy and filled with a suffocating stench. I thought about the 4,500 French people killed there during the four long years of Nazi occupation.

Walt and I found a couple of bayonets and a dagger or two before all three of Valerian's ex-prisoners said they wanted to get out of the damned place.

Marcelle wasn't home when we arrived, but there was a note saying she'd gone with a friend to the business district. When we arrived there, we found a crowd as deliriously happy as the group uptown; but here, there were only civilians.

We found Marcelle, talking with a friend. As we walked toward her, we saw two women with shaved heads being marched down the middle of the street, naked to the waist, the crowd jeering and shouting at them. One cradled a baby, supposedly the illegitimate child of the cook at Fort Valerian.

We all went back to the house to get the two big picnic baskets Marcelle had already packed. We loaded them in the car and headed for the Etoile about noon. We made good time until we reached the bridge where the streets were so packed, we barely crawled until we reached the official parking area. Louis had a pass so we didn't have far to walk to reach the Arch of Triumph.

Walt and I each hoisted a basket while a gendarme checked Louis's pass. He escorted us to the elevator in the Arch and held the door for us and we rode to the top.

As we stepped out of the elevator, other people were already waiting at the balustrade, looking at the scene below. Every street leading to the Etoile was choked with people. On the other side, the Champs Elysees was wall-to-wall celebrants as well.

Marcelle found a shady spot near the elevator and we left our baskets there. From our 160-foot elevation, the scene below was magnificent.

The rumbling of the crowd filled the air with a hum of happiness. A group of British soldiers and non-comms, along with some French civilians sat near us. Most impressive was a dapper old gentleman in a scarlet uniform blouse who introduced himself as the former Paris fire chief. One couple in particular caught my eye; a French captain about 30 years old and his wife. He said he'd returned to Paris yesterday for the first time since being evacuated from Dunkirk.

He was wearing filthy tank corps coveralls when he arrived, but his wife had been expecting him and had his dress uniform, cleaned, pressed, and waiting for him in the closet after four long years! He was probably the best-dressed soldier I saw that day and his wife was definitely the happiest person around.

Marcelle opened the baskets and we were joined by Bill and Martin and the family they'd stayed with - minus their little boy. Jack and Stone were with the Besses of course, so we had a good-sized group. But when Marcelle learned the British non-comms had no food, she asked me to bring them over. They were surprised at the invitation, but joined us eagerly. They added a couple bottles of Scotch to our supply of cognac, Armagnac, and wine.

We looked down on the Champs Elysees, waiting to see General De Gaulle. The crowds thronged around the base of the Arch and we saw gendarmes clear the area several times anticipating the start of the General's march.

Occasionally, a shot rang out and we saw people hit the deck, lying flat a moment before getting up to walk again. Around 3:30, heavy firing broke out. We watched silently as soldiers began shooting at rooftops ringing the Etoile. Suddenly, a shot ricocheted off the masonry only two feet below us. That was all we needed. Either they thought we were Germans, or Germans were doing the firing. We ducked down and sat on the blanket, drinking our booze, relaxing, talking with the others until the firing ended. When we went back down in the elevator, we were told by the gendarme that De Gaulle had just departed on his march.

The huge crowd started to break up, some heading for their homes to continue the celebration, other groups remaining to whoop it up and have a ball.

Traffic was so congested it took forever to reach home, but when we arrived, some neighbors invited us to a party at the school. Walt and I carried a case of cognac between us while Louis and Charles carried a case of champagne. The Besses were there with Stone and Jack but neither Martin nor Bill showed up.

The place was packed, and Walt and I shook hands and drank toasts with everyone there. The neighbor lady, who had thought we were so impolite before, came over and kissed us, laughing and happy. The champagne was chilling on ice, but the cognac flowed freely. The young guy who set up the party made a speech, after which he introduced others, including Louis and Raymond Besse. Then the crowd joined in singing the "Marseillaise," tears streaming unabashedly down the cheeks of many. Walt and I sang a duet, "The Star Spangled Banner." I'm afraid we didn't do very well, but we were enthusiastic. Musicians arrived and the speeches ended. By 11:00, the place was jumping. Marcelle led Walt and me to an anti-room where some girls, 16 or 17, were passed out cold after drinking too much cognac. We hoisted them over our shoulders, their arms dangling behind us.

Marcelle led the way for me, Madame Besse leading Walt in another direction. The first one lived about three blocks from the hall. I dumped her on the bed and Marcelle undressed her and covered her up. Then we went back to the hall. Walt was just getting back, too. For the next 30 minutes, we were kept busy packing drunken teenage girls back to their homes. When the war started most of them were just kids and everything caught up with them when they had a few drinks to celebrate for the first time in their lives.

Finally, we settled down to some serious drinking ourselves and danced with the best looking ladies in the place until the lights went out - every light in the area, not just in our building.

We heard the drone of aircraft engines and knew the Krauts weren't going to let Paris forget they were still around. The young party organizer announced the gala was over, then changed his mind, and decided to call someone to see what was going on. When we learned a northeastern suburb of the city was being bombed by the Germans, we cancelled the festivity out of respect to those killed in the bombing. But then they decided the heck with it, we can't let the Germans run our lives anymore; we'll drink a toast to the people, light candles, and go on with our party. It was settled.

I was just about as loop-legged as some of the teenagers by the time we finally got home and fell into bed. The next morning Walt woke me, shaking me by the shoulder. It didn't make much sense to me and it took him awhile to finally wake me up.

"What is it, Walt," I mumbled.

"We have to go. There's a Tank Corps officer in the parlor and he's come to get us."

I sat right up.

"You gotta be kidding."

"Nope, he's already given me the word and now he wants to talk with you—personally."

"Tell him to go to hell. I'm not going anymore. I've got too much to do before I go anywhere."

He tried to argue, but I rolled over and was already asleep when someone else started poking me.

"Lieutenant Woodrum, you have to get up and if you don't get out of bed, I'll see you are court martialed immediately."

I turned over and looked at him. He was a couple of years younger than me, maybe 5'-8", and he looked even madder than he sounded. He was a 2nd Lieutenant.

"Where in hell do you want me to go?"

"We have to go back to headquarters. You must be interrogated."

"Can't that wait awhile? I've got a lot to do here."

"Don't give me a hard time. We will leave in 10 minutes."

That made me mad. I thought I might start evading all over again.

Finally, I got up and shaved, taking my time. Then I put on my uniform and went into the kitchen. Marcelle poured a cup of coffee for me, raising her eyebrows questioningly without saying anything. I shrugged. About that time, the lieutenant headed down the hall to the bedroom, but when he saw me sitting there, he turned into the kitchen.

"Are you ready?"

"No, I'm not ready. What the hell is all this about?"

"Well, you are still in the United States Army and they are waiting to interrogate you at the hotel right now."

I sat there sipping my coffee, trying to figure out what was really going on. "It seems to me the Army is in a might big hurry. What's the rush?"

He started giving me a snow job about how important it was to get details during interrogation while they were still fresh in the memory. Besides, they didn't want downed pilots scattered all over France. Finally, he settled down a little, telling us where we'd be taken. He was from an intelligence unit, gave me its designation, and said the commanding officer was a British lieutenant colonel.

Then Walt and I laid it on him. We said we had a lot of friends who'd saved our lives. What would they think if we just took off without even saying goodbye?

"Besides," I argued, "we have a car and can check in for a few minutes this afternoon to talk it over."

Finally, he agreed to go back without us if we gave him our word that we'd come by later. We told him we would and he gave us the address and the name of the British officer. I had a sneaking suspicion that we'd been taken pretty bad.

"Walt, we have to find that French General."

"It's too late; Andre's the only one who can find him."

Andre's phone had not been answering.

As I finished my coffee, we talked it over with Louis. He listened carefully, then went out to his warehouse and came back with a bottle of brandy, some of the best scrounged from the Krauts.

"Go see the British officer. Tell him you must have two weeks to say goodbye to friends." Then he said, grinning, "Take this rare brandy with you and tell him you know where more is available."

Louis was droll, not really joking, but indicating such an approach might work. Marcelle nodded. It was worth a try.

"Walt, did he know about the other guys?"

"Yeah, all of them, and he said there were two other groups: the one where the kid from the RAF was taken, and another big place, with about six guys."

We took our time, and walked around the neighborhood saying goodbye just in case. The old taxi driver was over his illness and thrilled about the liberation.

Finally, we were able to see everybody except Denise and Andre. After lunch, we went into Paris, but decided to check into the hotel before we went to see the colonel. The Windsor-Reynolds was a few blocks off the Champs Elysees. Mr. Besse had come along with Jack and Stone, and Marcelle and Coco were also with us. The lobby was vacant and I remembered somebody saying it was used by German Staff officers until the last few days.

Finally, we found a man who took us to the manager's office. He was flabbergasted at first when we told him we were Americans, then Louis explained everything in French.

He managed to make part of the hotel staff materialize out of thin air, and escorted us to the second floor where he showed us each to a suite of rooms. We set our canvas bag on the table just as a waiter came in with a bucket of ice and a bottle of chilled champagne. Louis pronounced it to be at the perfect temperature and popped it open. The manager joined us in a glass, offering a toast: "Vive l' Amerique!" I was beginning to like this hotel. He excused himself and asked us to meet him downstairs on our way to our next appointment.

We looked around; Louis said we'd picked out a good place to stay. When we went downstairs, more champagne was waiting. The manager had already assembled the entire staff in the lobby. He stood at the head of the line and made a little speech.

We clinked our glasses, refilled them, and offered our toast.

"Vive la France!"

We shook hands with each staff member as we were introduced to everyone: the chef, waiters, chambermaids, the secretary, bookkeeper, and the doorman. We were the only guests, he said, but when we told him we might not be back for a day or two, he said it made no difference, there would be a staff member standing by to take care of whatever we needed, at any time. We booked rooms for Bill and Martin just in case. Then we went to see the British colonel.

Five minutes after we arrived, an American 2$^{nd}$ lieutenant stepped out of an office and escorted us down the hall to a darkened room. A massive desk in front of the window was flanked by British and American flags in standards, the window blinds were drawn. The colonel sat behind the desk and began the conversation by remarking that he understood we wanted to talk with him before we went back to the UK.

He said he hoped that we understood it was important to get debriefings accomplished while everything was still fresh in our memories and before important facts were forgotten.

"I'll never forget any of it, sir," I said. "But I've been down for three months already, and I don't think a few more days will make any difference." I leaned over and reached into my bag for the brandy. I pulled it out and held it in my hand as Walt picked up the conversation.

"We have a lot of friends, sir, and we want to say thank you before we leave. Louis Berty was a prisoner in Mt. Valerian until the 23rd or 24th, and others who helped us have been captured. We want to learn what happened to them."

"That's right, Colonel," I jumped in, "One place was hit just after we left. Also, we want to help our friends drink some of this good brandy." I put the bottle on the desk. "We know where there's a lot more like this."

"How long do you intend to stay in Paris?" he asked.

Oh, two weeks will do it, maybe a little more," said Walt.

"I'll give you three days. You won't be able to leave Paris during that time anyway, so that'll give you plenty of time. You'll be picked up by truck on the 29th or 30th. You are staying at the Windsor-Reynolds?"

"Yes, we are."

"In the meantime, there's a debriefing this afternoon you must attend. We'll take you there."

"We have transportation," I said quickly.

"It won't be needed. We'll take you back to the hotel."

He went back to the lobby with us where we introduced him to Louis and Marcelle. He explained in perfect French what was happening. We told them we'd call that evening and let them know our schedule. A corporal arrived and said he'd drive us to the debriefing.

Walt and I jumped in one jeep, the others in two more. I don't know what happened, but enroute our driver became separated from the others. Suddenly, we found ourselves in the midst of a continuing liberation party; a crowd of people packed the narrow street so tightly the jeep couldn't move. Women leaned into the jeep and kissed us wildly. Bottles were handed to us. As we stood and tilted the jugs, the crowd cheered. We noticed two girls looking at us from a first-floor apartment window and called to them. They smiled and the crowd began to shout to them. An old man leaned into the jeep and said, "I think she's married."

"Tres bien."

He grinned as Walt and I jumped out and ran up the stairs. The girls opened the door and let us in. One said she had been married, but her husband was killed in a German prison camp. The other was single. We were just getting acquainted when our driver knocked and said we had to go. We got their names and addresses and left. It took another ten minutes to reach the debriefing.

When the first person I saw in the room was Mr. Paris, I knew why they'd sent that lieutenant directly to the Berty's house. There were several American and French debriefing officers, but the interrogation took less than 30 minutes and little of importance was asked. Just more damned paperwork.

When it was finished, they took us into the dining room where a spaghetti dinner was already being served. There were seven RAF people, one from Montreal, who spoke French like a Parisian. There were also a few other Americans.

One was a staff sergeant who didn't say much. He was found by the FFI locked in a boxcar in a marshalling yard. He hadn't eaten in four days. He was a ranger, captured six times since the Normandy landings, and had escaped five times. The last time, they swore they'd kill him in revenge for the Germans he'd killed.

Another was a 2nd lieutenant P-47 pilot shot down on his first combat mission during the Falaise battle. An SS tank battalion commander had worked him over in the basement of his headquarters with two big goons nearby to make sure he couldn't get at the commander.

Unconscious, he was tossed into the back of a truck going to Paris. The German Intelligence Officer questioning him treated him kindly, had his wounds attended to, and kept him under guard in a big hotel when the surrender came. This kid was a mess.

When we finished the meal, we scrounged a case of 10-in-1 rations and took it back with us in the jeep to the hotel where we met Bill and

Martin. Their rooms were smaller than ours. We went with them to a hotel bar and it turned out to be quite a party. Bill's host lined us up with some real dolls.

We returned to the hotel the next morning and found a note from the French general inviting us to a party. But we were pretty busy with a party of our own, which seemed to keep going and we simply never reached the general's place. A day or two later, we met him and his wife for cocktails in the lobby, and apologized for missing their invitation.

During that time, we also received notes from Ernie Pyle and Earnest Hemmingway, inviting us to the Scribe Hotel or the Ritz, saying they'd like to interview us. We never found the time.

When we ran out of food, the four of us found a QM supply center in a downtown garage and were able to draw rations, five big cartons. We took them back to the hotel. We gave one to the chef, showing him what some of them were when he was unable to translate. He had never seen powdered milk, but we showed him how to mix it and he asked us to let him take some home to his little boy. He whipped up a meal from those 10-in-1 rations that was fantastic. What he could do with a can of GI plum pudding, just by adding a little cognac to the sauce, was almost magic!

While we were there, I tried to call both the Filipottos and the Brenners. The Brenner's number rang once with no answer, but the rest of the time, circuits were jammed. The next couple of days were one continuous party.

The last day, we went to Nanterre and spent the time with the Bertys and Besses. They came back to the hotel with us around noon as we prepared to leave.

The manager fixed some snacks and brought us some champagne. We talked and reminisced until the truck arrived. We slung our bags over our shoulders, mine pretty well loaded down with the two bayonets, a dagger, and the Luger I'd liberated the same day we'd picked up that first load of booze in Neuilly.

Downstairs, we drank a toast to our friends and said goodbye. It was a very tough moment for all of us. We all had tears in our eyes. Walt and I had become very fond of these two families, especially Louis, Marcelle,

Charles, and Coco. It was like leaving home all over again. Finally, we had to climb into that damned truck and leave. We stood waving from the back until we rounded the corner and they were out of sight.

As I sat down, I wished I could see the Filipottos and the Brenners again - and of course, we were both thinking of the guys in the camp, and old Marcel.

As it turned out, we could have spent a couple of more hours with them. Only a couple of blocks away at the Champs Elysees, the 29th Infantry Division was parading down the big old boulevard for the citizens of Paris. The reception those guys got was amazing as gals ran out to march along with them, kissing them all the way. People dashed from the crowd with open bottles, marching alongside as the GIs drained the jugs.

Cheers went up all along the boulevard and when the crowd learned we were Americans, included us in the festivities. But about half the people in our truck were Britishers who were interned throughout the war and hated the Germans. Most of them could speak French fluently and they called to the crowd.

But finally, the parade ended and we drove through intermittent drizzles to Le Mans. The guards at the gate thought we were German prisoners and put us in the cage until we realized what was going on and yelled to get out. Off to one side there was a whole gaggle of German generals, one with a monocle. One of the Britishers said, "They can leave me in here awhile if they'll just give me a few minutes alone with that chap!"

We slept in GI tents the next two nights, and ate at the GI mess hall. We were briefly interrogated again, sitting in the back of a command car in the rain, and finally hitched a ride to an airfield on Normandy, A-2.

I found a B-26 from my outfit on the ramp there: the Empire State Express. The pilot and co-pilot were hut mates of mine back at Stansted.

Then we flew back to England in a C-47 and spent the next three days being debriefed by a SHAPE Headquarters personnel intelligence team. A sharp-as-a-tack WAF captain interviewed me, helping me remember things I thought were long forgotten, but I couldn't remember the markings on that Mustang in the Versailles dogfight.

On the second day, they took us to the PX for new uniforms. As I was being fitted, I heard somebody holler, "Hey Woody!"

It was Lou Offenberg, the guy who gave me the ride to the flight line on May 28th. He said he'd tell the guys at the base that I was back. He did, too, because nobody was surprised when I walked in a couple of days later.

There were a lot of new faces at Stansted, and a few old timers. Al Freiburger, my old buddy and the guy I always liked to fly formation with, was still there, flying his 64th mission the next day. So was E. R. Bowers, with whom I'd flown a lot. My radio operator, who was on R&R when we were shot down, didn't make it back from a milk run to Brest a few days before it was captured.

Corporal Tancardo, who was drawing my idea of a mountain home, went ahead with the plans even after I was shot down. He handed them over to me when I returned - three months late! Even though a lot of people tried to talk him out of them, he'd saved them for me. Major Wallace, our executive officer, and a World War I fighter pilot whom I greatly respected, pinned me down and made me tell him all about it.

I found some of my stuff they never bothered to ship home, even my trench coat and my 60-mission crusher. Col Vance, our Group Commander, invited me to visit him and asked for details of my evasion. When I finished, he told me to keep the .45 pistol as a permanent issue.

A lieutenant colonel in the group took me off to one side and said he heard I'd been telling some pretty tall tales, and suggested I knock it off. I looked him right in the eye and said, "Colonel, I haven't said much, but everything I did say was 100 percent true. I was down for 90 days and some strange things happened."

Back in London, I saw Walt and Bill who were going to finish their tours. I wasn't allowed to switch to fighters and I didn't want any more bomber runs. The last night I was there, I was in London having a drink in the Reindeer Club when something exploded nearby, demolishing an entire block. The concussion blew half the bottles off the bar shelves. Later, somebody told me that was the first V-2 to hit London. That was the last shot the Krauts got at me; I sailed from Plymouth on an Italian liner, the Saturnia, and returned to the States a few days later.

This is front view of the house I landed on. My parachute caught on the right side of the house. Photo taken during my return in 1948.

Another view of the house I landed on
taken in 1948 during my visit.

Photo of me, Louis Berty and Jacqueline
Besse taken in 1948 during my visit.

Louis Berty and Jacqueline Besse in 1948 during my visit to France.

Mr. and Mrs. Besse. Photo taken during my visit in 1948.

Bert and I enjoying an evening out. Photo taken
in Bavaria at the Post Hotel in 1948.

Pierre, Marcelle, and Louis Berty in late 1950's. Berty family photo.

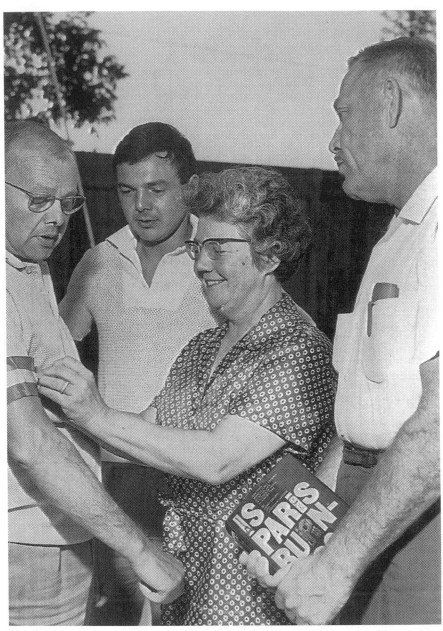

Louis, Pierre, and Marcelle Berty with me during their visit to Redding, California in 1966. I am holding a copy of "Is Paris Burning". We are all mentioned in the book. Photo used with permission of the Redding Record-Searchlight.

# Chapter 19

# PIERRE'S CHILDHOOD MEMORIES

After a journey of over 50 years, a man turns and looks behind him down the furrowed road. It is strewn with a multitude of memories which jostle for his attention: faces of friends, some of whom are dead and others who have sunk into that other oblivion of forgetfulness. So many details, from the most important to the most trivial, flash before his eyes. School friends, student pranks, then other friendships during military service.

Then there are the women, first love, fleeting encounters, a wedding that never happened. After that, a carefree, careless life with a few unimportant flings, and at last the encounter with the girl who was to become his wife and lifelong companion. Marriage, the immense joy of having two beautiful children, the worry of seeing them safely through their schooling, and the great pride of their happiness in life, the birth of five wonderful grandchildren, the health problems here and there along the way, community life, leading to a form of political and philosophical militancy.

The sixty-year-old thinking these thoughts was a child during the Second World War, and at the time his parents affectionately called him Coco. He was three years old when the war broke out, a skinny little boy with brown curly hair. He hated being mistaken for a girl when his grandmother tied red ribbons in his locks! During these tender years, Coco was lucky enough to have, almost despite himself, some unforgettable adventures. A very brief passage of his life is packed with more inextinguishable memories than the whole of the rest of his existence.

14 July, 1944. The previous evening, Coco and his friends had marched all around the neighbourhood until late, with a very loud drum, singing the Lorraine marching song (all about Jeanne d'Arc), with bravado, making the passing soldiers smile. Because of this nocturnal activity, Coco is off colour that morning, having got to bed much later than usual, and then having had a very troubled night. Excitement was thick in the air in the household, strange shadows tiptoed through his bedroom into the next-door room. Luckily, his mother is there to calm his fears – his nights are still haunted by the strange and sudden departure of his friend David whose family had been taken away by the Germans.

First thing in the morning, his parents call him into their room, and he snuggles happily into the bed between them. His mother begins by praising him for the way he acted during his Father's spell in the *maquis*. Now, they are counting on him even more. His father speaks up.

"You see, Coco, I've always known I can trust you, but this morning I'm going to ask you to promise me something: you must never, never tell anyone what we're about to tell you.

"I promise".

"Here we go then. Yesterday evening, with your Mummy, we went to fetch some American airmen who had been shot down in France, and who are hiding out before making their way to England to be able to continue fighting. They have fake French identity cards, which say they're deaf and dumb, to cover for the fact that they can't speak a work of French. You should know that there are also two of them at Raymond Besse's house, rue des Luaps, two more at Madame Lemoine's in the rue Volant, one of whom is a French-speaking Canadian, and two at Verdier's garage on the rue de Suresnes – a right little colony, in fact!

His heart is bursting with joy and excitement, mixed with a little fear. Coco will finally meet some real Americans, who he has heard so much about for months. The closest he has been before is to see the silhouette of their aeroplanes passing very high up in the sky during air raids.

"I promise to keep the secret", says Coco solemnly, proud that his parents have confided in him and placed their absolute trust in him.

"Run and say good morning to them", he says to his son. Coco draws a star spangled banner and runs into their guests' room, where he is greeted with friendly grins. Coco's heart is racing and his head is spinning, as he imagines everything these men have lived through during their last assignment. It's the best 14th of July of his whole life.

One of the Americans is of Scottish origin, born near Sacramento. He is a tall red-head with an uncontrollable mop of hair and a big moustache. Everybody calls him "Albert", but his real name is Henry C. Woodrum. Before the war, which began for Henry in Pearl Harbour in December 1941, he was a musician. He's a B26 pilot, shot down in May 1944 over Carrières sur Seine, while he was attempting to bomb the Maisons Laffite railway bridge. From link to link, the escape network had carried him to Coco's house *via* Versailles, Montereau, and Melun. His trip has been a veritable odyssey. Wherever he stayed, people have been arrested and shot after his departure. The Melun *maquis*, his last hiding place before Nanterre, had been partly wiped out.

Although the orders from the Network were that the airmen should remain hidden at all times, it's only understandable that young men have a need to go out and enjoy themselves – otherwise they will suffocate. They arrange to meet up sometimes, each family taking it in turn to host a little gathering. Coco likes showing them the way to each others' houses. He particularly likes going to Madame Lemoine's, since one of her guests is a French-speaking Canadian with a hilarious accent. He's the only one that can take the risk of going out on the town alone, and frequents Parisian cabarets. When he gets back, he makes sure that the cabaret tickets stick out of his jacket pocket a bit, in order to arouse the envy of his housebound friends.

"This morning, we're going to the Naval Museum – get the bikes out", announces Coco's father. Coco runs to prepare the bicycles for the outing. Five cyclists leave Nanterre, head for the Puteaux bridge, cross the Bois de Boulogne, past the lake, and arrive at Porte de la Muette. The airmen are most impressed by the Georges Mandel and Henri Martin avenues that they cycle down, they hadn't imagined that there were so many trees in Paris. When they arrive in Place du Trocadero, they admire the view of the Eiffel tower and the Ecole Militaire, from the viewpoint between the twin Palais de Chaillot buildings.

The little group enters the museum, carefully locking the bicycles up just outside. Inside, they decide to split up, and they all wander here and there in the museum taking in the exhibition. A few other visitors comment about the exhibits in hushed voices, in a silence broken only by the creak of the parquet. The cyclists from Nanterre are scattered all around the building – Coco's father is with his mother, and André is a few yards away from Albert, that impressive figure with so many exciting tales to tell, that Coco follows around like a little shadow. Another group can be heard in the distance, first of all by the door of the museum, but then progressing rapidly through the different rooms, judging by the sounds of footfalls on the parquet. Coco turns his head and realises, to his panic, that it is a group of German soldiers, and that they are heading his way. His heart begins to pound. André moves a little way away from Albert, Coco's parents cautiously observe from a distance, only Albert stands firm. The Germans are drawing closer. "They mustn't stop by us" mutters Coco to himself, with an imploring, sidelong glance at his parents. The soldiers head straight for Albert. Coco could almost touch them now, and they're stopping in front of Albert, who isn't showing any visible signs of panic.

"Papieren bitte!"

The words of their leader ring out loudly in the silence, resonating in Coco's ears – quickly he turns to the Germans, and on an impulse, says "My Daddy is deaf and dumb", while slipping his hand into Albert's, who has in fact understood nothing of the exchange.

"Gut" says the German, apparently satisfied, and they move off to continue their round.

As soon as they can, the five visitors discreetly slip towards the exit and out of the museum; unchain the bicycles and start back home for Nanterre. Coco has had a big fright; he is shaken by great sobs and can't summon up the strength to pedal, for his heart is already racing as fast as it can go. The group stops for a long while in the Bois de Boulogne to recover. His father uses the time to good effect, explaining to the bemused Albert and André the details of Coco's courageous lie to the Germans. When they get back home at last, he tells his son how proud he is of him.

The 26$^{th}$ of August 1944 is a day of national festivities, and the whole of Paris flocks to the Champs Elysees to see General de Gaulle. Around nine French and American revellers pile into a car to drive there, but it breaks down at Porte Maillot - the tyres give in under the sheer weight of the passengers! They carry onwards on foot, walking up the Avenue de la Grande Armée. On the left of the avenue, armoured vehicles are lined up facing inwards, and on their right, small reconnaissance planes have been displayed. When they arrive at Place de l'Etoile, Coco's father suggests climbing up the Arc de Triomphe for a better view. Everybody agrees to this proposition. From up at the top, the view is indeed fantastic, and Albert enviously cranes his neck to watch a squadron of Marauders fly past above their heads, saying that he would give anything to be there with them at the controls of his own plane.

The top of the Arc de Triomphe is jam-packed with crowds of Allied soldiers and civilians. A soldier is fast asleep on his back amidst the general uproar, his helmet balanced carefully on his stomach. Coco is over the moon to be there with his friends. He has high hopes of seeing General de Gaulle going down the Champs Elysees.

Suddenly, shooting breaks out down below them. Coco wants to see what is going on, so he scrambles over the parapet which surrounds the top of the Arc de Triomphe, and which is blocking his view of the action. Before he has the time to take it all in, his father drags him down to the ground as bullets ricochet off the stonework around them.

After all these events, it's time to head back home to Nanterre. The nine of them are now without a means of transport. Albert takes the situation in hand. He approaches a group of American officers, and tells them his story, turning frequently towards Coco's father as he does so. The officers approach Coco's father, shake his hand and offer him the use of a Jeep and a driver to take them home.

Coco climbs proudly into the Jeep. The Americans have told him so much about these mythical vehicles over the past few weeks that he feels at home straight away. The rejoicing goes on for days, in a whirl of new experiences: the welcome given to the American soldiers, young girls climbing up onto the tanks with flowers, and hugging the tank drivers of the Leclerc division. Jacqueline Besse, 18 years old with her superb white skirt decorated with the Ally flags.

Coco can't tell how long the non-stop post-war party lasted. He remembers the barrow-loads of Champagne arriving, recovered from villas in Neuilly occupied by the Germans, the impromptu dances, Roger dancing on his wooden leg and asking his partner if she wouldn't mind revolving in the other direction, for his leg is starting to come unscrewed.

# POSTSCRIPT

Many times between May 28, 1944 and the Liberation, I wouldn't have bet a dime on my chances of successfully evading the enemy---or even surviving. But when it was all over, I wouldn't have traded the experience for anything.

Beginning with the little man who gave me a cigarette and showed me where to hide for that first hour, virtually everybody I met provided assistance. The lone exception was the man who waved me away from his front gate on the morning of the second day.

At various times since, I have tried to establish contact with everyone in France whose names I could recall or whose home I thought I might be able to find again. In 1948, just before the Berlin Airlift, my wife, Alberta, and I visited the Bertys in Nanterre. It was my first trip to France since the war. We traveled to Carrieres-sur-Seine, and I quickly found the house I had landed on. As soon as I got out of the car, I was recognized by the elderly woman who'd come out of the same house in 1944 and spotted me shrugging out of my parachute harness. She sent her daughter-in-law out to greet me and invited us into her home where she described being interrogated by the Germans regarding my whereabouts. She said my likeness on the poster they prepared later was accurate. She knew Nicole and the old man, but said they moved immediately after the war and she didn't know where they were.

The person I contacted at the garage knew of the incident, but would not go into details. She was not one of the participants and seemed reluctant, for some reason, to talk about it. Since I didn't know their real names, the names used in the narrative are fictional. The butcher shop where the little man in the straw hat worked was no longer in business.

In Carrieres-sur-Seine, we also met Jacques, now a truck driver. He was still wearing the bracelet I gave him, but as a matter of practicality, he removed my name and engraved his own on it. At the bar, I learned that the Filipottos had sold the place and were living in the south of France. We exchanged letters with them. In the early 1950s I learned that they had both passed away.

Unable to contact the Brenners, I continued to write but lost contact in the fifties. Leslie Atkinson, the representative in France of the Air Force Escape and Evasion Society, located them for me in 1963. During a visit in 1964, I went to their village and was dismayed to discover they were away on vacation. I talked with their neighbor and left a note. Shortly after I returned to the States, the Brenners sent a long letter. The following year, we visited France again, only to find that Charles died prior to our arrival. Henriette was well and as spunky as ever, but Charles' death affected her deeply. She died a year and a half later.

In 1946, shortly after I returned to active duty, I received a letter from the twin daughters at whose home I stayed for two days. I replied, but never received an answer.

During my 1964 visit, Pierre (Coco) drove me through Versailles, Provins, and Montereau. In Montereau, a young gendarme listened carefully as Pierre related my experiences, and went out of his way to help me. He called several people to learn the real name of the man who was chief of gendarmes in 1944. After several calls, he was able to get him on the telephone. I talked with him at length and learned that Marcel was killed just as the story had been related to Marcelle. The Chief said none of the men from the camp in the woods ever returned. It was the Chief's opinion that none survived capture. And, he told me something surprising: of all the Allied flyers his group assisted, I was the only one who had returned since the war.

As we finished talking, I told him I intended to visit the village. But when I arrived at Valence-sur Seine, I realized immediately that it was not the place I was taken to by Marcel in 1944. I hadn't asked the chief the name of the village; I'd assumed the one they gave me was correct. Obviously, it was a false name, or the name of another village to prevent possible disclosure if I was captured. I am certain those stock certificates were never recovered after Andre buried them in the box. Nobody else knew he had them, and only Walt and I knew the general location of the treasure.

The people in the house at Lagny, which I located easily, knew nothing of the wartime occupants. I learned from Walt that Paul, the British agent, was killed in action in an ambush set up by the Germans three weeks after we left when someone informed on him.

I saw Mr. Paris three times during my visits. He was active throughout the war and took part in some risky missions.

I remember sitting with Walt in the camp and talking for hours trying to bring him up to date. Among other things, I described the dogfight in detail. I hoped he would recognize the squadron or group from the aircraft markings I described—but he couldn't. Two months later, in London, I couldn't remember the three-letter marking. Years later, I spent three days at the Simpson Historical Library at Maxwell Air Force Base, tracing the daily reports of every fighter squadron in the ETO during that time. I found 22 names of pilots who might have flown the Mustang. Fourteen of them were killed later in the war. I have been told that the only way I will ever be able to identify him is to find a good hypnotist and relive the experience. I'd try that if I thought it would work, because that guy was terrific.

When the Bertys first visited Redding, California in 1966, Walt and his family also stayed with us for a couple of weeks. It was a nice reunion. I kept in touch with Walt through the years, first spending a few days together in Chester, Pennsylvania, on my way to an assignment in Germany in 1947, then by phone after my return to the States. Later we lost track of one another. During the writing of this book, I looked him up again and talked to his wife, only to learn that Walt was in the hospital. I wrote a long letter to him, and three weeks later received a reply from his stepdaughter informing me that Walt died of post-operative complications.

In June 1983, I received a letter from Pierre telling me of Louis' death. He had no previous illness, but died of a sudden heart attack while working in his garden. Alberta and I were saddened to hear of his passing, for no one ever had a better friend than Louis Berty. Alberta first met him in Nanterre in 1948 and became very fond of Marcelle, Louis, and Pierre, and, later, of Pierre's wife Joselyn and their children. During my visits to France, we saw the Bertys and the Besses—and Charles who was in business for himself as a chacutier. In 1965, we met Raymond Besse, his wife, and daughter Jacqueline in Normandy. Pierre informed me that Mr. Besse died before our last visit in 1984. At that time, Pierre. Joselyn and their two wonderful children, Alexander and Christine, were living in the same house where Walt and I were grateful guests in 1944. Pierre had modified it extensively.

Last May, Pierre visited us for two weeks. Shortly after his return to France, he called to say Marcelle had become ill and was in the hospital. Ten days later, she died. We were just planning a visit to see her.

I served with Bill during the Berlin airlift and we kept in touch for a few years, but gradually lost contact. In January 1986, I picked up a copy of the Retired Officers' Association magazine and learned that Bill died the previous month.

Bud Morgan got out of prison camp, and returned to civilian life in Burlington where he joined the Air National Guard and retired a few years ago. He and his wife, Thelma, visited us in 1984. Every May 28, we call each other to talk things over.

Hickey died from flak wounds after bailing out. Zagorski spent months in a POW camp with the other captured crewmembers, but was reported missing during a forced evacuation in the face of a rapid advance of Russian troops. No other word of him was ever received. I was in brief contact with Burton and Griffith after the war but have lost track of them since.

I put off writing this book for a long time. When I retired as Director of Airports for the City of Redding in 1983, I remembered a 1956 conversation with a distinguished author. I was stationed at

Tachikawa Air Base in Japan then and I called James A. Michener, a guest at the Imperial Hotel. He graciously agreed to talk with me and when we met, asked me to relate some of the story. I did, and after a few minutes, he smiled and asked "Why not write this book yourself? Everyone has at least one book in them. All you have to do is sit down and get started." Nearly 30 years later, I did exactly that.

During World War II in the Pacific Theater and the China-Burma-India area, the Korean War, and in Vietnam, shot-down flyers had virtually no chance at evasion and faced terrible consequences when captured. Compared to them, I had a "country club" existence behind enemy lines. In France during World War II, if you could stay free for the first 24-hours, you had a 50-50 chance. From then on, you were sure to get a lot of help from the French people. I certainly did, and they have my everlasting thanks.

Henry C. Woodrum
Lt. Col. USAF (Ret.)
Redding, California
September 1987

# ADDENDUM 2021

"The Walkout Trail"
By Michael Woodrum
A journal of Remembrance and Reflection
Dedicated to my parents Henry "Hank"
Woodrum and Alberta Woodrum,
and my wife, Laurie, who allowed me to chase a dream

Dad's letter to Mike explaining he realizes his book will never
be published but passing the story on to us. Mike holding
a copy of Walkout in "Jack's Grill", Redding. 2011.

## "I know my book will never be published."
## H.C. Woodrum, Late 1980's

In the summer of 1966, Louis Berty, his wife Marcelle and son, Pierre, visited our family in Redding, California. I was 16 years old and chomping at the bit to see the world. These were the people who hid my dad during World War II. They were from a small village adjacent to Paris, Nanterre. As soon as I graduated from high school I was going to backpack across Europe, using their home as my base.

My brothers were working that summer as U.S. Forest Service firefighters and I was the only kid at home when the Bertys visited. Pierre was interested in American music, especially country and western, and we hit it off from the start. Pierre was about 30 years old. He had a passion for sailing and owned his own sailboat. He promised to take me sailing on the Mediterranean. He had a lot to show me and I looked up to him. Life has a way of interfering with plans and it wouldn't be until 2011 that I was able to make it to Paris.

Pierre was able to visit twice more in the ensuing years, once on his honeymoon with his wife, Joseline, in 1972 and once more by himself in the mid-1980s. My dad was able to visit France multiple times, sometimes with my mom, after World War II.

My dad wrote of his experience of being a downed pilot, on the run from the Nazis for 105 days. He finished his book "Walkout" in the mid-1980s. My dad died in 1990, never seeing his book published. He gave each of his sons a manuscript, so that we could understand what had happened during his journey.

In 2010, twenty years after he died, my brother, Henry "Hank" Woodrum IV, and I were able to realize dad's dream of seeing his book in print. The publishing of the book started a new chapter for myself and my brother, and new associations with people in France. In 2011 we were on our way to visit with the Berty family.

## "April in Paris"
## Count Basie

April in Paris! I was about to embark on the biggest adventure of my life. My wife, Laurie, and I flew out of San Francisco and met my sister-in-law, Pat in Houston, Texas. We were flying with her and would meet up with Hank in Paris. Hank was a marathon runner and coach and his team was already in Paris, where they had run the Paris Marathon a few days earlier. We had a wonderful but long flight. I had a window seat as we crossed the English Channel and the farm fields of France come into view. Much the same view that dad might have witnessed on May 28, 1944. My excitement was palpable.

We arrived at Charles De Gaulle Airport and the adventure was underway. We navigated the airport and found a cab. Our destination was the Pont Royal Hotel in the Saint-Germain Arrondissement or district of Paris. We hurried to check in and grab another cab; we were running late to meet Pierre. We were meeting Pierre at a tobac shop near a central metro station. We ended up missing our connection to meet Pierre and Joseline, arriving an hour late at the shop. With no way to reach them, I was getting anxious. While we were waiting at the shop, hoping that they were running late as well, who should pull up but the cab driver who had taken us from the airport to the hotel. In a city of millions, we ran into the same cab driver twice in the span of three hours. It was just the start of amazing coincidences that seemed to figure large in all our trips to France. We didn't meet up with Pierre that day and we headed back to the hotel. Jet lag had reared its ugly head and it was time for sleep.

Pierre called in the early evening and we made arrangements to meet again at the tobac shop the next day. The next morning, we were waiting anxiously at the shop. Would we recognize Pierre? Then he came around the corner and there we all were, somewhat speechless for a moment and then grateful that this moment had arrived. Joseline was waiting in the car and we had to hurry to get there because she was in a no parking zone. Pierre was no longer able to drive due to health reasons so Joseline was doing the driving. We all piled into a small French car;

four Americans, who had no idea where we were going, and our two French hosts.

After about an hour we arrived at the house in Nanterre. It was how I pictured it: stone walled, gated, leading into a driveway, with the butcher shop on the left and the house on the right.

We were treated as welcome guests; sangria was poured along with a light appetizer tray. As soon as that course was done, it was on to champagne and a different set of appetizers. Finally, it was red wine and dinner time. It was a typical French kitchen, tiny by any standards, let alone American standards; an apartment-size refrigerator, and the cooking space enough for only one. We ate a wonderful meal, one of many at this table in the next few days. When the cheese course arrived, we thought the evening was winding down.

All of the sudden, Pierre announced that we were going on the Seine River sightseeing cruise. Over the next 10 days it was like that. We balanced our time between the Bertys and when they were busy, we were on our own. They took us to the Notre Dame Cathedral, the Sainte-Chapelle Chapel, the Eiffel Tower and the museum where dad and Pierre had their run-in with the Nazis. It was closed due to renovations.

Hank and I, with our wives, went to Shakespeare and Company bookstore. It's an English-speaking bookstore that was a haven for all the writers and artists that flocked to the Left Bank in Paris after World War I. Hemingway and Fitzgerald had spent days and nights there. A treasured place, indeed for all expatriates and now we had arranged to have dad's book for sale on the shelf of this storied place. His book was now on the shelf in the city and country that he had come to consider his adopted homeland. Paris was turning into everything we could have imagined.

But for all the wonderful sights in Paris, the most memorable were the moments that we shared with the Berty Family. On our second night at their home, Christine and Clement arrived, Pierre's daughter and grandson. They lived in Moisson, a village about 50 miles west of Paris. Along with them, two large dogs were in tow. A friend of Pierre's who grew up in the neighborhood as a youth, Paul Blanc also visited.

Paul was a businessman, who lived in the south of France, but traveled to Paris during the work week. He had met my dad on previous visits, dating all the way back to the 1960's. The little room was overwhelmed with people, speaking a language we couldn't understand, the hustle and bustle of another great meal being prepared, and of course wine and more wine.

One afternoon Pierre asked if we wanted to watch a home movie that had my dad and Walt in it. Amazing! Yes! Soon enough they had an old projector and a can of film that dated back to the early 1930s. Neither had been used in years and Pierre and Christine had difficulties getting it rigged up. Pierre finally called a neighbor to come over and help. It was quite a scene, the three of them, speaking in French, trying to get the movie going, all the while the film is pooling at their feet and a cat getting ready to bat the film with its paw. I was fearing the worst but the movie came on. It started with a visit to a zoo and worked its way forward. Finally, the war years, Pierre and friend playing on a scooter, then playing with a homemade wooden machine gun. Then members of the local underground were at the house playing ping pong and generally cutting up. Then my dad and Walt came out of the house, the same house I'm sitting in. They were only on film for a short time. My dad had just turned 26 years old while in France, he was rail thin. It was an emotional time for all of us but especially for Hank and I. We were seeing our dad not as our father, but as a young man, frozen in time.

**"Michael, you came too late."**
**Pierre Berty, April 2011**

Pierre at one time had a very passable knowledge of English, but with the passage of time, he had to search for the right words. Sitting around the same wooden table where our fathers had broken bread over 60 years ago, not much was lost in translation. It was the universal language of friendship and emotion. Paul and Christine were helping translate when needed, the topics were far ranging, both in English and French. We talked about his trip in 1966 to Redding and how I was going to visit. With the decades taking their toll on all of us, Pierre broke my heart when he said, "Michael, you came too late." The fleeting passing of youth and time had indeed passed us by, the days of dreaming of sailing boats were long in the past.

We were able to visit the beaches of Normandy and the cemetery of Colleville-sur-Mer. And we were able to be tourists in the City of Lights. It was very difficult to leave. We had come to visit friends and had instead found family. We promised to visit within the next two years. This was one promise I wasn't going to break.

## Red Taillights...... dawn, leaving Redding
## May 26, 2013

In the early winter of 2012, Hank and I were starting to plan our return trip to France. At first, our wives were planning to go, but somewhere that got changed to just the two brothers going. It was now much more than a journey; it had become a pilgrimage.

We had a block of days that my wife, Laurie, had to reserve in advance as vacation days, to lock them in for her work. So, we did and then the wives decided to stay behind. Hank and I booked the plane and hotel reservations in early February. Pierre knew we were coming and now we were just counting down the days. When I saw the dates on the reservation paperwork something clicked in my head. I got my copy of "Walkout" and confirmed what I had thought. We were due in Paris on May 28, 2013, 69 years to the day that dad had bailed out over the outskirts of Paris.

In April, we received news that Pierre had suffered a heart attack and was in the hospital. Sadly, he passed away three weeks later. One week before we arrived, his service was held. The Bertys assured us that they still wanted us to come.

We had heard of a Frenchman named Franck Signorile through my parents' best friends, Bill and Anne Nicol. Anne had sent a copy of "Walkout" to Franck in 2010 and Franck had taken it upon himself to research the book. He had retraced many places and events and we would meet him soon.

I left my home in Redding, California at 5:45 a.m., May 26, 2013. It was cool in the dawn air, as morning clouds filled the sky to the east. Streaks of red and orange sunlight filtered in. As I stretched and looked skyward, the whole experience washed over me. A lone small plane flew east, framed by two trees, its red taillights blinking into the clouds.

Had a day to myself in San Francisco, so I took in a San Francisco Giants baseball game. They got down 0-2 in the first inning but came back to win in the ninth inning on an Angel Pagan inside-the-park home run.

It had been a long rainy season in France and the Seine was swollen to nearly flood stage. Hank and I were staying at Hotel Luxembourg in the Montparnasse Arrondissement. Many nice restaurants and bistros in the area. Le Select was a great old place and I felt like an expatriate, sitting outside and watching the world flow by. We ate there several times and struck up a friendship with our waiter, Jeremy. He asked what we were doing in Paris and he loved our generational story. Before we left, we gave him a book.

The trip was very hectic and bittersweet. We alternated between Joseline and Franck being our tour guides. Christine was also a constant. She and Clement were staying at the house in Nanterre, helping Joseline. When we first saw Christine at our hotel, she told us more of the circumstances of Pierre's passing. I had forgotten how much English she knew. We let her talk and get her emotions out.

We met Franck on our first Saturday and he had a full itinerary planned. He greeted us as close friends which we were soon to become. He had found the apartment in Versailles and several other places, the most significant being the room above the bar where dad stayed in the first part of his journey. It was still a bar and restaurant, Canadian Corner, in Carrieres-sur-Seine. We had a wonderful meal and after the lunch rush we had a conversation with the owner. Well, Franck did. The owner didn't know much about the history of the place, but he knew enough to confirm that we were, indeed, at the right place. We still found it hard to believe that we were sitting in the same place where my dad stayed almost to the day some 69 years before. The upstairs was now the office so we weren't able to go upstairs.

Both Joseline and Franck took us on side trips to find the house where dad's parachute landed but we could never locate it. One Saturday, Joseline picked us up and we headed for Moisson where Christine lived, about an hour outside of Paris. It was one of those spring days that takes your breath away. Drove through a part of Paris that was mostly parks with families walking and biking, enjoying the bright sun after a long winter.

The house in Moisson was built by Pierre and Joseline as a summer retreat in the 1970s. It still had the thatched roof, one of the very few left in the area. It was on the banks of the Seine. Christine and Joseline cooked a simple meal outside on a hibachi grill; rice, beef, potatoes and of course cheese and bread. Of all the meals that I've eaten in France I think this one was the best. Very simple, very magnificent! Christine had much to do because she not only helped cook but she also had to translate.

That evening Joseline was tired and asked if one of us wanted to drive back to Paris. Having a love for driving I jumped at the chance. I drove the whole way back and even navigated the Arc de Triomphe roundabout. Only got lost once, close to the hotel.

## "A Free Man in Paris"
## Song by Joni Mitchell

On the sixth night in Paris, lying in bed at the Hotel Luxembourg, with the windows open, I drifted into sleep. The noise from the street, cars and motorbikes, formed a rush of sound like water flowing down a stream. The foreign language, that was foreign only to me, drifted into the room, and filled my mind with an intoxicating feeling. I was alive. I was in Paris.

We had entered "Walkout" in a book competition and the awards dinner was in Paris. We invited Joseline to go with us. It was a great evening, about 10 authors were there from all over the world. Interestingly enough, Hank and I were the only men. We all told stories about our books. They were all captivated by our story and very caring toward Joseline. It turned into a dinner among friends. We stayed about an hour past the time it was supposed to end. Joseline wouldn't let us take a cab back to our hotel, insisting on driving us back herself.

The next couple of days were a whirlwind of activity. We were still trying to track down the house where dad's parachute landed. Also, in the 60's Pierre had sent dad an article in the newspaper about a museum in Cormeilles that had wreckage from his place crash. When we visited the museum, they had no knowledge of the crash site wreckage.

We visited an old French fort that the Germans had taken over. This was the site that they used to launch their flak attack on dad's plane. It was now a relic of another era, open only at certain times of the year. But that didn't deter Franck. He knocked on the fort's wooden doors and got the attention of a caretaker. After telling him our story, we were allowed in for a quick tour. We were able to see the flak bunkers.

We met the Busnel family. Antoinette and her two step-brothers, Remi and Alain. Antoinette was a young girl during the war and she remembered going to view the wreckage the day after the crash. We had a wonderful lunch with them at a café, where we sat outside and watched the swollen Seine roll by.

When we had some free time, we were able to cross some items off our bucket list; Went to a jazz club in Montparnasse; took in The French Open, where we watched Serena Williams win her semi-final match; she later won the championship; and we took a trip by high-speed rail to Lyon. My co-worker, Denise Rapinoe, was visiting her daughter, Megan, who was under contract for the Lyon soccer team. Megan had just won the Gold Medal with the US Women's National Team at the 2012 London Olympics. It was early in her career, which would turn out to be an illustrious one. Denise, her sister and sister-in-law, were visiting Megan and we went for a daytrip to visit them and to see Megan. We explored the old section of town. A beautiful city, all the charm of Paris but not all of the crowds. We had a great visit. Megan was enjoying being with her family. Another example of how small the world actually is.

Sadly, this trip would be the last time we would see Joseline. She passed away in 2016 after a brave fight with cancer. She was a loving and caring woman and will be missed.

## Redding, California, 2014

In early 2014, Franck was planning a family trip to the United States. I was eagerly awaiting their arrival. Hank and Pat and their grandson, Connor, were also traveling to Redding from Arizona.

Franck had never stopped doing research of "Walkout" and we were excited to learn of any new finding.

We had a wonderful visit. A day on a patio boat at Whiskeytown Lake and many side trips, including a visit to an old mining town, French Gulch.

French Gulch is home to a bar, E. Franck and Company, which is more of a museum than bar. Filled with all sorts of western and local artifact it has been owned by the same family since the gold rush days.

I've found that foreigners appreciate the U.S. West and the national park system. This was true for Franck as well. We could have spent much longer in French Gulch but dinner was waiting.

Before he left for home Franck gave Hank and I each a binder that contained the day-to-day details of our dad's time behind enemy lines, all that Franck had compiled at that point. What a gift!

I was working as a bartender and part owner of an iconic Redding restaurant, Jack's Grill, which has been a Redding landmark since it opened in 1938. I've been there since 1979.

In December of 2015 a high school French teacher, Tami Bennett, and her husband Chad came in to buy a copy of "Walkout." It was my first night back after a three-month recuperation from shoulder surgery. Tami wanted to send the book to her former student, Mady Dubre-Beduneau as a Christmas present. Mady had been a foreign exchange student about ten years before. Now married to Charles, she was an English teacher living in Carrieres-sur-Seine, the same town where dad's parachute landed. Both Mady and Charles read the book and speculated on the location of the house. We began to correspond and were able to meet in February 2017, when they visited Redding.

**Bargemaster Report**
**Athis-Mons France, April-May 2018**

Hank and I went back to Paris in April of 2018. With every trip we felt less like tourists and more like pilgrims. Franck had done more research and had much more to show us.

About a month before we left, we ordered tee shirts commemorating "The Walkout Trail" that we were about to go on. We ordered enough for our French family.

We booked an Airbnb in Athis-Mons, a suburb of Paris, close to where Franck lived. Orly Airport is near Athis-Mons, so that's where we were flying into. The Airbnb was part of a large brick house. A small apartment with a large balcony overlooking the Seine. What a view. I could sit drinking wine, beer or whatever else was on hand and watch the plentiful barge traffic that plied the river. In France, barges do much of the work that trucks do in America. I was soon fascinated by watching the coming and goings of barges.

I had arrived a few days ahead of Hank and it was a hard journey this time. My flight from San Francisco had been delayed and when I landed at Orly, my bags didn't. At least Franck was there to greet me. Franck had a car for my disposal and after a hurried driving lesson and a trip to the Food Mark, I was now at the Airbnb.

When it was time to pick up Hank he was nowhere to be found, but my bags had arrived. I had missed Hank by minutes and our cell phones weren't in sync yet. I drove back to the Airbnb and Hank was waiting on the doorstep. Christine and Clement arrived the next morning and it was a great reunion. Clement was now a young man of 16 and Christine was the same as ever. We were going to spend the day in Paris.

The section of Paris that we were in was an area that Christine had spent her university days, living in. It was a beautiful Saturday and the small streets were bustling. We ate at a small café that was a favorite of Christine's back in the day. It was an old-style café with an old neon sign of a martini glass and an old Coca Cola sign, looked like something from the '50s or '60s. Had a great meal of chicken and rice.

My wife and I loved the Pelforth beer brand, it reminded me of my favorite beer back home and Laurie liked it because its logo was a pelican. Later that day we passed another sidewalk café when there was a Pelforth glass on the table. I was soon on a mission; I was on a hunt and wouldn't be denied. I went up to the first employee I found and asked if I could buy the glass and another one as well. She had no idea and didn't want to get involved. I went to the barman and I explained that I needed to buy two glasses. He said he would have to call his boss and get the okay to sell the glasses to a crazy old Americano, who hadn't even bought a beer. The boss gave his okay and said just give them to me. After 42 years of bartending, I felt a brotherhood. I too have been in similar situations at Jack's when people want to buy an ordinary glass as a remembrance of a great time. With a nod of my head, I would give them the glass. I appreciated the young barman and the anonymous owner, a band of brothers united by the code of the bar. I gave him a hearty handshake along with 5 euros and my Jack's Grill business card.

We had a great day with the Bertys. I marveled at how much Clement had grown, both physically and emotionally since we had met him in 2011. He said he had learned much of his English from reading "Walkout." He also said he learned much more of his family's history through the book too. Like men of that era his grandfather, Pierre, hadn't talked much about the war.

Walking back to the car, we saw a poster in the subway announcing the revival of the play "An American in Paris." We were struck by that and then noticed the date the play was to open, "May 28". Seventy-four years to the day my dad became an American in Paris. Just another in a series of coincidences.

**Clement and Christine with the poster announcing opening of the play on May 28, the day dad became an American in Paris.**

We drove back to Athis-Mons and had dinner in a 1960s classic-style restaurant. Big, many dining rooms, a suburban oasis. You could chew the atmosphere. Lines of people, big parties of multi-generational families, noisy and fun. After dinner Christine dropped us off at the flat, an end to a perfect day. Tomorrow we walk with the ghosts of World War II.

Woke up at 6:30, had my coffee on the balcony before sunrise. What a morning. Streaks of pink from the east, a few clouds in the sky and the river below. The section of the Seine where we were, the river is a lazy stroll except for the current leading into the diversion dam. The barges pass through the locks in the calm water while the rest of the river flows over the dam.

Franck was due in a couple of hours and we would start our Walkout Trail in earnest. We were going to duplicate, as much as possible, dad's trip to the camp. We stopped in Montereau, the town where dad spent the night in the police station. It was across the street from where the Germans had set up regional command headquarters in a historic magnificent hotel. It's a beautiful river town, it's also where dad witnessed the attack on the three German barges by the Canadian fighter planes.

Further along we came to the village of Valence. We pulled into a driveway and met a wonderful couple named Daniel and Danielle. They were local historians who knew of the maquis camp and of the memorial to Andre Taboulet.

We talked over a four-course lunch. Listening to Madame Danielle and Franck speak rapid French was like watching two jazz musicians trading riffs back and forth. They were excitedly exchanging information on what they knew. Every so often Franck would interpret for us. Demitasse coffee was served, strong and slightly bitter. We would need the caffeine because after a two-hour lunch, our task was at hand, we were going to do what we had come to France to do. Remember and honor our dad and the courageous French citizens who had sacrificed so much.

We drove east through a much smaller village. A village that played a major role in the story, it was the village closest to the maquis camp. We continued down a side road; off in the distance you could see a memorial nestled between the fields and the woods. We stopped and made our way on foot towards the memorial to Andre Taboulet. Andre was the leader of the camp and was killed the day after dad and Walt left the camp. We had purchased flowers and we placed them there with Andre. It was an emotional moment in a long emotional process. One that would be played out many times in the next two weeks.

The next few days we spent in Angers and Nantes. Mady and Charles now lived in Angers and they are from Nantes. Separated by about an hour, they are both charming old-world cities. They both have castles in the old section of town. We visited both of them. They have been restored to their glory. While in Angers we visited Mady's English-speaking class, where we told our dad's story to three different classes. They seemed interested and at the end of the class a student from the first class came back and talked with us. He was very interested and wanted to get a book. I promised I would send him one, which I did.

We left Angers by car with Mady, heading back to Athis-Mons and then to Paris. She and I had a long conversation about many and all things. She had much the same ideas that I had at her age. In Paris, we were to meet Charles and his mother, Nicole Dubre-Chirat, an assemblywoman from the Angers district. The assembly wasn't in session and she had arranged a tour of The Assemblée Nationale. A city in itself, the Palais Bourbon, dates back to 1728. It was a magnificent maze of buildings. Everywhere you look was an amazing example of art and architecture, in the style of Versailles. We were very fortunate to tour such a place.

The following day, a Saturday, was to be a very special day. We were to visit what we had been searching for all these years. Franck arrived in the morning and we headed to the Canadian Corner restaurant, where we met up with Christine and Clement. We started walking and soon we were joined by Mady and Charles. We all just happened to be wearing our black Walkout Trail tee shirts. For indeed we were on the trail. After about 30 minutes of walking, we found ourselves at the gate of the house where my dad's parachute landed. We stood and soaked up the moment. It was across from a metro station that Mady and Charles had used many times. Franck rang the bell and soon we were greeted by the owners. A couple in their 30's, they welcomed us with open arms. They let us tour the house and yard and gave us a history of their ownership. The house was very similar to the picture that we have from 1947, when dad visited on his return to France, while he was stationed in post-war Germany. Franck kept looking at his watch anxiously and hurried us along. We had much to do. We started walking again. Hank and I lagged behind the group and were talking about what we had just seen. Up ahead Franck was talking to some residents of the neighborhood. We caught up with them and were introduced to Daniele, the two-year-old girl from the book. Her mother was the first person to help my dad. She had fed and hid him in her basement on his first night in France. What an unexpected moment, Franck had told us nothing of the day's events except for the house visit.

The house that Daniele lived in during the war was no longer her home but she still knew some of the neighbors. Since the old house was vacant, we couldn't go onto the grounds, so one of her friends let us onto her deck so we could see into the yard. The yard where my dad hid much of his first day. Suddenly, this old man, Henri, came from the house and saw us peering into his son's yard and asked us what we were doing.

He had just turned up that day to check on his son's house. When he heard our story, he allowed us in to tour the yard and property. The basement was off limits because it was full. Daniele showed us where dad hid from the Germans, huddled under a shrub next to the fence. We spent some time there and when we were getting ready to leave, I think it was Charles who again asked if we could visit the basement. Henri agreed to let Hank and I go down and spend time in this sacred place. It was more of a cathedral for me. I felt my dad's presence. Not as my dad but as a young man.

After we said goodbye to Henri, we started back to Canadian Corner, when Daniele said she couldn't have lunch with us. She had to visit her mother, Simone, who was a resident in a nearby convalescent hospital. Yes, she was still alive at 98 years old. Daniele said she would talk with her mother and see if she would be up for a visit next week. Couldn't believe the events of the day and it was only lunchtime.

Franck had called ahead and they had a table set up for us. Two other families were there and when we came in wearing our Walkout shirts, they were very inquisitive. We told them our story and we bonded immediately. Hank and I recognized the owner from our visit in 2013, and he welcomed us with open arms. After a few beers and great lunch, we thought the day was over with.

We wouldn't see Mady and Charles again on this trip. Mady and Charles, who I had known only a short time, but we had shared so much in that time that I felt like I was saying goodbye to family.

Mady, who was an exchange student in Redding 14 years earlier, fell in love with the area. Then reads a book while living in Carrieres about a downed pilot from Redding who parachuted into the village of Carrieres and a kinship is made for life. Charles and I had a conversation and said goodbye and then it was time to say goodbye to Mady. It was an emotional long hug, the traditional kisses on the cheeks and then we spoke of staying connected and how much we meant to each other. I have come to feel like she was a daughter in some ways. A poignant moment and I know our paths will cross again.

As Franck, Hank and I were driving away in his van with Christine and Clement following in their car, I could tell Franck had more up his sleeve. In 2013, we had visited a museum in Cormeilles-en-Parisis, which is the town where his plane actually crashed. We again arrived at this museum and out comes Remi Busnel and a couple in their late thirties, Xavier and Stephanie. Huge smiles and I'm trying to remember if we had met them before. We hadn't but Franck had found them through his research. Xavier was Bill's French grandson and Stephanie was his wife!! What's more, in all the towns of France that they could have lived in, they resided in the same village where dad's plane had crashed.

After the greeting we were ushered into the museum by the curator. She showed us a new exhibit that they were proud of. Then we were taken into a smaller room, where a small table was set up. Several small items and a manila envelope were sitting on the table. French writing was on the envelope and on placards next to the items. Franck asked if we knew what we were looking at. It took me a moment and then yes, I did indeed.

When we visited this museum in 2013, they didn't know about the wreckage. Stephanie who knew Franck and lives less than a mile from the museum worked with another curator and they had located the wreckage in storage.

When I realized what I was looking at, tears and emotions welled up. It was a small piece of sheet metal, a piece of my dad's plane. Along with the piece of metal were fragments of bullets and flak. The notice on the envelope had description of the crash, along with the date and names of the crewmembers.

A sense of private and public reflection. I felt much the same way as I did in the basement, a sense of peace and inner jubilation. I caught the eye of my new friend Xavier and I could tell he was very happy to be sharing this moment. I also, caught the eye of Christine; our fathers had shared moments and now we had one. Pictures were being taken as Hank and I passed the metal back and forth. A shared moment between two brothers who had started this journey ten years before, never knowing where it would lead. Never imagining it would lead to this. The day where it all started for my dad, to the house he landed on, to the toddler who saw my dad hiding in her yard, from a dark, dusty cellar, walking from that cellar and following a bicycle up a hill, hoping it would lead to a safe place. And now holding part of his plane. As we were leaving the room, I touched the metal one last time, it was in a safe and lasting place, a place of honor and respect.

After leaving the museum we went to Xavier and Stephanie's home about a mile away and had a short visit. We toasted champagne and talked of the events of the day and thanked them for working with the museum.

Then we started the long reflective drive back to Athis-Mons. On the way through Paris Hank mentioned that he had seen what looked like writing etched on one side of the sheet metal. Neither Franck nor I had noticed it. In checking my photos, I was able to enlarge it and sure enough it was there. Franck translated it, "Plane shot down by German flak on May 28, 1944. Cormeilles-en-Parisis," there was a name also, but we couldn't make it out.

Hank and I were drained emotionally. Franck had to drive and stay alert but the day's events had taken a toll on him as well. He takes great joy and pride in helping people connect and discovering their family history.

Arriving back in Athis-Mons, Hank and I talked into the night. A few beers and a shot of Jack Daniels later, we finished off the day. And what a day it was.

After resting on Sunday and Monday we went to the Berty home in Nanterre, where we were to meet Christine. After the passing of Joseline, the house had been put up for sale. Now the house was in escrow but we would have one last visit. The house was still intact but some of the outbuildings were already being torn down. Gone were the garage and Louis's butcher shop, which Pierre turned into his painting studio. Some of his paintings were stashed in one room. The rooms were mostly empty, with little evidence that this house was once full of much joy and history. We walked the property, trying to soak up all that we could. A final bittersweet photo of the three of us in front of the gate.

We followed Christine to Moisson, where we were to spend a few days. It was a long and winding road, no freeways for Christine. Followed her for about 40 minutes and then we came to a bakery. Christine went in to buy some bread. There was a roadside flower stand set up in honor of May Day so I went over and bought some flowers for Christine. In the next three days, we were constantly busy but never rushed. We would soon visit Les Andelys, Normandy and the home of Claude Monet.

Christine would drive and we had great talks, much like the talks that Mady and I had.

The castle in Les Andelys, Chateau-Gaillard, sits upon a bluff above the picturesque river town. It had a commanding view of the Seine and of any army forces going down river to Paris. Unlike the two other castles that we visited, this one sat in arrested decay.

The next day we set off for Normandy. It was going to take about three hours under rainy and windy conditions. We stopped at the Pegasus Bridge, a key component in the D-Day invasion. It was the duty of the British paratroopers to take the bridges out in the local area.

We soon arrived at the American Cemetery in Colleville-Sur-Mer. My second visit and it was still humbling to walk its hollowed grounds. We went to the visitor's center, reading the history and personal stories of the men who perished there on the beaches. The scope of the invasion, the bravery, the toll that it took and the price that was paid.

The moment I walked outside into the cemetery I was struck by what I didn't feel; the wind. The wind and the rain had stopped. The dark clouds were giving way to the sun over the English Channel. Walking the cliffs above the beaches, the green lawn and the white crosses, we paid our respects to the fallen. As we were leaving the wind and the rain resumed.

The next day we went to Giverny, the estate of Claude Monet. With its beautiful expansive gardens, home and artwork, it was a visual feast. Painting played a part of both my dad and Pierre's lives. I have numerous paintings of both in my home and so does Christine.

On Friday, Hank and I had to go back to Athis-Mons, Saturday we were to visit with Simone. Another long goodbye to Clement, he was leaving to go on vacation on Saturday.

On Saturday morning Franck met us at the apartment. It had been an emotional trip, beyond anything that I could have envisioned and this was going to be the encore. We stopped at the Canadian Corner but they were closed. Found another place and had a great lunch. Tried to buy the beer glasses, but the barman said no. I guess he didn't understand the code.

I was nervous entering the convalescent hospital. I didn't know what to expect. A beautiful older woman was sitting in a big chair. Wide-open pleasant face. Introductions were made by Daniele. Simone was immediately back in 1944, when she came out of her back door and found an American pilot hiding in her shrubs. Simone started speaking in French, telling how my dad wanted to smoke a cigarette and she had to tell him no. The Nazi's would smell the smoke. Then a story that my dad didn't know about; how the Germans lined her family against a wall and threatened to shoot them all if they didn't tell what they knew. I was holding Simone's hand as she was telling her story, attempting to hold back tears. By the end of her story, she and I were both shedding tears. We talked as much as time would allow. Daniele had brought champagne and cookies to celebrate the occasion. We left Simone and had a longer visit with Daniele in the parking lot.

The visit with Simone was on our last full day in France, which seemed only fitting. We were to fly back to the United States the next day. That evening Franck and his two daughters came for a visit. We talked on the balcony about all the amazing things that had happened during our three-week visit. This whole journey and this trip especially, was filled with one last times and tremendous coincidences. Landing in Paris on May 28, 2013, the date on the "American in Paris" poster; Mady's connection to Redding and Carrieres; the old man emerging from a vacant house; meeting Xavier and Stephanie in the same village where the museum was located. So many coincidences I can't even speak of them all.

World War II is still very much a part of the fabric of lives in France. From the murals on the walls of the homes and buildings in Normandy, to the streets named after famous and obscure heroes. Almost everyone who heard our story, related one of their own. It's only a generation removed for most people.

After Franck and his daughters left, we finished packing and cleaning up our apartment, of course that meant finishing up the beer, wine and Jack Daniels. Franck and Christine were driving us to the Orly Field in the morning.

Franck dropped us off and said goodbye, but Christine stayed with us as long as possible. Then it was time to say goodbye, another in a series of long goodbyes.

When Hank and I started this project in 2009 we had no other objective than to publish our dad's story. We never could have imagined what was to happen to both of us. Three trips to France and the wonderful friendships that have evolved. How events from 1944 played such an important part still. Something magical happened to us in the last 11 years. It has taken on a story of its own.

In June of 2018, I enrolled in an oil painting class. I thoroughly enjoy the process of painting. Not sure of the talent but the passion is there. Many of my paintings have depicted my memories of France.

In August of 2018, we got word that Simone had passed away. Daniele said our visit was one of her last good moments.

Also in August, Mady visited Redding, California. We had a disastrous fire in and around town and Mady came back to check on her American families. She is now translating "Walkout" into French. When she is done Hank and I are determined to get it published in France.

In the fall of 2019, the house in Moisson was sold and no longer in the Berty family.

Franck has gone on to help numerous American families retrace their father's or grandfather's time in France during World War II.

I want to thank all of the French citizens who risked their lives in helping my dad and the many other airmen and soldiers, who found themselves behind enemy lines in World War II. In particular, Louis and Marcelle Berty, an ordinary butcher and his wife, a heroic couple as ever could be found. And their little boy, Pierre, who grew to be a man as soon as he was born.

I want to thank the wonderful people of France who reached out and welcomed us with open arms. The historians, Daniel and Danielle. To the owners of both the houses that figured so prominently. To the owners of the Canadian Corner restaurant, to Daniele and Simone, from the first day to the last day of the journey. To Mady and Charles Dubre-Beduneau. To the Berty family, Christine, her brother Alexandre and her son, Clement. And last, Franck Signorile, a man whose unstoppable determination brought this group together. I will always be grateful.

Michael Woodrum
March, 2021

Dad in his old bedroom of Berty home, 1964.

Pat, Hank & Mike with Joseline and Pierre Berty in 2011

Front of Berty home in Nanterre, 2011

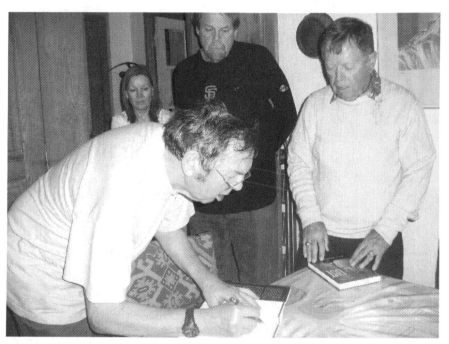

Pierre signing copy of Walkout at dining table
with Laurie and Mike and Hank, 2011

Mike in dad's bedroom with Pierre's paintings, 2011

## Mady's Story

August 7th 2004 - A few days after my eighteenth birthday I boarded a plane and flew halfway across the world, leaving everything and everyone I knew behind to start a new adventure. I was on my way to Redding, this little town in Northern California I had never heard of before.

I was glad my twenty-hour-journey was over when the small plane landed, but that feeling didn't last very long. I stepped out of the plane and it suddenly felt like I was entering an oven. It was about 110°F. At that moment I felt completely panicked at the thought of spending a year in this little town. I panicked even more when I tried to communicate with people who spoke a different English than the one I had learned in school. They spoke so fast; I just remember hearing sounds but none of them made any sense to me the first few weeks. I didn't have to tell people I didn't understand what they were saying; they already knew, so instead, I smiled, feeling like a complete idiot.

I was an exchange student with the Rotary Club (Redding East) because I wanted to learn English, go to an American school, discover a new culture and meet new people. I had no idea how much this year spent in Redding would change my life and have a major impact on me.

Shasta High School's graduation ceremony took place on June 3rd 2005, and two days later I was on a plane on my way back to France.

This American chapter never ended because I am still in touch with some friends and the parents of the two host families I lived with became my American moms and dads. Redding still feels like home.

In 2014, my husband Charles got a job in La Défense[1] so we moved to a little town we didn't know called Carrières-sur-Seine.

In July 2015, our friends Tami and Chad B. visited us in Carrières-sur-Seine. Tami was my French teacher at Shasta High, but over the years we became close friends. Chad started telling us about a book he had read. The story was about a USAF pilot from Redding whose mission was to bomb bridges along the Seine River during the second World War. Chad said the book made him think of us because the pilot

---

[1] The Business District in Paris

had landed on the roof of a house located in Carrières-sur-Seine. What are the odds?

I made a mental note to read that book.

Christmas Eve 2015 - I unwrapped a present and there it was, "Walkout". Charles couldn't help reading it before he wrapped it for me. Mike (whom I didn't know then) had signed it.

The story really moved me, mostly because it reminded me of all the stories my grandparents told me when I was younger. Two of them were teenagers during the Occupation and the other two were about ten or so, but they remembered everything, the good and the bad.

I decided to translate the book without telling anyone. I sent a long letter to Mike along with a mediocre translation of the prologue and the postscript. Mike and I communicated through emails for about a year before we met on February 14, 2017 in Redding. That day, we had lunch at Corbett's. I can't remember who got there first but I remember seeing a giant. I was so overwhelmed that I couldn't speak a single word of English. Suddenly it was August 7, 2004 all over again, so I just looked at him and his wife Laurie, smiled and once again felt like an idiot. A few minutes later, I handed Mike a dozen pages stapled together. Mike doesn't speak French but he understood right away what "Chapitre 3" meant. His eyes filled with tears and I saw how important the book was to him and his family.

We talked about my year in Redding as an exchange student, and we realized that their daughter and I attended the same school at the same time, but since she was a junior and I was a senior, we didn't have any classes together. Funnily enough, it didn't feel like I had just met Mike and Laurie; it felt like I was having lunch with friends whom I hadn't seen in years.

In April 2018, Mike and his brother Hank came to France for a visit. I asked them if they would like to come to my school and make a presentation about the book. They liked the idea. The day before they came, I organized a game in class. My students had clues and they had to guess the surprise I had prepared for them. The groups whose guess was correct thought it was a joke. How could it be true? Two Americans would be coming to their school to talk about their dad, a former USAF pilot who served during World War two - impossible. Five minutes before the bell rang, I told them about Mike and Hank. I remember how excited they were; that was exactly what I was hoping for.

That same afternoon, Mike and Hank arrived in Angers, where I now live with my husband. It was the first time we met Hank.

The following morning, we went to school together in my small - French - car. I was so grateful they had agreed to come. We had prepared a Power Point for the students with pictures. Mike and Hank spoke slowly so that my students could understand them and I eventually translated a thing or two. I loved seeing how captivated they all were. Many of them told me Mike and Hank's visit was their best memory of that school year.

A few days later, we went to Paris where we met Franck, Christine and Clément. Franck had planned an amazing day for all of us in Carrières-sur-Seine, starting with the visit of the house Henry landed on in May 1944. I realized that I had passed this house almost every single day for two years without knowing it was "THE" house. It was the same thing for the Canadian Corner.

Franck's extraordinary hard work paid off because he managed to find many people and places mentioned by Henry in the book.

Four months later, in August 2018, I went back to Redding to visit my friends and family. Of course, the Woodrums were on my list of people I really wanted to see. Mike, Laurie and I got together for lunch at Woody's, then Mike took me to visit his dad's grave at the Redding Memorial Park. It was very peaceful. A few deer were enjoying the shade provided by the trees on this hot summer afternoon. I was really surprised because that is not the kind of thing we see in France; deer are at the zoo or out in the mountains but not in a cemetery.

I asked Mike if I could read a chapter I had translated. He chose the postscript. We sat by his father's grave and I read the French translation while Mike tried to follow with the English version. I was so overwhelmed that both my hands and my voice were shaking. I was also dizzy from the Redding heat. I treasure this memory because it was a very special moment. I do hope I'll come back and read the whole book in French one day.

I speak English but I'm not a translator so this project has been a real challenge for me. Reading and translating the book brought me more than I expected. I knew next to nothing about aeronautics and the German artillery. I met some people I never expected to meet and I made friends along the way. I don't have a faith and I don't believe in destiny either. However, when I think about all these coincidences, I can't help reconsidering it all.

Mady Dubre-Beduneau

**Mady and Mike on her visit to Redding in 2018.**

Mike and Franck at the apartment building in Versailles, 2013

Franck at the Canadian Corner, 2013

Antoinette Busnel pointing out the crash site where
she saw the plane shortly after it crashed. It narrowly
missed the school building behind her. 2013

Mike and Hank with Christine, Clement, and Joseline
Berty after our last lunch together, 2013

## Reflections of Hank Jr.

As kids, we grew up on Air Force bases surrounded by men who had served during World War II and were still actively serving. I just assumed that everyone's dad had served in the war, just like my dad and all the other dads that I knew. I became aware of dad's experience during the war, that he was a pilot of a B-26, that he had been shot down and managed to evade capture and stayed with friendly, helpful French civilians. I recall over the years visits by men who served with him during the war and I recall while I was in high school, he began writing his account of what happened to him during the war. Reader's Digest had a first-person story in each issue of the magazine and I remember he submitted his account of the dogfight between the lone P-51 pilot and the German fighters. I remember that Reader's Digest liked the story but wanted to verify that it was a true account and submitted a list of questions for dad to respond to. As part of his attempt to authenticate the story, he traveled to Maxwell Air Force Base to review records and try to identify the Mustang pilot. As he stated in the book, he was not able to identify the pilot and his account was not published in Reader's Digest.

During that same time period, he traveled to France to visit the Berty family and attempted to locate additional people and sites from his travels while in hiding from the Germans, this was at least the second trip to France to visit those who helped him so much in 1944. Both he and mom made another trip in 1965, he as a guest of the French government, to celebrate the liberation of Paris. The book "Is Paris Burning" was also published then and details the events surrounding the liberation of Paris. The experiences of the Berty family, Louis, Marcelle, and their young son, Pierre, were provided in the book as was dad's experience. The French edition of the book has a photograph taken about 1963 or '64 with them together with the Eifel Tower as a backdrop.

After dad retired from the Air Force and moved back home to Redding, California, the Bertys, Louis, Marcelle and Pierre, now a young man about 30, came to visit. I was attending college at the time and while they were there, I was working with the U.S. Forest Service and was gone fighting forest fires for most of their visit. But I do recall that there was an obvious tight bond between dad and the Bertys. There was still the language barrier but there was no trouble communicating and I could see that they all enjoyed each other's company again. That was the only time I saw Louis and Marcelle Berty and it would be more than 40 years before I would see Pierre again.

After graduating from college and serving in the Army from 1969-1971, I began a career with the federal government, a career that took me around the world and to the east coast and back before I retired. It was while I was in Bangkok, Thailand, that I first read a copy of dad's manuscript that he had sent me and only then did I become aware of the full story of what happened back in 1944. Dad had bought a brand-new Radio Shack Tandy computer with dual large floppy disks and wrote his story. He contacted several literary agents but none were interested in publishing his account. I remember, while home on leave one time, I rode with him to San Francisco when he had an appointment with an agent. At some point he told me that since he was not famous, like Chuck Yeager for instance, and because his story revealed nothing new about the events of World War II, he believed that it would never be published. He made sure that Mike and I had copies of the manuscript so that we would know what happened. He felt it was important that the world not forget how ordinary people did extraordinary things during a critical time in world history to defeat evil.

The Japanese attack of December 7, 1941 did not kill him nor did flying 35 combat missions over France and getting shot down. But multiple myeloma was something he could not defeat and he passed away in 1990. Mike and I and mom all felt that his story needed to be told somehow. After mom passed away in 2008, we began seriously pursuing getting his story published. His old Radio Shack Tandy computer was now long gone. All we had were the hard copies of the manuscripts. At some point I started the process of retyping it into Word and was surprised at the level of emotions I had while re-reading and re-typing it. It was as if I was hearing the words, not of dad while an older man, but of a young American boy from a small town in Northern

California facing uncertainty not knowing if he would see the light of the next dawn.

Over the last 30 plus years of my parents' lives, their best friends were Dr. William and Anne Nicol. Dr. Nicol was an ENT specialist but was also an Air Force reservist and a pilot. Their oldest son was a close friend of Mike's and the parents bonded from the start. When Mike and I began searching for a publisher, it was Dr. Nicol who suggested IUniverse, a suggestion that we accepted. It turns out that was not the only contribution the Nicol family made to bringing "Walkout" to life. Their son, Jim, played a major role.

Jim Nicol was involved in international business acquisitions and, through one of those business dealing, met a young man from France named Franck Signorile. Dad and Dr. Nicol had both taken an interest in painting and dad had given the Nicol's a painting that was of a street scene somewhere in France. Jim mentioned this to Franck and that began a quest that continues to this day.

Franck began to search for the location of the street scene and, eventually, found what he believed to be the location. Jim also mentioned the story of an American pilot who was shot down, hidden by the French and made it out of German occupied France. Once the book was published, Anne Nicol sent a copy to Franck and he was off and running.

In the meantime, I became involved with Team in Training, a fundraising branch of the Leukemia and Lymphoma Society that trains individuals to compete in endurance events. I became involved with Team in Training as a result of dad's battle with multiple myeloma. After several seasons I was asked to be a coach and, in 2011, I was asked if I could coach a team for the Paris Marathon. I jumped at the opportunity since we had been talking about "someday" going to France and seeing the Bertys. We contacted Pierre and told him of our plans and he was thrilled that we could come. After the marathon, my wife Pat, Mike and his wife Laurie, joined me in Paris. I hadn't seen Pierre in over 40 years but recognized him as soon as I saw him approaching the tobac shop where we were waiting for him. He, and his wife Joseline, welcomed us with open arms and treated us as family.

And we felt we were with family as well. One of the first things we did when we arrived at the Berty home was to toast Louis, Marcelle, dad, and mom with chilled champagne that Pierre had waiting for us. We had several fantastic meals at their house, the same house where dad stayed while in hiding in 1944 and enjoyed great meals in the same kitchen, probably at the same table. We were shown the room where dad stayed and were taken to the museum where Pierre and dad had the encounter with the German soldiers but were not able to view the same painting as the museum was closed that day. We attempted to find the house where dad landed after bailing out but Pierre was not able to remember exactly where it was. We felt lucky that we were able to see their house and I think both Mike and I felt that we would likely not see any other locations from his movements back in 1944. We enjoyed our time with Pierre and Joseline and their daughter Christine and her son Clement. They took us to Normandy to see the D-Day landing sites and the cemetery and we met their son, Alexandre, who lives near the Normandy area. We left France with the sense that we truly had family in France, a family that we hoped we would have the opportunity to visit again soon.

Dad mentions Louis Berty having quite a sense of humor and on our visits with Pierre and Joseline, it was evident that Pierre had inherited that trait from his father. Pierre was suffering from the effects of Parkinson's disease but there was still a twinkle in his eye and reactions from Joseline and Christine whenever he made a funny comment.

After our return from France, we said that we would return to visit the Bertys but life kept getting in the way. Meanwhile, Franck was busy reading the book that Anne Nicol had given him and hard at work searching for the locations mentioned in the book. We began communicating with Franck and made plans for our trip in the spring, early summer of 2013. Franck told us he had some places to show us. After our plans were finalized and coordinated with the Bertys and with Franck, we received word that Pierre had suffered an apparent heart attack and was in the hospital. Several days later Christine informed us that Pierre had passed away. She told us that we should still come as they wanted to see us so Mike and I went ahead with our plans.

It was a bitter-sweet reunion with Joseline, Christine and Clement. There was chilled champagne awaiting us at their home and we toasted as before, now adding Pierre as one who we remembered and missed. We had entered Walkout in a writing contest and it won an award. There was a dinner honoring all the books that had received awards and we invited Joseline to attend the dinner with us. It was a special feeling to be at that dinner in Paris, recognizing dad's account of what transpired in that city in 1944 and to be there with the widow of the young boy who had saved him from the German soldiers that day at the museum.

During this trip, we met Franck Signorile who had been busy since he first received the book. On our first day with Franck, he took us to the apartment building in Versailles where dad had stayed with the Brenners. This was where he learned of the D-Day Invasion and where they alerted the allies of the tanks in the railyard that were bombed and destroyed in the nighttime raid. While we did not go inside the building, since we did not know which apartment he had stayed in, we did see the railroad tracks near the apartment leading to the railyard which was not far from the building.

Franck also explained to us that he had done a lot of research and had found the bar where dad met Carlos and Maria and where he encountered the beautiful Austrian German soldier, Lisa. It was our next stop and as we approached, I was a little disappointed or skeptical since it did not look at all how I pictured it and the interior of the main floor did not match dad's description. We had lunch there and Franck talked with the current owners but they knew nothing of the past history of the bar, now known as Canadian Corner. It did have a second floor and the doorway was on the corner and that matched dad's description. I was still unsure but when the owner said that the post office used to be across the street, I knew that this was it. This was where he stayed in the second floor looking out onto the street at the German soldiers going into the post office. Franck had hit a homerun!

We made plans to meet again in a few days and Franck took us to the home of people who knew of the plane crash. We had gone previously with Joseline and Christine to locate the crash site and the house where he had landed but without any luck. After meeting the family, named Busnel, we went to the site, now a residential area full of homes. At one end of the street is a school which the plane passed over and narrowly missed before impacting in what was at that time a vacant lot or field. Their sister, who was a young girl in 1944, met us there and explained that she saw the crashed wreckage within a day or two of the crash. We had heard that a nearby museum had pieces of the wreckage and Franck took us all there. We spoke with the staff at the museum and toured the facilities but they knew of no such items. Franck also told us that he believed he knew where the German guns had been that shot down the plane. We made plans to all meet and to also introduce Franck to Joseline and Christine and to include them in our plans.

Franck picked us up and drove us to the Berty home where he met Joseline and Christine and we then all drove to a French military facility where he believed the guns had been located. It was locked when we arrived but after Franck and some of the others caught the attention of someone entering the facility and explained why we were there, the gates were opened and we were allowed in. The fort had been built after WWI, as I recall, and appeared as if it hadn't been used in quite some time with some old trucks scattered around and a lot of ivy and vines overgrowing some of the walls and sides of buildings. There were some gun emplacements still there and you could see the river off in the distance and the bridges which were the targets that morning in May, 1944. It was eerie being there and imagining the Germans storming out of the barracks, manning the guns and attempting to blow the bombers out of the sky.

Towards the end of our visit to France, we spent time with Joseline and Christine and were invited out to their second home in Moisson where Christine and Clement now lived. The drive took less than an hour and the home sat on a large lot overlooking the Seine River. They told us that they built the house about 40 years ago and it was their summer home. It was peaceful and beautiful. We went on a tour to a rowing club where Pierre used to be a member and also saw where Monet painted some of his works of art along the river.

They drove us back to our hotel that evening and we said our goodbyes. They were waving as they drove off and I believe we all had tears in our eyes. We didn't know then, but that was the last time we would see Joseline.

In 2014 Franck and his family came to the States for a visit. Their first stop was to visit Bill's family in Florida. Dad stated that he received word that Bill had passed away but that was incorrect; he lived for several more years after dad passed away. Franck was able to locate Bill's son and his family living in Florida and was able to show them places in France where Bill was hidden and introduced them to some of the people who helped him back then. After the visit with them, Franck traveled out to California and visited with us in Redding. The local TV station interviewed him about his efforts researching downed aircrew and those who helped them. He also made a point of visiting the cemetery and paying respects to dad.

Connor, my grandson/adopted son, enjoyed spending time and playing with Franck's two daughters, Juna and Lou-Ann. He was four and they were at least two years older and spoke different languages but that didn't seem to be a problem. They played and swam together the entire time they were together in Redding. Franck surprised Mike and I with a binder for each of us which outlined dad's travels after he was shot down, from landing on the roof of the house and all the other locations up to staying with the Bertys. This step-by-step retracing of the events from 1944 made it much easier to visualize his travels, the distances involved, and their relative position in regards to Paris. After our visit in 2013, Franck located the house where dad landed, and had included a photo of the house taken before he left for his trip to the United States, and also located the area where the camp was where Walt and dad hid. Now we had more places to see on our next visit. He also discovered that Carlos Filipotto, whose bar dad stayed at for a few nights, had sailed to the United States as a younger man and, while living in New York, he shared an apartment with a young Italian who later became famous – Rudolph Valentino.

For various reasons, our next trip to France didn't take place until 2018, but, now, we had one more person to see. One of the people who bought a copy of "Walkout" from Mike was a teacher in Redding who sent it to a former exchange student from France who had come to Redding for one year during high school who she had maintained a friendship with. She was now a teacher herself and was living in the town of Carrieres-sur-Seine, a town near where dad's plane crashed. Through the Redding teacher connection, she met Mike on a subsequent visit to Redding and was given Franck's information so she could learn more details of locations in France discussed in the book. Once our plans were made to visit France, she asked us to do a presentation to her English language class of dad's story which we readily agreed to.

On this trip, we stayed in an Airbnb apartment near Franck's home and he loaned us his van for our use. One of the first things we did was spend the day with Christine and Clement Berty. Christine showed us some of the sites from her college days and some tourist attractions. While exiting one of the Metro stops, we noticed a poster advertising "An American in Paris" and the date that it was to open – May 28 – the day dad was shot down. Coincidence? Of course, our visit with Christine and Clement was mixed with sadness as Joseline had passed away after our last trip.

Franck had a trip planned for us the following day. He took us to the town of Montereau where dad stayed in the police station across the street from city hall, the German Headquarters. The city hall is still there but the police station has been demolished and a new building is going in. On the way to our next stop, Franck pulled over to the side of the road and we walked to overlook the river. He told us that this is where the car stopped when the Canadian fighters came overhead and destroyed the barges in the river. I could imagine the fighters screaming overhead, making their attacks, and pulling up and around to go in again.

We then continued on, heading for the location of the camp and the memorial to "Marcel", but we had a lunch stop first. We visited a couple, named Daniel and Danielle, who have researched the history of those events in 1944 and are instrumental in maintaining the memorial. They told us that the Germans learned of the camp after two men went to a local café claiming to be hiding from the Germans and looking for the location of any resistance camps. A farmer and his son indicated that they may know of one. The two men were actually working with the Germans and reported this to the Germans. That night, the Germans raided their farm and the man and his son were arrested, taken away and both were later killed. "Marcel" was warned that he and the camp was in danger but decided not to go into hiding and was later arrested by the Germans and killed as described in the book, either when he shouted a warning to the camp or when he told the Germans he was not taking them to the camp. In either scenario, he was a hero trying to prevent the capture of his men.

After lunch, we drove to the site of the memorial to "Marcel" whose real name was Andre Taboulet, and Mike and I placed flowers on the monument to honor him and the others. We did not visit the actual camp as it is on private property and Franck was not certain of the exact location, but it was nearby.

The town of Lagny was the next stop on the Walkout Trail. This is where Walt and dad had the hot bath in the kitchen of the house and where they helped move a cart full of guns past the Germans from the garage at the home to another location in town. Franck told us that he was never able to find anyone home at the location but, just as he said that, someone looked out from the window and asked what we wanted. Franck explained why we were there and the owner and his wife came out and gave us a tour of the house, which they purchased from the owner who was there in 1944. They explained that they had remodeled it and that the kitchen used to be where the living room is now. There is a plaque on the side of the house honoring "Paul" the British agent who met with Walt and dad there and asked them to help move the guns. He was later killed in an ambush by the Germans. We discovered that Walt went back to England, as Paul asked, and later married Paul's sister. The current owners told us that they were planning on redoing the garage within a few days but that it was unchanged from 1944.

We detoured from the Walkout Trail on our next stop to give our class presentation to Mady's class, the teacher who studied in Redding and lived for a time in Carrieres-sur-Seine, a town near where the plane went down. We met her and her husband, Charles, in Angers, where they now live, for dinner and went with Mady to her class the next day. Mady had talked about dad's story but didn't tell them we were coming until the day before our visit. We gave the presentation in English and Mady interpreted it into French but it seemed as if most, if not all, of the class were able to follow us in our English presentation. We impressed upon them that the story was about friend helping friend and that because of that, we have the freedoms we enjoy today. They seemed to take it to heart and appreciated the presentation. One of the students came up after class and talked to us and explained that his grandfather had recently passed away and that this reminded him of his grandfather and what he had done. I think we got as much out of the presentation as the kids.

We learned that Charles's mother was a member of Parliament and had offered to give us a tour of Parliament and, of course, we said yes. We thoroughly enjoyed it. Here we were just two guys following in the footsteps of our father from 74 years earlier and now we were getting a personally escorted tour of the French Parliament. Quite impressive! And Charles's mother was very gracious and humble and made sure we went to a nice café for lunch after the tour.

But there was still more to come. Franck had organized a walking tour to take in the route that dad followed from the house where he landed, to the café where he stayed with Carlos and Maria. Christine and Clement joined us and also Mady and Charles. We walked from the café towards the train station, which is no longer a small quiet station, but has grown into a bustling busy commuter station for those going into and out of Paris. The house where he landed was a short walk, maybe two blocks from the station. The gate looks as it did in the 1940's. Mady told us that she drove by this house every day when she lived in the area. What a small world – A young student comes to a small town in Northern California, the hometown of a young man who was shot down and landed in the town near where she lived in France.

Franck had arranged with the owners for us to visit the home and they were very gracious. They gave us a tour and explained that they were planning some modifications to the exterior but that it hadn't been changed at all.

We then walked the route from the house towards the bar with one stop. Franck introduced us to a woman, Daniele, and told us she was the young girl who first saw dad hiding in the bush. She pointed out to us where the bush was and she and Franck explained that it was her mother who brought the food to dad. This was the first person, besides the Bertys of course, we had met who was part of the events back then and who we could thank in person. It was an emotional moment. She explained that her mother was not well and in a nursing home but she would check and see if she was up to meeting us at some point.

We were shown the house where dad hid in the bush and where he spent the first night in the basement of the garage or shed, but were told nobody was there at that house and hadn't been for a long time. Just then, an elderly man appeared in the back yard of the house walking in from the street. Everyone was excited that someone was now home and Franck explained why we were there and the story of the young American airman hiding there in the bush and then the shed or basement. The gentleman welcomed us and took us back to the garage and showed us the basement, which now has concrete walls and floors, and let us go in. It had a musty odor like most basements and probably just as it did in 1944. While it had been upgraded, it was the place where he spent that first night. Mike and I were overcome with emotions.

As we were beginning to continue our walk back to the bar, Daniele said she had to leave to be with her mother. We thanked her very much again for all she and her mother had done as she left and we moved on towards the bar.

A short distance later, we stopped and Franck pointed out signs indicating that this was the entrance to a French military installation. He explained that this was a secret site for the German military back then, heavily guarded and near where dad landed. It was also the work place for Lisa. He almost landed on a secret German facility making weapons. Wow!

We soon arrived at the bar and had lunch. Christine and Clement were sitting in the place where their grandfather/Great-Grandfather, had arrived by bike to retrieve dad's .45 and saw where he then went to find it and bring it back to show Carlos and to get dad's uniform. Louis Berty did so at great risk to himself and to his family.

Franck still had more surprises for us and after lunch we headed off to the next stop as Mady and Charles caught the Metro heading back to Paris. Mike and I didn't know where we were going as we rode with Franck and Christine and Clement followed in their car. As we pulled in to the parking lot, we recognized it as the museum in Cormeilles we came to on our last trip. Franck introduced us to a group of people gathered to meet us, including Remi Busnel, one of the people we met on our second trip who showed us the fort and took us to the museum on that trip. Franck introduced us to a young French couple among the group, Xavier and Stephanie, and explained that Xavier was the French grandson of Bill who Franck had located after much searching.

Once inside the museum we took a quick tour and then were brought into a room with items laid out on a table. As Mike and I were looking, Franck explained that the items were pieces of shrapnel and bullets found at the crash site and then pointed to a piece of metal and said "That is part of the plane." I think Mike and I were in shock. Here was an actual part of the plane that he flew that day and that went down with the loss of Sgt. Hickey. Franck explained that Stephanie, a volunteer at the museum who was familiar with the story, went through the museum looking for the pieces and found them. We each held it and took photos of us holding it. What a find! We are forever grateful!

Over the next few days, we visited with Christine and Clement at their home in Moisson. We first stopped by the Berty home in Nanterre which was being sold. It was sad to see it like this, bare of furniture, with some of Pierre's paintings leaning up against the walls being the only items in the house. While Mike and I only had memories of good times and great meals at the Berty home going back just a few years, the Bertys and Woodrums had enjoyed many good times over the last 70+ years here, and now it was coming to an end.

The days we spent with Christine and Clement were very rewarding. We sat around their table in the mornings drinking coffee and munching on toasted baguettes with butter or honey and in the evenings eating her home cooked meals with beer and wine. During the day they took us on tours of the area, including Claude Monet's house and gardens which looked exactly like his paintings. In the afternoon, we sat outside around a small table snacking on cheese, wine, beer, listening to stories of the house and the times the Berty family spent there, and watching the dogs, cats, and chickens chase each other around the yard overlooking the river. Our last day we went into the small town-center area that we had not visited before and had lunch in a very nice crepe restaurant, and then we said our good-byes to Clement, as he was going to be visiting his father, and Christine would see us off at the airport in a few days when we left.

Franck had one more adventure for us. He told us that Simone, the young woman who brought food to dad that first night while he was hidden in the bush, felt up to seeing us and we would meet her and her daughter Daniele at the nursing home where she was staying. Mike and I were nervous about the meeting since she was in her late 90's and frail and we did not want to cause her any discomfort. We met Daniele outside and she led the three of us to her mother's room.

Simone was sitting in a chair next to her bed and Daniele reminded her who we were. She looked at Mike and said something in French and Daniele smiled and told her something again. She and Franck then told us that she said "You wanted to smoke and I told you no, no smoking. The Germans would smell the cigarette and find you." She was thinking that Mike was the young pilot she saw that evening in the bush, so she clearly remembered the events of that day. Daniele explained to her that we were the sons of that pilot. Mike and I were both overwhelmed and told her that we owned our lives to her and that we wouldn't be here without her and her daughter and all the others who helped. We knelt next to her and both held her hands and thanked her.

Daniele had some cookies and champagne for us all to enjoy so we toasted the two of them, thanked them again profusely, and enjoyed a few minutes together. Daniele told us some of her family history and brought out two photos taken back then, one of Simone holding a young baby, Daniele. We left after a few minutes and again thanked Simone and told her how much we appreciated what she did and we told her that dad had tried to find her after the war to thank her but was not able to.

The meeting was very emotional for Mike and I. When we got the book published, we thought we would renew our friendship with the Bertys, see their house and probably the house where dad landed and nothing more. Meeting Simone and Daniele and being able to thank them was something we couldn't have imagined. Our meeting was even more meaningful when we received word from Daniele that Simone passed away about 3 months after our visit. We felt truly blessed and fortunate to have had the opportunity to thank her in person.

In addition to locating and visiting many of the locations mentioned in the book, Franck helped answer a question, actually two questions that I had. Dad and Walt believed that the two men claiming to be Americans who appeared at the camp were actually Germans who had assumed the identify of two captured or killed Americans. Franck was able to locate records showing that Lt. Robert Brown and Sgt. Charles Roberson were captured by the Germans after being betrayed by double agents to the Gestapo. But I was still not convinced that it was really them that showed up at the camp. Well, Franck was able to locate family members of both men and he and Mike and I have spoken with and communicated with them. Both men wrote their account of what happened years after the fact and tell a story of being in resistance camps and being on the move after their camp was attacked by Germans. After passing through the camp where dad and Walt were, they made their way via the Underground to Paris where they were betrayed and captured by the Gestapo. What then happened to them and a small group of Allied airmen was kept quiet for many years. Hitler declared these Allied airmen to be terrorists and not prisoners of war subject to the Geneva Convention. They were moved from Paris in crowded rail cars, some of the last to leave as the Allies were liberating Paris, and endured the long ride, as did thousands of other political prisoners, to the death camp of Buchenwald. There, they were treated horribly with little food, shelter, or medical care and were scheduled to be executed. After several weeks, by one account, the factory next to the camp was bombed by Allied bombers and destroyed. Within a day or two,

German Luftwaffe officers came to inspect the damage to their factory. One of the allied prisoners spoke German and got the attention of a German officer and explained that they were Allied airmen and should be Prisoners of War and not in a work/death camp. Apparently, the officer agreed and they were later moved out of Buchenwald to POW camps, but not before at least two of them had already died in the camp.

I had wondered over the years what would have happened to dad if he had been captured. I think this answers that question. I suspect that if he had been caught, he would have been part of the group slated for execution and sent to Buchenwald. This part of history has not been talked about much and I have seen accounts written by some of the airmen stating they were told not to talk about it and some were called liars when they did. Why? One answer is that the US Government wanted to bring German rocket scientists to the United States to help with our rocket and space program and if the American public knew how badly our airmen were treated, they might object to bringing these people in, some of whom may have been Nazis.

Mike and I, and my late wife Pat, met Lt. Brown's daughter, Suzanne Price, who lived in the Phoenix area. During our discussions, I mentioned why Walt and dad were leery of her dad and Sgt. Roberson-Lt. Brown making a point to talk about baseball with the latest stats, asking about their experiences and the map that her dad had. Suzanne explained that her father was a real fan of baseball and was also very interested in geography and maps so it was natural, for him, to talk about baseball so much and to draw a map. While we have communicated with Ginger German, Sgt. Roberson's daughter, we have not met her in person. Both provided copies of their fathers' account of what happened back then and it would be an understatement to say they had a very harrowing experience, one that they were fortunate to survive.

There is another resource that has proven to be a wealth of information. Carl Carroza began researching the plane that his dad flew in during the war, a B-26 named Shopworn Angel. He contacted me about the time we were getting the book published. While I thought that dad was flying the Shopworn Angel the day he was shot down, he was in another plane that day because Shopworn Angel had sustained damage while being flown by another pilot on an earlier mission and had not yet been repaired. After dad and his crew were shot down, there were two subsequent crews assigned to the Shopworn Angel and Carl's father was in the second crew and flew on the D-Day missions. After he and his crew finished their required number of missions, a third crew was assigned to the Shopworn Angel and that was to be the final crew. On February 14, 1945, the Shopworn Angel was shot down and suffered the loss of several crewmembers. Carl has an extensive record on the history of the various crews and of the 344th Bomb Group and the 495th bomb squadron. As a result of his website, shopwornangel. imaginarynumber.net, he has gathered much information from family members of aircrew who flew back then who have contacted him either seeking information, or providing information about their family member. One of the people who contacted him was the daughter of Sgt. Hickey's widow. After the war, she remarried and her daughter reached out to Carl and Carl put me in contact with her. Sgt. Hickey was the "new guy" on the crew that morning but he was not a rookie. He had been in another plane that went down after being damaged and survived and was awarded a medal for his actions that day. She shared with me many letters between her mother and the military officials, and family members of other crewmembers seeking information, and a letter that dad wrote her after his return to the United States. She also shared copies of many letters her mother wrote to her missing husband over the course of months in which she held out hope that he was still alive. It was not until several months later that she was informed that he had died that day. It is heart wrenching to read her letters to Ed Hickey holding out hope that she will see him again, and the letters from the family members of the other crewmembers', and dad, after he returned, offering her hope with little or nothing to back it up. It truly brings home the personal cost of war.

Through various sources I was able to locate one of Bud Morgan's daughters. I sent her a copy of the book that she shared with her sister. While her father's experiences were much different after being shot down, she was able to learn what that last morning was like and get a sense of how they lived at Stansted. While there is a mention of them flying from Brazil to Europe via Africa, I also sent her a short story about the trip that provides more detail.

Recently we learned that a group in Cormeilles, the town where the plane crashed and where the museum is located, is attempting to have a monument erected at the crash site honoring the crew. We have been told they are in the process of obtaining permission and funding for the project. If this does come about, Mike and I plan to be there and to let the survivors of the other crew members know so they may attend if they choose to.

As I stated earlier, Mike and I never could have imagined what our project of getting the story of one young man from a small town in Northern California who survived with the help of many in a foreign country united in the fight against a common enemy would lead to. Our family ties with the Bertys have been renewed and strengthened; Thanks to Franck we have been able to walk in dad's footsteps and see the locations and meet people who helped him back then; We have met a young school teacher who lived in the hometown of the pilot, lived in a town near where he landed that morning and is now passing that story on to her students and translating the account into French; And, thanks to Carl Carroza and his efforts, we have learned of the history of the Shopworn Angel, it's crews and have been in contact with the families of various crewmembers. It has truly been a rewarding experience. Mike has stated that we thought we were giving a gift to dad by getting his story published, but now realize that we were the ones receiving a gift from him.

Hank Woodrum Jr.

Mike, Hank and Christine at the Berty home one last time.

Mike and Hank with the current owners at
the house where he landed, 2018

Daniele, Mike and Hank at the site where she
saw dad hiding in the bush, 2018

Henri exiting the basement where dad hid that first night, 2018

Our group in front of the Canadian Corner after our walk and lunch. From the left, Charles, Hank, Christine, Mike, Clement, Mady, and Franck, 2018

## Franck's Journey to The Past

### Jim

I met Jim Nicol for the first time in June of 2005. Jim was my new manager, and I was to report to him going forward. He is American, I am French, and it was my first business meeting in English.

As a software Engineer, I have spent the first ten years of my career building a new technology. The small startup was gaining success in Europe, and we were getting a lot of attention from a US-based company. A merger was concluded during the spring of 2005, and leadership teams from both companies were organizing meetings in Paris.

As the Vice-President of Engineering, Jim wanted to have a "one on one" meeting with me, as he called it. I found the expression amusing as it does not translate well into French.

It was a rainy day. I was sitting in a typical French Café located inside Paris, waiting for him. I was wondering which questions he would ask me, which subjects he would want to cover. Jim eventually showed up and sat down in front of me. "Franck, you will not believe how excited I am to be in France!" he said. He was smiling, and I immediately liked him.

I was prepared for an intense business meeting, but obviously Jim had something else in mind. During more than an hour, he told me about the incredible story of a World War II bomber pilot named Henry Woodrum, the French people who helped him avoid capture, the Berty family, the maquis camp, the liberation of Paris, and much more. He also explained the strong bonds between the Nicols and the Woodrums that have existed for decades.

When he was younger, Jim would listen to the adventures told by Henry Woodrum himself, and it had become a family legend to him. Coming to Paris was like bringing a 60-year-old story back to life.

He was speaking very fast, and I was struggling to adjust to the American accent and the specific vocabulary he used. This was all new to me. But I understood most of the story, and his excitement was contagious. What a great story, I thought. Jim quickly left the Café as he had other commitments. The meeting was over, and I was puzzled. It was not exactly what I had expected from that very first meeting! I even wondered if Jim was trying to "test" me.

Now I know that it was not a test. He was genuinely thrilled to be so close to where the story took place and he wanted to share it with someone, and that was me. When I left the Café, I had no idea that Jim had just triggered a chain reaction that would later change many things in my life, both from a personal and professional standpoint.

I worked with Jim for several years, and at several occasions, either in Paris or in California, we would talk about the story of Henry Woodrum. He was my manager, but that story initiated a very special bond between us. When Jim left the company, we decided to stay in touch as friends.

## The Book

When the first edition of Walkout was released in 2010, Jim thought that I would want to read it, and I got a copy sent to me. It was probably the first copy of the book sent to Europe. Needless to say, I was excited when I opened the book for the first time. It was a special gift from a special friend, and I was under the impression that I had a personal connection with the author of the book himself. And I did not even know Mike and Hank Woodrum at that time.

I took my time to read the book, as I was not familiar with the terminology and expressions. Opening a dictionary was often needed. I did not want to miss a single piece of it. After several chapters, I was stunned by the level of details used to describe the places and people. As a reader, it seemed like the story was written a few days after the events, not several decades afterwards.

When I finished the very last page of Walkout, I was stuck in the year 1944. A couple of hours were necessary for me to come back to the present time. I then realized that I wanted more of that story. The book was opening so many questions with no answers: Where are all these places he was sent to? Who were these people who helped him? Why did they risk their own lives to help someone they did not even know?

The good news is most of the places mentioned in the book are located in a 20-mile range from where I live, and all the city names he recalled are familiar to me. Soon after I finished reading Walkout, I went to the city of Carrieres to find the house where he landed. All I had was a picture of the front gate and a street number. I thought it would be easy. I wandered in the city a whole afternoon, but didn't find the house.

The inhabitants of Carrieres were watching me scrutinizing their houses with my book in hand. They were probably thinking that I was mentally deranged, but I did not care. All I was doing was connecting a bit of History with my own world. It was important for me to do it. I did not achieve my goal, but that was ok. I eventually found the house, but three years later and with a little help from Google Street View.

Obviously, I wanted Jim to know about my adventures in Carrieres. I wrote a long email, telling him my impressions of the book and my visit to one of the main spots. Jim forwarded it to the sons of Henry Woodrum, Mike and Hank. It was the starting point of a new chapter beginning in the spring of 2013.

## Mike and Hank

Mike sent me a first e-mail on early March. He and his brother were planning a trip to France, and he told me that he would be pleased to meet me. He had heard about my interest in the story of his father.

I was happy to meet them, but at the same time I was feeling a bit uncomfortable, because I did not feel "legitimate". I am not a family member of someone who helped the airman in 1944, as the Berty family was. That feeling disappeared immediately as soon as I met them in Paris. Both were very friendly and it was obvious that my interest in that story was very welcome.

During several weeks before their visit, I had spent a lot of time researching special spots mentioned in the book. I had also made contact with witnesses of the plane crash in 1944.

We had a wonderful time visiting all the places that I had located. I will always remember Hank's reaction when we discovered that the restaurant where we were having lunch in Carrieres was actually the bar where his father was hidden during the first days after the landing. When I made a reservation for lunch in that restaurant, I was not sure it was *the* place, but we had it confirmed by the owner of the restaurant after we told him the special reason why we were there.

I felt emotions that were completely new to me. The past was suddenly connected with the present, and it was like seventy years of time were reduced to a second. When I met Mike and Hank, they were complete strangers to me, but when they left France, we were special friends. I wondered if their visit was the end of the story. Actually, it was just the beginning.

## The world of Escape and Evasion

That trip had left behind a huge number of open questions. I wanted to know more, and I felt a surge of energy to continue the research. Thanks to the Internet, it is now easy to do research from home, and that's what I did. After finding places, I wanted to know more about the characters from the book. I realized that I knew very little about the organization of the *Resistance* during the war, and *Escape lines* were unknown to me as well.

Woodrum's story is unique in many ways, but he was definitely not the only airman shot down during the war. It is estimated that nearly 10,000 airmen were shot down behind enemy lines and made a successful evasion. And these men were the lucky ones, many more were arrested or killed during these highly dangerous bombing missions.

Evasion could not be successful without the help of locals. Either sympathizers of the Allied cause, or members of Escape Lines, these helpers were key players in each evasion story. Woodrum was directly assisted by more than thirty people. I soon learned that in France, there were more than 20,000 helpers of evading airmen during World War II. They were identified by the British and American authorities after the war. Many helpers were recognized and awarded for their actions.

The internet gave me access to great resources, as a number of Historians had already researched these WWII-related questions, and I made contact with some of these experts with many questions. They were all very helpful and were happy to welcome a new member into their "world".

But not everything is available on the Internet. One has to go out and seek for information that is not reachable from a computer. I discovered that many documents were held in archive centers, and I visited many of them, all located in the Paris area. I also met local historians whose knowledge proved to be very helpful when I started preparing for the Woodrum's visit in 2018.

In the meantime, I kept myself busy studying the story of the other airmen that Henry Woodrum met when he was in France. All of them had a similar fate: they bailed out of a damaged plane and landed in occupied France. They were lucky enough to avoid immediate capture. Bill was one of them, and his name pops up in the middle of the book. Woodrum met him in Melun. They share the same story until the end of the book.

What had happened *before* they met was far from ordinary, and I had no idea what I was going to discover when I contacted Bill's family.

## Jane and Stew

I wanted to get in touch with Bill's family for two main reasons. First, I was looking for more information about Bill, as I thought he had shared his adventures in France with his children. And second, I was pretty sure they would be interested to hear about the book.

Jane quickly answered my contact request on Ancestry.com, where her family tree is posted. She is Stew's wife, and Stew is Bill's elder child. No family names will be exposed for privacy reasons.

Jane's first reply was enthusiastic. She told me that her father-in-law never said a word about his evasion story. He would easily share his war-time experience, but anything related to France was taboo. I did not understand why, and of course I was disappointed.

But Jane and her husband were eager to know more about my research, and asked me a lot of questions. We soon became "e-mail friends". A few days passed, and Jane told me she had a document I absolutely needed to look at. It is quite special, she said.

The document was a letter found in Bill's personal archives after he and his wife passed away (respectively in 2006 and 2009). Their house was to be sold, and Stew's sister went through his military archives and found that letter. It was dated 1946, and it came from France. A young French lady wrote the letter to Bill and asked him about his intentions regarding the *baby girl* she had with him during his stay in her house.

OMG… I read the letter several times and realized that a family secret had been kept for nearly seventy years, and was only revealed posthumously. Jane told me that Bill never went back to France. His life and career were in the U.S. He had a wife and raised four children, all born after the war. Nobody needed to know, and the well-kept secret was not to be uncovered. Stew had a sister in France.

Jane and Stew also told me that they would love to know more about the baby and her mother. I had my first phone call with them soon after and it became obvious to me how important it was for them to reconnect with what they considered to be their "French family". In case the now grown baby girl was alive, they would respect her decision, whether she would agree to make contact or not.

## Searching for Christine

I remember sharing all these unexpected events with Hank Woodrum, and we both agreed that the release of "Walkout" had triggered a strange chain reaction.

After a few days, my decision was made: I wanted to help them, and I was going to research the baby girl. That would be my next mission, and I could feel a surge of energy needed to accomplish such a difficult task. I knew I would need to overcome a number of hurdles, and I anticipated the potential consequences in case of success. Was she alive? And if so, what would be her reaction? What did she know? Would she be willing to get in touch with her siblings in America?

I asked myself all these questions at a time I did not even know her first and last name. Her mother - the author of the letter - was probably dead, but her daughter would now be 68 years old.

I did not have much as a starting point for my research. The letter was signed with the most common family name in France, and there was no mention of a first name. Google could not help me at all… But there was an old address, and that information proved to be extremely helpful.

By trial and error, I first managed to collect quite a bit of key data related to the mother. She was a member of the French Resistance, and her chief had asked her to shelter the American airman until he would have to move to another place. He stayed two or three weeks in her house, and left early in the morning of July, 12$^{th}$, 1944.

I visited the old address, searched several cemeteries, asked questions in City Halls, requested vital records and visited archive centers. I discovered that I was not too bad as an investigator, and I really enjoyed that kind of research.

After two months, the research was nearly over and it was successful! I found out that the baby girl was still alive. She is now a grand-mother. Her name is Christine, and she lives in Brittany. I even found her address and e-mail.

During those two months, I kept in touch with Jane and Stew. Each new piece of information was very well received and our friendship grew stronger. They wanted to know everything, and they were thankful for all I was doing.

I remember my first phone call with Christine as if it was yesterday. It was a stressful moment for me as I had no idea about what she knew and how she would react. Fortunately, she was very happy to learn that her family was finally looking for her. She told me that all she knew is her father's name and nationality. That was it. When she was younger, she wanted to find him and meet him, but it never happened. After so many years, she had lost hope that he would ever want to make contact with her.

I felt mixed emotions during our conversation: bitterness and joy. She was thrilled to learn that she had two brothers and two sisters living in America. She said she would love to know more about them. But she was sad when I told her that her father had died a few years before. He had a long life and never tried to reach her.

The following day, I had another phone call, this time with Stew and his wife. They were so happy when I told them that I had found her and had a call with her. It was a very emotional moment when I added she would be happy to meet them someday.

Two weeks later, Stew and Jane landed at Paris Charles-de-Gaulle airport. I was there. Christine's son was there too. We had met in the meantime, as he lives not too far from where I live. Christine could not be at the airport, but the plan was for me to drive the "Americans" to Brittany, which is about 200 miles west of Paris. There was no way I would miss the reunion of a brother and a sister who, at the age of 70 were to meet each other for the first time.

It was a long drive, and I remember that Stew wanted to learn a few words in French. He wanted to introduce himself and say hello in *her* language. He probably repeated the sentence a hundred times and got it right when we reached the small village where Christine lives. We could see her, waiting outside the gate of her house.

Who could have imagined that reading this book would give rise to such a family reunion? Even now, I cannot think of it without a surge of emotion.

Christine was a bit shy but Stew was not. He hugged her as if she was a long-lost friend. The language barrier did not seem to be a problem at all. It was only tears and laughter. They have very common features, and we all agreed that there was no need for a DNA test. During the following hours, they shared their own story, and there was a lot to be told. I could see new bonds appearing between a brother and a sister separated by the war. These bonds were strong, and the years to come would prove it.

That first visit was too short, and they all decided to meet again as often as possible. Since that day, they have seen each other in person at least once a year, in France or in the USA. Both Christine and Stew made it clear that I was to be part of the reunited French-American family.

After the family reunion, I went back to my research and started to uncover a very sad side of Bill's story. My adventures with Walkout were not over. The following year, Stew and his wife came back to France for a very different purpose.

## The sacrifice of Helpers

Before he met Christine's mother, Bill had been helped by a group of French patriots who did their best to organize his evasion. Unfortunately, right after Bill left his first hiding place, all the patriots were denounced by a traitor working for the Gestapo. Fifteen men and women were arrested and brutally interrogated. Nine of them were deported to a concentration camp in Germany, and six never came back. Six lost their lives to save one.

The story was told to me by a man called Daniel, the son of one of those brave men who gave their life for him. Daniel was only seven years old when his father was arrested and died in Germany. Telling the story was not easy for him, even after so many years. I met Daniel several times, and I told him everything I knew about the pilot and his family. He was glad that the pilot made it back home, as he did not know what had happened after he left. He said he would be happy to meet Stew.

A new reunion was organized several months later, and Daniel went out of his way to locate and contact all the families of the men and women involved in the story, seventy years before. What was initially planned as a private reunion with a small group of people became a major event with more than fifty attendees and got national TV coverage. The event was planned during the week of the 70th anniversary of D-Day.

Despite the terrible story that affected all the village in 1944, the reunion was a day full of joy and emotion. Stew was the hero of the day, and he made a remarkable speech – in French – to say thank you on behalf of his father whose life was saved by the sacrifice of so many.

## More stories...

During the summer on 2014, I went to the U.S. with my family for an extended vacation. We visited Bill's family in Florida, and then went to California to meet Mike and Hank Woodrum and also the Nicol family. It was a great visit, and we shared a lot of new information.

Hank and I started a discussion that would – again! – be the starting point of a new major research. Walkout raised the following question:

Who were the two airmen that Woodrum met in the maquis camp? Were they real evading airmen, or were they spies working for the Gestapo? Woodrum and Walt, the other American hiding in the camp, seemed to believe that they were spies, which would explain why the maquis camp was discovered and destroyed soon after.

After some research, I discovered the names of the two airmen, and their escape story is unique in many ways. Many documents were necessary to retrace their escape route, with exact dates and places. I came to the conclusion that they were in the exact same area as Woodrum was at the exact same dates: they were not spies!

Unfortunately for them, they decided not to stay with Woodrum, as they wanted to move on and go to Paris. When they finally reached Paris, they fell into a trap set by a double-agent working for the Gestapo. At the beginning of August - two weeks before the liberation of Paris – they were arrested and sent to a nearby prison, where many other airmen were gathered and were awaiting their fate.

What intrigued me the most is what happened next: instead of being transferred to a Stalag in Germany, which was the usual consequence for the vast majority of arrested airmen during the war, these two airmen were deported to a well-known concentration camp: Buchenwald. They left Paris in crowded cattle cars, with a group of other captured airmen: there were a total of 168, from various countries (UK, USA, Canada, Australia, New Zealand). They all stayed two months in that camp, which was a direct violation of the Geneva convention, and suffered from terrible living conditions. But a senior officer from the German Luftwaffe was made aware of the situation and managed to transfer them to Stalag Luft III. Most of the 168 men survived Buchenwald, but their health was impacted and most of them suffered post-traumatic stress disorder for the rest of their lives.

In 2015 and 2016, I contacted the children of the two airmen that Woodrum had met. They were very interested in my research, as they had many questions and no answers for them. We shared a lot of information and documents, and both families came to France in 2016 for a wonderful visit. They walked in the steps of their father, and that was a great experience to show them the places and let them meet families of helpers. There was a large party the last day, attended by half of the villagers.

The story of the 168 airmen is not well known, and I made it my next project. I wanted to know everything about them and understand how and why they were arrested. Many of them were on their way to a successful evasion, but they met the wrong people at the wrong time.

## Conclusion

Up to this day, I continue to devote a lot of my time into research, meeting families and making great friends along the way. The 2018 visit of Mike and Hank Woodrum made us even closer friends. The idea of a new edition for Walkout was discussed during that visit if I remember well.

The chain reaction goes on and on, and despite the pandemic, new projects are being planned. My passion for these stories is still vivid, and I am now in a position where I also help others who are interested in these matters.

This book has changed my life in so many ways. Even my career as a software Engineer came to an end, after twenty years. Switching careers is always difficult and risky, but I wanted to follow a new path which would be in line with my new passion. Little did I know that I would become a Probate Genealogist, making my living as a researcher!

Stew commented on behalf of his family after reading my account of searching for people and places related to the book:

"Franck's thorough but sensitive investigative talents changed our family's lives. Through understanding the incredibly brave actions by our father and Christine's mother and discovering our beautiful sister Christine, our lives have been infinitely enriched. Each and every visit with Christine yields even more loving understanding. There are so many other families with similar stories- my wish is for them to become united while their family members are still alive and able to successfully search."

Franck Signorile

Mike, Daniel, Hank, and Danielle at their home, 2018

Mike and Hank at the memorial for Andre, 2018

Hank and Franck with the owners of the Lagny house, 2018

Front of the house in Lagny with the plaque
to "Paul" the British agent, 2018

The garage in Lagny where the guns were hidden
that the group moved to another location, 2018

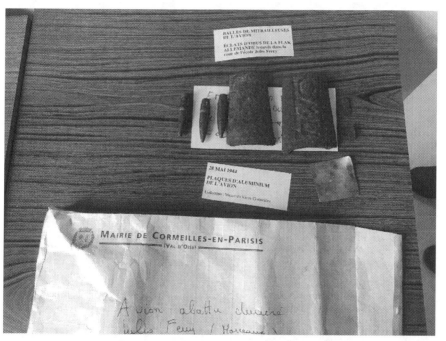
The table display at the museum with items
from the wreckage of the plane, 2018

Mike holding the piece of the airplane, 2018

Simone and Daniele during our visit to her room, 2018

Simone with Mike and Hank thanking her for what she did in 1944 to help save a young American airman, 2018

Printed in the United States
by Baker & Taylor Publisher Services